Words in
Transformation

Words in Transformation

by

Carolyn Morgan & Robin Wells

2016

Courtyard Publication

Bembridge, Isle of Wight UK

Courtyard Publishing:

The Courtyard, Bembridge, Isle of Wight, UK, PO355SF.

www.courtyardalchemy.com

First Edition 2016

Copyright © Carolyn Morgan

Copyright © Robin Wells

Copyright © *Courtyard Publishing*

ISBN 978-0-9927453-4-9

Cover Art: Elaine Pattison for *Courtyard Publishing*

Contents

Page

Acknowledgments

When I began this book I had no idea how to get it published, I just knew it had to be written and the publisher would arrive when the time was right. It was my *Field of Dreams*, '*Build it and he will come.*' And so I started to build this book as Robin and I had been directed by the information with the given title '*Words in Transformation*'. I was in the   middle of building this dream when my daughter Sarah Rawlings had the opportunity to find accommodation for authors attending the 2014 Isle of Wight Literary Festival at Northwood House and asked me if there was anyone I would be interested to hear. One man's name stood out who was to speak on the subject of Alchemy and Hermetic Philosophy. Although neither were my particular field of thought this resonated with me, it was one of those opportune moments I have learnt to recognise, those synchronicities that occur when the universe is trying to get my attention. So at the selected time I joined others waiting to hear the talk given by Dr Robert Anderson Plimer. After his very intellectual discourse I was moved to speak with him when he finally concluded that after all his scholarly years of academic study love is indeed the answer. He had reasoned through his intellect what I had learnt through my open heart. Thank you Bob for appearing in my *Field of Dreams* and having the faith to edit and publish this book and thank you Sarah Jane for being the catalyst for our fortuitous meeting. My thanks too are extended to Elaine, Bob's very gifted partner, for all your hard work in getting '*Words*' from manuscript to book and showing your appreciation of all the stories I have yet to tell. My gratitude to you Mary Maddison for your sparkling crystal radiance, you have always been a beacon of light for me. And to Margo Williams with whom I shared a truly wonderful and enlightening friendship - we shall surely meet again. And to Robin who in the face of much adversity always had the courage to carry on. There is indeed much steel in your soul, for along with the choicest wisdom in your words, I believe there is more intrigue yet to come. And let me not forget all those un-named communicators whose wise words have changed my perception forever. Finally to all my family who have kept me grounded when I am away with the fairies as they so politely refer to my passion. Nevertheless my life with the unseen realms has given me an unshakable faith and fulfilled my destiny to be who I am.

Carolyn Morgan

Dec. 2015

Introduction

Introduction

The Way-shower

Robin Wells - *in his own words*

The Beginning

As a young child *fear* was my constant companion. I never knew why, but every night brought this dreaded feeling. There seemed to be no reasonable explanation of what frightened me. Could there be something under the bed or behind the curtain waiting to jump out on me? Finally, when drifting into that other state of consciousness just before sleep, my fears were more fully realised. Ghastly things visited me and the most grotesque terrifying *ghoul*-like things dragged me out of bed. My mother would hear a thud and then find me on the floor.

This torment continued for years but the memory vanished upon waking. Yet during those hours of darkness something did visit and frighten me. Eventually, my strengths and weaknesses matured but the nights were still a trial.

In my early twenties my girlfriend Melitta was living with me and one particular night as I drifted towards sleep something started dragging me out of bed. I was just conscious yet aware of her sleeping beside me. Bang! I was on the floor, panic stricken, and being dragged towards the wall. Conscious now I picked myself up and climbed into bed only to have a repeat performance. This was new and persistent and very unpleasant, and it was certainly frightening. But this time I used a different approach; instead of feeding this horrible apparition with fear I clasped my hands together in prayer and sent it love, whereupon it vanished. The realisation dawned that I had only ever fed it with fear, so it returned for more. Love and prayer seemed to be the answer!

Then one evening an apparition turned up, a ghoul, the usual nasty being! Saying the vanishing prayer resulted in a very different set of circumstances; it morphed into an angelic being of Light, at the same time saying, 'It has taken you all this time to learn the lesson of fear. Never fear, this holds you back as a man. Never worship fear when there is love.'

The first lesson in all spiritual work is overcoming fear, which can be very debilitating. I took my apprenticeship in fear to the extreme but learnt the lesson well. There are things out there to be afraid of but don't challenge them, always question whatever you are asked to do and where you need to put your energy. Check it out first, never accept fear when love is available.

Carolyn is my aunt and spiritual mother, she was my teacher when wisdom keepers were rare. When one speaks with love from the heart, no matter how the words come out they are meaningful, and she was always patient with my constant questioning:

Who is God? Who was Jesus and were there really disciples? Do you think there are people on other planets?

Carolyn would always take time to speak with me, even though she had a large old Victorian house to maintain and many mouths to feed. Anyone and everyone were welcome at The Grove; it was a sanctuary for the homeless, the sick, and the many young people that found their way to her home to be fed spiritually and bodily. For not only did she look after her own large family but, with her husband Reg, spent time caring for many others as well. I am indebted to them both for their wise counsel.

Books found their way into my life as my thirst for knowledge grew. Grace Cooke's teachings from White

Eagle,[1] the teachings of Ramala[2] and anything of a spiritual nature that could help me find my place in life. I wanted to fit in somewhere. With hindsight it is not necessary to fit in anywhere, just be who you are. When you are settled in the skin you have been given you no longer need to go outside to find fulfilment but are content to converse with your *self*, the spirit within, and the Godhead.

My mentor during my twenties was Ken Baker, a member of the Kent Healers, who trained me as a healer. But there was always a presence following me and when Ken attempted to lay his hands on me for healing my arms would get quite violent and throw him off. He knew something was amiss and it wasn't long before he realised he was dealing with an entity attachment that had been with me for some years. Entities attach themselves to people who have similar problems; it could be sadness, drink, anger, love, sex, passion, there is always something within you that is latent within them. Energy is always attracted to energy.

This was not a malevolent entity, it was just a frightened individual who had attached himself to me and was eventually released. This was a very strange experience because it turned out to be a young shepherd boy who was caught stealing and suffered torture by having his eyes removed with hot pokers and eventually hanged. How barbaric!

---

[1] www.whiteeagle.org
[2] www.ramalacentre.com

Over a period of time Ken and others unsuccessfully tried to remove my shepherd boy attachment, but eventually Ken sourced the right people. There was a circle of four involved, but every time they attempted to release him, as he could no longer see through the eyes of my body he was blind again and came straight back. He was frightened because he couldn't <u>see</u> the Light. We discussed the situation and he was told to <u>feel</u> the Light. Finally he did and the Light left along with the entity. But stranger still were the rope marks that appeared around my neck as I physically experienced his hanging, actually feeling the heat and the constraints around my neck. Very unpleasant but it soon passed.

Jill, the medium who released the entity, was from London and a friend of Ken Baker.[3] She revealed that something wonderful would happen to me when I reached thirty. This was a couple of years away and I was impatient to know but she just smiled and repeated, 'It will all begin when you reach the age of thirty!'

For months afterwards I felt incredibly alone, because having an entity is a strange experience. Always an awareness of the presence of someone so I held a conversation with it, not realising I was conversing with it mentally, it was just something I did. Today I refer to it as my inner dialogue and it has done me a great service in

---

[3] www.britishalliancehealingassociations.com

many respects. I realised my inner dialogue was inappropriate as I would discuss my inner angers, my inner anxieties, my need for sex, whatever it was would be discussed. I could have used a much better inner dialogue to enhance my wellbeing, I didn't then but do now.

I reached the defining year of thirty. Ken mentioned there would be something to do with channeling but I wasn't particularly interested, having witnessed the kind of mediumship used in the Spiritualist church it was definitely not for me, and certainly didn't understand what channeling entailed. My interests lay in finding out where we came from, what we are here for, what happens on other planets and do we really have extra-terrestrial visitors. Indeed a knowledge of a different kind.

1994

I was now married to Helen and living in Kent. As a self-employed builder I had an opportunity to work for friends in London, which meant getting up very early to avoid the rush hour traffic. Once home I looked forward to a long relaxing soak in the bath to relieve the stresses of the day and on one particular evening the pressures in my head had built to such a crescendo it felt as if my head was in a vice. Strange words began spewing out of my mouth and the terrible thought crossed my mind that perhaps I was going mad. What on earth was happening to me? Ludicrous words kept coming, over which I had no control and no idea what was occurring, but I was made aware that something was happening that day.

I knew something was desperately wrong. There was trouble in my life with anger issues and my temper flared very easily. The early years of marriage were very difficult because my wife has the hot temperament of her Greek ancestry that led to fiery outbursts between us. This was a hard lesson for both of us as we grew into our marriage.

1995

A chance came to visit the Isle of Wight in July 1995, a month after my thirtieth birthday, and my life was never to be the same again. As Jill had prophesied something wonderful did happen, the **Elders of Zor** made their presence known... Carolyn has written of what happened on that momentous day.

So the channeling began. I was just thirty and beginning my life's work, but totally unprepared for nineteen years of roller-coaster rides of emotions, discomfort, misunderstandings, misinterpretations and misperceptions. The fact that nobody really read what I was channeling, apart from myself and Carolyn and a few others, often made me question the validity of the contents.

What was the purpose of those reams of information? Who was channeling through me, and was it positive? Coming to terms with all this was not an easy task. There is no such thing as a happy medium! How true these words are.

The journey has not always been enjoyable. When channeling and working with those eccentric non-human energies you become something other than human. As you are incorporated by another energy that is moving down and working through your vibration you are no longer in human form at that point. Your cells change, you can actually feel yourself step aside as the words begin to flow, but you are listening to them as your apparatus is being used to bring these words through.

But you are only channeling for a short while and for the rest of the time you are a human being, housed in flesh and subject to the rules and regulations of being in flesh – the laws of energy, the laws of attraction, the flow and return, and so on. Regardless of being a gifted medium, healer or channel, the challenges of physical life are the same as for anyone else.

You do have to utilise the knowledge from the information, to become the information is the way it has been expressed. Many people are gifted with knowledge yet if not practiced they will only get so far and no further. I have had to re-evaluate my life with regards to my knowledge. It took me many years to realise I needed to listen to the importance of the information because it manifests a change within. Words are catalysts for change. There are words within the words that allow us to perceive a new understanding.

If we create a framework around knowledge it is tantamount to placing a castle wall and a moat around it. You then stay within the confines of that knowledge and don't stretch your mind to move with it. Knowledge has to be fluid, it needs to constantly change like water it should be fluid, as should your acceptance of knowledge.

My belief system has been pushed to the limit and there have been times when I haven't wanted to channel. In fact I almost spat the words out in disgust on to a tape for Carolyn to transcribe again and again. Only now do I understand these channeled words have immeasurable merit. Carolyn brings reference to the information, because much has been given out of time sequence in advance. Data given ten years ago is beginning to come to fruition now. She recently brought to my attention some material given on 1.3.1996 that is totally relevant to this point in time.

"You are well aware of the areas that will precede with the changes. **Egypt** and **Syria** are the places as and where the initial changes in Earth's structures will occur. Your element of humane being will be the initial changes, you must then realise that the changes will then be in Mother Earth's hands.

You are being given the information of the initial changes for your planet so we can start repolarizing the human mind.... Your group is being used for the information for forwarding man's advancement <u>after</u> the changes.... Your information is held within your minds and when you are ready to understand and talk and dictate on these levels you will be given the source to do so."

These words are categorically to do with the present time. Carolyn is the reference holder, I am the voice. She is the library and I feel very honoured to have a librarian, a curator of this knowledge who actually holds it for its worth.

At times I have definitely felt unworthy of this information, and sometimes it has made me so sick because of my refusal to comply and finally being compelled to speak. Being a channel has been very problematic and challenging and entailed experiencing a whole gamut of unwanted emotions. Helen is a lapsed catholic and does not practice the same set of beliefs as myself yet has been steadfastly loyal throughout, a very worldly person who does very worldly things. There were times I wished she could have been on my cloud but instead has been my balance and kept me firmly grounded. Her love and normality has kept me sane over the years.

When did I start really listening to the words? To be honest only recently. In the early days it was like thick soup and frankly I found the information quite boring and laborious to read, and when Carolyn returned the transcription I often didn't read it. The files stacked up and occasionally I would come across one, read it and remember the sensation of those words as they fell from my mouth. How things have changed for me as a channel in the last nineteen years.

The Preparation.

Prior to the commencement of the channeling there had been much physical preparation. I was being prepared to be a channel, prepared to be a voice. But prepared for what? Many times I questioned this, but when I read the information and finally understand the lucrative knowledge that stands between me and its words I know this has not come from my conscious domain of thinking. It may well have come from somewhere deep within me but certain words and explanations are not my way of using language, therefore I have to accept that it has come from elsewhere.

2002 Robin meets with Dolores Cannon

I first met Dolores Cannon, a regressive hypnotherapist and world-renowned speaker, in Glastonbury in July 2002 where she was speaking at the Glastonbury Crop Circle Conference.[4] Answers about my personal life had not been forthcoming via the channeling and I knew she was able to connect with information held deep within the subconscious. However as Dolores began the session an entity immediately started communicating some very difficult information for her. This was the first time she had regressed someone who had never had a human life so there was no karmic involvement with previous lives.

In Dolores' own words:

———————————

"This entity turned out to be different in several ways from the ones I was used to conversing with in this state. This one used words and complicated terminology that was difficult to understand and it created new words. It described Robin as a different type of human and it made me feel uncomfortable and was difficult and tedious to converse with."

The entity speaking through Robin explains:

"The child is a multi-dimensional frequency. He has so much relevance to do with the past, the present and the future. There is so much information to be had with regards to this. This information is so paramount and the burden it places upon the young child is sometimes immense, but the importance of this information needs to be transformed into a vibrational energy frequency so that the repolarisation of humanity and the poles in which he works can create a new process of free structuring.

The child is not a child, the child is a component of this energy. The child is a reality behind your human format but the reality behind the child is he is a composite of energy and that energy my children is the relevance behind the changes that man's body, spirit, mind and physicality is part of.

The fight between the three-dimensional and the non-physical is a very difficult one, because there is a fight within this humane frequency and until that fight desists the child will continue with the pain. The non-knowledge is what is required."

This episode referred directly to Robin's continued early reluctance to channel and explains the reason for his suffering.[5] Even Dolores had difficulty with the wording when transcribing her tape and had to condense and clarify some of it for her book but the complete transcription is in our files. It should be made clear, that Dolores is not a channel; she uses her own particular method of hypnosis by which she is able to contact what she refers to as the Subconscious, her name for it. She explains:

"It is actually like communicating with a computer terminal connected to a giant database. The database transcends time, space and all limitations of individual consciousness. I always seem to be speaking to the same part (or entity or whatever it is), a part that I have now discovered to be all-knowing. It not only has the answers the client is seeking, it has answers about anything I wish to ask. An all-knowing part of something that has access to all information. Some people may choose to call this the Total Self, the Higher Self, the Oversoul, Jung's Collective Unconscious, or God. These could all be relating to the same thing under different names. In my work it responds to the name of

---

[5] The whole session is recorded in *The Convoluted Universe: Book Two* under the chapter *The First of Seven.*

Subconscious... it is like having access to the grandest library of them all."

The Subconscious/Entity continued:

"There are not many of these children on this planet, we state the parameter of five to seven children doing the correct work at this point in time with regards to the elongation of the mind. We have sent <u>seven disciples</u> now to this planet to elongate, to stretch. There is going to be a three and there will be a four, they will all meet at some point but the three will not know the four and the four will not know the three. As and when you come across them Dolores you must not mention one to another in a physical sense, you can talk subliminally but you must not talk on a physical sense. It will interfere with the energies, because they are carrying the same energies but they are using different formulas. Bearing in mind, the ethnic breeding is different, they carry different energies so therefore southern and eastern and western and northern hemisphere energies are not totally conducive with each other on the planet, so therefore you must not mention. You will know subliminally immediately when you meet one of the others.

Energies interfere with energies. What you have is a connection via a subliminal thought-form process that is connected via one spiral of energy. If you connect one to the other you can fuse the two together and dilute the information and dilution would not be conducive to the thought format creational purpose behind the energy so therefore introducing one to the other doing the same work would confuse.

The seven are vibrating at a different frequency, they are not bound by karma and they are on a specific assignment."

Robin's reluctance to channel was commented on here.

'The resilience with which you abstain from your work is quite tremendous. Your abstinence has created an incorrect procedure within your body and you must understand that if you do not use one energy it will be converted to another so therefore you work yourself into a procedure. It is time to find that balance as you well know so as you move forward in balance the retribution for one action will not be the retribution for another. It is the law of cause and effect that you attract to yourself. As energy coexists within your system you will attract other energy of the same frequency, it is part of the laws you preach my child, but unless you teach them to yourself you will have these laws attracted to yourself.

The contact that you feel so many times are people jogging you in a direction you are not yet willing to go in but you <u>will</u> go in, and you will continue with abstinence until you realise this abstinence is there for a reason. You will not kick forward until you have kicked back and relinquished yourself of the angst of the past'.

I was still kicking and fighting and challenging whether or not to channel at the commencement of Words in

Transformation nine years later in December 2011 as is evident from the following:

"I have been feeling unwell today. Had a major collapse on the floor with spasms and all sorts of discomfort so something is amiss ... however we shall work this one out."

That is how I used to feel and often wondered if my body had a genuine illness that medical intervention could explain, or was it trapped energy within me that was not being released by expression? I need to comprehend what I do as a channel.

2005 The move to Ireland

After forty years in the UK life brought me to West Cork in Ireland. Having spent family holidays there in the 70s I loved this beautiful mountainous area of the country. In the early days there was little communication with the family because we had bought Gabriel's Return, a plot of three acres of land with three Irish ruins, a workshop with the only roof, no telephone lines and very little money. We had gone from very fast internet in the UK to a telephone in the house we rented for a short while as I prepared the workshop to be our home. Celebrating my fortieth birthday listening to music in a bar in Schull the realization came that I was happy, possibly for the first time in my life.

I never felt at home anywhere. Perhaps that is why we were constantly on the move during the early years of our marriage. We bought and sold houses and certainly didn't invest our money wisely but enjoyed ourselves having some fine holidays. Of course this was all before children. We now have two daughters and life is very different.

At last I had found my home and embraced life with vigour. Building Gabriel's Return single-handed, a large four bedroom family house, took an enormous amount of energy and I became a workaholic, setting myself impossible tasks to meet each day then another impossible task for the following day and did the same thing day after day. Sundays were my time off and all I really wanted was to spend the day in bed but the family needed my attention. I was so tired and exhausted there was no energy left to play or converse with them, I had lost my zest for life. But we wouldn't have a roof over our heads if I hadn't built it, there was no option.

This also gave me time off from channeling and there was a long period when I didn't channel very often at all. My whole energy went into the fabric of building Gabriel's Return, creating a vegetable garden, an orchard, caring for sheep, erecting a poly-tunnel, slating the roof, rendering the outside, surfacing the drive, and being a father and a husband. That was my life then and it is these mundane things that teach us the essence of being a human being.

Yes I am a human being. I may well have come from somewhere else, as we all have, but my flesh is no different – my fingers bleed when I work with them, my heart bleeds when I stop loving, and my head hurts if I drink too much beer, just like everyone else. I am also a channel and my body rebels if I don't channel.

Clonakilty Dreaming

In April 2006 I was so exhausted after building the house that Helen forced me to have some time out on my own. I went reluctantly on retreat to Clonakilty to refuel my energy and find myself again. It was during this time alone with nature these verses came as I lay on the beach.

When you have worked your fingers down to the bone
And every spit just hits a stone.
There is nothing left in the tank,
There is no one around to thank

And the time has come for you to lay down your arms.
Your loving life, your humorous charms,
They've gone in a gust of wind
Your life has blown so you rescind.

We walk in faith, our loving charms,

Our life becomes our own demands.
What is it that you sought dear boy
It is your life, your love, the joy?

When you've become what you are now
You have become nothing, just a plough.
The plough is the thing that sows the land
But you do not think or understand.

The residue that is now left
Is you, legs and arms with nothing but your breath.
So take away that feeling of lust
And go into your mind and think of your trust.

Your trust takes you on your journey,
It is your life my boy, your life. The tree,
The roots, the son of God
Is what you are here against all odds.

So you must but give the loving trust,
The one that was given to you, a must.
The must, my child, is where you go.
The trust, my child, is what you do not yet know.

So when you stand in your own might
You can but begin to understand the fight,
The fight that you chose from the spark of Divinity.
My child, you are not just from your family tree.

You are here to take on the loving charms,

The man, the boy, the boy in arms.
My child, as you take on your response-ability
You are here, not just part of that family tree.

Move in fight, move in chance,
Watch my son the way you demand
You are but here to move with trust
The fight is no longer a must.

Put yourself in the loving arms
That have no demands,
You are here to understand my child.
In a while my child, in a while you will
Understand you are here to thrill.
Take on the choice, take on the trust,
You are here my child, it is a must.

I had been fighting my destiny for so long and continued to do so until it became a matter of life and death when I literally had to pick up the mantle I chose to wear during this lifetime or return to Source. There really was no choice. Building Gabriel's Return had been a distraction in one way but now the choice was mine.

Source does not see the separation between life and death as we humans do. It is just a change of cells as our existence continues elsewhere.

After all this physical exertion my head began hurting again. Carolyn's wise counsel came to mind, '*Robin, if you fill a vase up too far it will spill over but if there is a lid on the top it will explode and that is what happens to your head if you don't channel. So start channeling again.*' I did, but not with a good heart, I felt forced. Why should I have to channel, it gets in the way, I wanted to do normal things, I wanted to be a human being and learn how to converse properly, I didn't want to pretend to imitate that mentality, I actually wanted to do it.

So I worked at being human. I learnt to become a sportsman, to go out running, cycling and swimming, became involved in triathlons and groups of people and friends with common interests and rekindled my relationship with my brother Tim. Until I could talk about sport I didn't really have a relationship with him as sport is my brother's life, we now have so much in common but he doesn't understand and has no idea what I do. I am not comfortable with my unkind treatment of my younger sister Rebecca as we grew up, too much sibling rivalry, but things are better now. My mother always loved and supported me throughout my difficult times but has only recently come to understand who and what I am.

I am yet to find on any gravestone '*I wish I'd spent more time at work!*' Money means nothing if you have no love; it matters not how well you have done in business, how much you have in the bank, what kind of house you own or how many cars you have in the garage. What really matters is how you treat others, how you look after yourself and your body, how caring you are and what thoughts you entertain. Love is the key to all transformation.

It is difficult to be constantly good and kind, after all we are human and emotions play through us all the time. We get angry during moments of stress and show a side to others that can be unkind and hurtful, it is just a matter of finding the balance. I now accept that being a channel is part of my life and recently my daughters have been enquiring about my work and what it is I do when I speak into recorders. They are asking some of the same questions I once asked Carolyn and they need an explanation as to what channeling is all about because it is my job. And finally, after twenty years, I have learned to love the words and verses spoken through me.

As previously mentioned the first communication came from beings that called themselves the *Elders of Zor* who were concerned that their planet was being affected by man's continual abuse of Earth, the skies above and the waters below. Yet, however, who else was communicating with us and what was the source of our information? The following was received in 1995 and gave us some idea:

"Your group is developing a following of entities required to give the relevant answers you will need as and when. There are the extra-terrestrials, the etheric beings, the gods and the Pleiadians, all of which are connected with the cosmic thinking that we are trying to project to you. The

medium Arris is the communicator to you, he will receive your questions and the answers will be given from the relevant beings. Many people enter your realms and many more wish to do so."[6]

The channeling has stated that I am an alien soul in a human frame and have come from another dimension where the process is that of love but am now on planet Earth and suffering the consequences of being human.

Earth is a planet of free will and the opportunity is available to do exactly as we please, and we do, but there are consequences to every action. This planet allows all things to occur in many places at one point in time. There are human beings experiencing every form of emotion, every set of evolutionary cycles or devolutionary cycles all at once. As a consequence we have been distracted from our original purpose and reason for being here and need some help to get back on track. This is the purpose of the channelled material.

Throughout the world there are changes occurring because we no longer have the ability to see what change we need. Our eyes only see the need for more money, more status, more adulation, we live in a celebrity culture and have lost our sense of reason, our sense of *being*. What is required is a prompt towards something important.

---

[6] Arris has never had a <u>human</u> experience but is referred to, as 'a brave man' so is obviously male.

And what is so important? It is crucial that the bees keep pollinating the plants, the rivers keep flowing along their courses and not flooding the countryside, the seas stabilise and don't encroach on the land, and that we don't have catastrophic changes throughout our planet that eliminate much of our population. This happened in the past with the Atlantean and Lemurian civilisations where just a few survived the sinking of those continents.

When individuals are overcome by catastrophes they become more compassionate and caring towards one another, but gradually, as more and more people return to the planet, the whole process of self will begins to surface once again. The disasters have always been external but it appears that internal cataclysms are also happening now. There are tumultuous changes going on within and outside our bodies that are needed. We need to change on a *cellular level* in order to have the ability to take on *new cells carrying new information.* Way-showers are necessary for this and it is said this is my job. Maybe the words that come out of my mouth, over which I have very little control, might have something to do with this and will be valuable to those who wish to listen and absorb these teachings.

I am given to understand that *I have had no previous lives on Earth and am alien to this planet.* I may have come from a different planet, where the blood was cold instead of warm, but what we are all doing is vibrating on some level of love, gathering experience for the Godhead.

There is mention of our cosmic family when speaking about different planets. They may be of a different shape, from a different dimension, of different breeding and thinking, but they are all under the guise of God's love.

The channeling for me has now taken on a new life and has very much become part of who I am, it is not a separate thing as I have tried to make it in the past. If you were a gifted artist or sculptor would you deny yourself this gift?

I am now becoming who I am and embracing this in a positive way. My channeling is no longer a chore but a chosen asset that I need to try and learn from and grow with. This I must do with love in my heart as well as the spirit of pushing my boundaries. The brave pioneers that travelled to unexplored lands must have felt much the same.

Part One

Chapter One

Enchantment by words

Story telling holds the Magic & Healing Power of Words!

Why *Words in Transformation?*

It is through words that we communicate with one another on a daily basis, and yet, there is much *power* in the spoken word. For not only do words have the power to heal and the power to harm, but also, and more importantly, words have the power to *transform*.

Humanity, as we know it, is on a downward spiral and requires help. To reverse the madness being perpetrated on the Earth today, these transformative words of wisdom have been relayed and received from an *extra-kosmic* dimension. These *words* are therefore from beyond our third dimension and offer to us a message of guidance – from out of this prison we currently understand as conscious reality.

I am a story-teller and long ago I *realised* that words are not just about what they appear to mean. They are letters placed together, and yet, when vocalised and vibrated in the correct manner, these words *resonate* within the listener and promote a profound alteration of the mind.

Mind-sets are the development and result of our *belief systems*, and yet, belief is not in itself *knowledge*. Belief is merely the way one thinks about something that has been acquired through education, religion, and indeed the society that one is living in at that particular point of one's journey through life. What is therefore a belief for one individual at one particular point in time, is not necessarily so for another. *Knowledge,* on the other hand, is however, something completely different altogether.[7]

When you experience a sense of *knowing within,* it is because your entire being resonates with that which is being received. For not only do the words enchant and enrapture the individual, but they are also predominantly to do more specifically with *spell*-ing. This preliminary manifestation will result in how an individual responds to the *Art.* However, not unlike a Painter, this extraordinary Art works itself out through Enchantment of the He*art.*

Enchantment and the Heart

Enchantment ... Chant ... to intone words in a particular way, through order and rhythm, words that speak to the heart, the heart then resonates with Knowing ... the heart becomes truly *enchanted.*

The heart is connected to the metaphysical light body and this in turn is connected to the *Source.* Knowledge at this heart level will create a profound truth, one that is relevant for you now.

---

[7] It has been suggested that *knowledge* is a form of 'justified true belief' – but one might ask of what?

What then is *truth*? Truth is a resonance within. There are as many *truths* as there are individuals. And yet, what may have been true for you at one point in time may no longer ring true today, because the *ascent* to knowledge brings with it a greater understanding, and this in turn alters one's perception of truth. Truth is then ever present, but our ability to see it clearly has become shrouded through misperception and this can only lead to a certain misunderstanding.

We were instructed via the *channel* about the use of resonance and words by organised religions. This method of control was perpetuated in order to keep people in their place! Priesthoods have not only understood the power and resonance of words, but have been taught how to project sounds in order to gain the maximum effect and response from their congregations. This has enabled them to maintain and maximise their power as so-called intermediaries between God and individuals.

In-divide-you-all! We are all *individual* particles of the same God-source; yet, we are all as such *in-divide*. We are all *in-divide*, that is, until a state of realisation is reached; whereby, unity with the *One* releases the need for the priest. However, this is not expedient for religion to teach as such. The *spelling* of the *individual* has been maintained thus leaving humanity enslaved to a false god.

The Pen is Mightier than the Sword

Words in Transformation is part of a record of knowledge obtained via the voice of Robin Wells over a period of twenty years. Robin is a medium, a psychic-healer, poet, musician and an oracle through which teaching is received.

"He is a multidimensional frequency that carries an immense amount of knowledge which is gradually being transduced down via the levels, through to a three dimensional frequency. This child can vibrate this knowledge in a vocal format."

By way of a short explanation, Robin therefore receives extra-*kosmic* vibrations and channels them through to the mundane level. However, the 'message' retains its extra-*kosmic* originality, and hence through the voice to pen and paper become in essence *words in transformation.*

The title of this work *Words in Transformation* was channelled through him one evening after the source of these words suggested it was time to write a book. We had prepared manuscripts in the past about previous information – *Beyond the Clouds* and *The Evolving Spiral* – but nothing transpired, possibly due to our lack of knowhow as to getting them edited and published, so they are still collecting dust on my bookshelf. But now, the voice insists that it is time to get these words to print and out into the public domain. The reason we have been given the task at this point to publish a book is that many changes are imminent both for the planet and indeed mankind.

Humanity needs to be made aware of the possible timelines available and given the choice. We understand that the source of this knowledge has come from beings that dwell in realms above and beyond our limited three-dimensional *Kosmos* and who have the welfare of our planet and mankind in their best interest. They are therefore our kin from beyond the clouds and we are part of their family, hence their concern. The reason for their intervention is that because somewhere along the line we have been led astray and veered from the path originally set for us. There have been many distractions and it is now time to get back on track.

So, *Words in Transformation* is about the transformative power of words to alter the mind-set of man. It is proposed that these words will bring about a change that is so desperately needed. That is, if we are going to be able to survive the atrocities that are happening to our planet – we need to absorb and become the information that is transduced because knowledge is mere empty words, that is, if it is not exemplified.

Fundamental to this message is that of the restoration of the *divine feminine*. This is of paramount importance, especially in a world that is dominated by the negative imbalance, created through a masculine and logic-driven current. It is therefore about bringing love, care and compassion into a world of greed, anger and perpetual war. And most importantly, it is about the restoration of our *soul* into the *tri-unity* of *mind, soul and body*. In so doing, we can reconnect with the source of the Godhead and the original from whence we come.

Chapter Two
Who am I?

...Just a Storyteller

For myself, I am the storyteller, a teller of tales of the magical and mystical world that we live in. Many people are unaware of this realm and it seems that I have been given this job in order to acquaint them.

One evening Robin was channeling with Mary Maddison (see further) in her cottage on the Beara Peninsula in West Cork while I was at home on the Isle of Wight tuning in at the same time. When transcribing the tape a few days later

I heard these words of explanation about our work together.

"The lady (Carolyn) that sits so gently with you this evening is the transcender of information. She transmutes this into the written word. She does it so well with beauty and love and care and she rejoices in the words and sounds that are created by the verses. We rejoice my child with the work that you provide, it is like butterflies of rainbows flying out into the universe when we hear your rejoicing with the love and compassion that these words offer you and those around you. The two (Robin and Mary) that sit here are the workers, they are like the worker bees in the hive, they go out and get and gather and transcend. The mother that sits, she is like the Queen Bee, she gathers that information and holds it tight to her and allows it to transcend into other formats. That is your job my dear lady."

Influences from the Past

In ancient cultures knowledge was understood and handed down from generation to generation by word of mouth by the story tellers, the wise men and women who carried the information within their very cells. They taught the Way of wisdom and love and became exemplars of the knowledge.

Sadly, the Caesars and the Roman Church decided they alone would be the repositories for ancient world knowledge and gradually those who held this sacred and true knowledge regarding the wisdom of the stars along with that of the ancestral masters and true teachings of Jesus were sacrificed to the will of a vengeful god.

And so a socio-political religious institution was brought about that tortured and slaughtered those who held the truth of these original teachings such as the ill-starred Cathars of the Languedoc area of France. They held similar beliefs and practices to the Neoplatonists, Hermeticists and Gnostics that predated the so-called innovations of the Catholic Church. For example, Hermeticists' believe that divine or self-knowledge (*gnosis*) is granted only to those who can dip themselves in the *krater* or *monad*, which is full of *nous* (mind).[8]

The Cathars were an anathema to the established church of Rome and their teachings were considered heretical being based on Gnosticism. Jesus had taught these sacred or hidden teachings to an inner circle of disciples, which included women.

Legend has it that Mary Magdalene, the favourite of Jesus, brought these pure teachings to the Languedoc after the 'cruci*fixion*', where they continued to be taught orally. As knowledge spread, it undermined the power of the church and the Languedoc saw the first act of European genocide when over 100,000 members of the Cathar heresy were massacred on orders of the pope during the Albigensian

---

[8] Cf. **Corpus Hermeticum IV** *A Discourse of Hermes to Tat: The Krater or Monad.*

crusade in the thirteenth century, which was to ravage the area for forty years.[9]

The cultures of the indigenous peoples were annihilated, their sacred lands violated, their children stolen and their way of life destroyed, forcibly replacing it with a false god (compare the Christianisation of the Amerindians, the Australian Aboriginals and the Native American Indians by the missionaries sent out by the Catholic Church, and all the associated abusive horrors that are re-surfacing today).

The Church persecuted the pagans and took over their holy sites. These sites were 'vortices of power' and it was from these sites that the so-called pagans had communed with *beings from the stars*, and from whom they had received secret wisdom teaching.

Avebury Henge is a fine example of the destruction of a major sacred power point of the early inhabitants of Britain. There is now a village built right inside the circle of power so the ancient energy frequencies are no longer working as they should, many of the stones have been removed, broken up, and re-used in the construction of local houses and streets.

The earliest part of Avebury church dates from AD 1000. The Saxons feared the magical powers of the stone circles and carefully sited their church near to them in order to counteract their supposed malevolence.

---

[9] Cf. *The Templar Revelation* by Lynn Picknett and Clive Prince.

When Margo and I visited Avebury in 1992 she walked past one of the monoliths and experienced a time-slip into the past where, as a priestess, her assigned task was as keeper and protector of one of the very large remaining stones that she had to keep clean and polished so that it shone. Each stone had a custodian responsible for its wellbeing and these were the priestesses who assisted in the ceremonial worship enacted there.

Roman churches were built over these pagan sites to procure the power for themselves and then the true knowledge was intentionally misrepresented to create power and wealth for the people running them, and to instil fear in the masses. The church has held sway over the minds of the people for far too long and today we see a falling away in the congregations as people are no longer fed spiritually by those who say they have the authority to feed their flock.

According to John Matthews:

"When a received tradition begins to petrify, losing its original cutting edge of truth in a tangle of dogmas it becomes time for an esoteric tradition to arise by which the great truths may not perish but be revivified and transmitted to further generations. When the established hierarchy fails in its duty it is as though the angelic powers inspirit humankind to produce those who will continue them. These are the people who stand in direct communication with the will of God... the mystics... the storytellers... the

heretics... who formulate alternatives to the established ways of belief."[10]

Compare the following from our own received words:

"*How can we expect teachings from two thousand years ago to be of real relevance today when things have changed so drastically? Can we surely not understand why your disciples of your churches are becoming rather... I can't describe the words I feel for some of your shops. Shops! Yes* shops, *for the teachings of our Lord the Christ. Are they not selling a product now rather than giving of free will? Are they not asking you to give yourself totally to a cause when you need to give of yourself within yourself to understand yourself so that you can then understand others?*

We have not mentioned before the Christian beliefs and understandings but I believe that Christianity and the belief structure of humanity is an important thing. None of the manifestations of the Christ-force were put here to misdirect humanity's thinking, they were always put there at the right time to provide a catalyst for humanity to develop from.

The Christ Consciousness is within the changes. Can you not understand the Christ Consciousness within this new millennium will be in your conscious thinking to be tapped into. The Christ realised on his last visit that he was wasting much energy in trying to teach many deaf ears when only a

---

[10] Cf. *The Grail Tradition* by John Matthews

few very bright ears were prepared to listen, and unfortunately misinterpretation of many of the teachings were created, hence your book the *Christ Bible*

We do not have time nor the inclinations for this 'children's bible' as I would put it. Much has been altered and changed to suit your shops called the churches to interpret what they required for the manifestation of well-being for the people that run these shops. I bid you that these unfortunate fellows will not only have a further 2000 years of the re-creation of the physical form, I think they may have 4000!

Can you understand that the misguidance of the masses by the singular being cannot be accepted in any form?

The Christ Consciousness is now within the spiritual movement that is working towards the transitional change. He is there in every molecule of positive thinking. You are all now disciples following the Christ Consciousness.

We must always never venture too far away from the fact that spirituality runs always along the lines of God Consciousness and if it develops away from these two single lines then you are off the rails. Always remember the Christ Consciousness is behind the manifestation of the changes. He is not the creation of the changes; he is behind the thinking of the changes. The Christ is born in each individual mind of Light and is available for that thinking."

Inspiration is needed

So once more we are back to the mind-set of humanity and conditional thinking that through no fault of its own has been perverted from the true teachings of the Christ. Jesus carried the consciousness of the Christ, as did the Buddha and Muhammad. Jesus admonished the people to *love* God and *love* one another, but we have been manipulated by this socio-political religious system towards a path that has led to power and wealth for the few and very little joy for the remainder. This was not the purpose for man and it is the time for the mystics, the storytellers and the heretics to be heard.

The inspiration from the God-source is within these channelled words and the Star Beings are communicating to this *mystic* 'child':

'They bring non-knowledge to feed the soul of man, which is not available to humanity at this point in time. It is going to give consciousness a whole new sparkle within those that mix with you and those that venture into the realms of your conversation and your divine thoughts that will be given to you in the future, the past and the present."

What is the change?

The words speak of the transition that is bringing great changes within our bodies and upon the earth, they speak of how we have lost the Way and need the Way-showers, they speak of care and compassion and Love, they speak of Jesus the man, and they speak of the Christ.

One of the universal laws is non-interference with what beings on other planets are doing, consequently as they cannot intervene from outside some of these *Star Beings* have chosen to incarnate in human bodies to work from the inside for the purpose of altering man's consciousness and aggressive mind-set. We understand that Robin is one of the *Way-showers* who has come with this specific purpose.

Who are the Star-beings?

Star beings have been watching all that has been happening on Earth since time began and communicating with their chosen ones. They come from other planets, dimensions and galaxies and at times have incarnated to assist in the spiritual development of man. Those extra-terrestrials who visited during the time of the Egyptian Dynasties have been called gods, for want of a better understanding, as their life span can be hundreds of years in comparison with that of humanity. They know and utilise the process of rejuvenation through light-works.[11]

---

[11] Mary witnessed this in the crystal work we did with Margo where both slipped in time and experienced the effect of light on individuals within a pyramid where those individuals were transformed and rejuvenated.

Robin's soul has been visiting and observing Earth for millennia but this time it was necessary to incarnate in human form. A foetus was therefore prepared as a vehicle for his soul. The child that was born has an 'alien' soul and its purpose here is to carry out a specific task at this particular time.[12]

The communicators bringing this information are beings, not necessarily physical, from other star systems that have contracted to teach humanity through the voice of one of their representatives here on Earth, one such as Robin, but he is not the only one.

However, Earth remains a planet of choice and free will where we can choose to experience anything from extreme wickedness to supreme goodness, and everything in between. Yet, there are always consequences to our actions. So perhaps it is better to *do as you would be done by* rather than *be done by as you did* as Charles Kingsley wrote in his work *The Water Babies.* This is the biblical principal known as the *Golden Rule 'Do to others as you would have them do to you'* (Luke 6 v.31).

A time for choice

So every individual is being asked to make the choice as to whether they are willing to accept a new value system, a

---

[12] Cf. Dolores Cannon *The Convoluted Universe* Book Two, with specific reference to Robert (who is actually Robin) in Chapter 13.

change of consciousness towards love, care and compassion rather than selfishness and greed. The whole of the solar system is looking down upon planet Earth wondering what will happen next and waiting to see whether man can make this step-up in consciousness. Will he choose to transcend from one spot to the next and take a new energy field, a new understanding, by allowing his cells to extend into a new matrix of thinking or does he stay exactly where he is?

The time is fast approaching when we will no longer have a choice. It is the time of the *quickening* when those who choose to raise their vibration will move to the new frequency and those that don't will remain behind with the old vibrational power structure of self before others.

The revealed information speaks of change in every respect. Humanity has veered from its original purpose and requires a new directive to get us back on track. This directive is coming via the souls of children who have chosen to incarnate in human bodies but originate from other star systems with the sole purpose of assisting in the evolutionary consciousness of man towards the balance of nature.[13]

The Balance of Nature:

"What is happening is the balance required for nature is becoming out of balance by some of the needs that were

---

[13] See Dolores Cannon's *Convoluted Universe* Series

originally formatted and required. Man is overbalancing, overcompensating for the need for nature so therefore nature will overcompensate and bring man into balance and will eventually create the balance it needs. How can it do that?

We will tell you how nature eventually creates the balance it needs.

Look at man as furniture. Furniture is required within a household to supply comfort and need but if there is too much man will remove it or strip it down to basics. Understand that man is surplus to requirements if he pushes the boundaries of what nature needs, so nature is just requiring a balance.

The thought patterns of man were originally created to serve the balance of nature. But man has become disconnected from nature, from his nutritional connectivity to the planet, and is nullified but still living yet without connectivity to our life source. So as a human race we need to reconnect and re-join the joy and love processes we came in with originally. This will all happen when we decide what it is we are going to be."

Choices and a Course of Action – the Return

That is the choice we have and the reason why so many star-seeds are incarnating here. Humanity requires help to restore its original purpose as keepers of the garden of Mother Earth and move to a new vibrational frequency.

Man has abused her (nature) almost to the point of destruction and this cannot continue. Therefore the story needs telling.

History – *his story* – has been told long enough and his story is the wicked lies and deceit of the war-mongering victors. It is time for Mystery – *my story* – to be told of the connection we have to the stars, to love and to the God-source, the fountain of all truth that feeds our soul.

It is the return of the feminine to balance the masculine that has run amok. The Goddess energy that the old cultures understood so well was removed by the Church and is required to be reinstated to bring Mother Nature back into balance. And if we are not prepared to listen to her she has the power to give mankind a pretty hard and uncomfortable ride.

Fore-warned is to be fore-armed, and time is short. It is all about consciousness and our conscious choice as to which side of the fence we choose to be on. Love or hate, care or indifference, compassion or hard-heartedness, those are the choices we have and here is the information from the star people. Their words are here to transform you. Therefore my task as the storyteller is to simply give these *words of transformation* with love.

Glimpses of a mystical Life

This story began with my conception and I learned many years later it was a life ordained by my own choice.

According to the channeling I needed to be here and took the first vehicle available, which was in a feminine body conceived out of wedlock...it seems I was in that much of a hurry!

There were people already incarnate and I needed to meet them. My path was therefore set and so began my spiritual and cosmic journey to seek information and teach it to those whose consciousness was open.

Time was of the essence so it was vital for me to be born at that precise moment – on the sixth of December at six minutes to midnight 1936.[14] Although my mother may not

---

[14] Born under the sign of Sagittarius, the seeker, and programmed with the Jesus consciousness at birth according to the channel
ing 19.8.1997. I asked the question "Where does Jesus stand in all this?" and the answer I received was: *'Thank you my child for asking the valid question. As at Christmas time all children expect their saint, St Nicholas to visit, this was a formula that was set in their mind programming on the very first day of their birth, Jesus was programmed within your subconscious before your birth to allow you to tune into the energies that he left, and I might add he left in many places, for you to tune into. Many people will be working with the Jesus consciousness because he left much information for the peoples of the planet if they so tuned. Remember my child that if you do not tune into the consciousness that he left, the knowledge, the words, the keys, you cannot use that as a catalyst. We wish you to know that very few are tuning into the consciousness that he left. The keys and the programming that allowed you to access this information has been monitored, has been encapsulated by unfortunate people who are very blocked in their childish views. They know where the information lays and encapsulate it with their negative thought-forms which block you*

have understood it this way it was necessary for me to reconnect not only with my father, but also with *Margo Williams, Mary Maddison* and my nephew *Robin Wells.* So my soul *re-entered* the world on December 6th, the celebratory day of St Nicholas, known as Santa Claus, *the giver of gifts.*

My gift has been knowledge. The wisdom accrued from that knowing is the gift now presented in these words. Sometimes the words are mine, most notably when inspiration floods from my mind, yet others however come through friends and companions who are in touch with their higher selves. Some words come from *earthbound spirits* and *extra-terrestrials,* but the greatest source is that of *Kosmic knowledge,* which comes directly from those 'knowingly', working with the *Divine Source* we know as the Godhead.

This mystical information has been gleaned over the past four decades and it is time to reveal the secret and sacred unseen worlds that surround us. This is, after all, where we receive our inspiration from, and indeed our very breath ... the Godhead.

---

from going to these places. These thought-forms are being retracted now due to the consciousness and the polarity changes within the planet. Beware of false doctrines and dogmas my children and also leave yourself open to the positive consciousness that will be allocated to many if you choose.

Chapter Three

Oracles & Influence

The Oracle: Margo Williams

To be clear, I owe a great deal of my received knowledge to the powers of three specific *oracles.*[15]

Many years ago it was my good fortune to encounter and become friends with the first of my *oracles - Margo*

---

[15] In classical antiquity the term '*oracle*', such as Delphi, refers to three specific features: a) the place, b) the priestess and c) the actual message from the god(s). Our 'oracles' therefore reflect a person who provides wise counsel or prophetic prediction, inspired by the gods, and as such, represent a process of divination with entities, including extra-dimensional beings. Oracles also refer to portals through which these entities speak to certain chosen individuals.

Williams, an extremely gifted psychic and astral traveller who shared much mystical knowledge with me.

Margo first heard a disembodied voice speaking to her in 1976 and was impressed to write down every word. The words were all joined together with no dotted 'i' or crossed 't' which she wrote at great speed. This is known as *automatic writing.*

We met in 1978 and remained close friends until 1994 when she chose a different path. Margo had the gifts of *clairaudience*, hearing a voice directly in her ear, *clairvoyance*, seeing clearly into another dimension, time/space, and *healing,* the ability to diagnose and treat ailments with the help of her guides. When using these gifts she appeared to be in a slightly altered state of consciousness. Our work covered many aspects of psychic phenomena, particularly the rescue of *earthbound souls*, including those *terrestrial* and *extra-terrestrial* in form. This became her life's work.

From these souls we were given information on many subjects, often verified by Margo's initially sceptic husband, Walter, known as Wally, a retired chemical engineer.

Margo wandered and worked in many *realms*, not just that of the *astral* of the earthbound, but also those of the *faery* realm, *angelic* realm, and that of the *extra-terrestrials*.

Extra-terrestrials are beings that dwell in other planetary systems. Margo's guide *Jane Taylor* always referred to them as *those enigmatic men from the stars.*

Jane Taylor lived from 1783 – 1824 and with her sister Ann wrote *Rhymes for the Nursery* that included one called *The Star*, better known to all children as *Twinkle Twinkle Little Star*. Jane told Margo that she now knew that the star she had seen was a spaceship from another planet with the men from the stars who often visit planet Earth. Jane not only taught us about UFOs but Crop Circles also. We had amazing learning experiences with many extra-terrestrial beings.

Mary Anning, another of her guides, joined Margo in the 1950s when she was living in South Africa and had influenced her to fine the fossilised skeleton of a Bottle-nosed Dolphin now displayed in the whale gallery in Capetown museum.

Mary lived in Lyme Regis in the nineteenth century and discovered many large fossils of creatures on the beaches there, including an Ichthyosaurus now exhibited in the Natural History museum in Kensington. She said it was similar to the dolphin Margo found on the lonely beach in South Africa.

As Margo's guide Mary had that rare ability to explore the *Akashic Records* and give a certain insight to an individual, not only about their present incarnation but also about their own past lives. Mary used the words *gazing into the reflective lake* when reading past lives as in the following example.

"Once again I enter into the circle of enquiring minds to tell you of the incarnations of the young lady you know as

Sarah. I gaze into the reflective lake and I see back to the year 1881 when she was born the daughter of a wealthy barrister. She was a strong character and had a mind of her own even when young. She was sent off to a good school but only wished to dance and sing, her aim in life was to go on stage. Her parents refused but eventually she left home and her father would not receive her again.

She went into the choir at a theatre and eventually went on to a big London stage where she became very friendly with another dancer who is a sister in her present life. They shared a room together, a flat they called it, and were very happy in their stage careers.

In 1904 Sarah did another self-willed thing. In those days well brought up British girls rarely married coloured men, but she did and was very happy. She had three children and left this life in 1915 in an accident when the train she was travelling on was in a collision.

Now I go further backward to such a short life. She was prematurely born. Her mother, a hosiery worker, took part in the Peterloo tragedy and was injured in the massacre. Her child was born at seven months. That was Sarah. This was in 1819 I believe and she only survived for two months, she was too weak to live.

Now further backwards to the eighteenth century in India. The wife of a wealthy Indian with much happiness, three daughters, one being her mother in her present life, the other two she knows, and also had two sons who she does not know of yet but will meet in due course. Her husband is a man she will have great affection for. As a wealthy Indian's wife Sarah loved jewellery and fine saris. She had many grandchildren, two are related to her in this life now.

I gaze deeper back to 1603. A poor woman scratching at the soil in Ireland. Her husband tends the horses of a rich man but receives no money, only a shack to live in. There are many children, all are dressed in rags. She is an old woman at thirty-six when she passed over with another baby.

Then I see nothing for a long time but the year is 1124. Sarah is now a man and earns a poor living from the soil. It is not very clear but there are times of hunger and sorrow.

Before this I see her a long way back as a Jewish woman in Jerusalem with a good husband who is a trader in metals. She has six sons and seven daughters. Their religion means much to them and she lives to be very old with great grandchildren who treat her well. Now I can see no further and I hope that Sarah leads a happy life of peace and love before she goes on as I hope she will not have to reincarnate yet again."

This ability led us to holding reincarnation evenings at The Grove with invited guests interested to know of their past lives and a great time was had by all. This was just another one of Margo's divine gifts. Margo had many articles written about her, including those by: Stuart Holroyd, who wrote of her in his book *Alien Intelligence,* 1979; Andrew Collins investigated *The Margo Williams Phenomena* in the magazine *Anomaly,* issue 5 June 1988; Hayley Mills and

Marcus Maclean asked her to contribute to their book *My God, letters from the famous on God and the life hereafter*, October 1988. Margo privately printed several small books about her work with the earthbound including *Ghostly Gifts, Out of the Mist, Ghostly Adventures, Fairies at my Fingertips, Mystical Memoirs* and *The Answer*, the last, on the subject of crop circles, we co-wrote. Unfortunately these are no longer available but I do have my own personal copies for reference.

The Oracle: Mary Maddison (picture of Mary)

The second oracle is that of *Mary Maddison*, who I have known since moving to the Isle of Wight in 1971. Mary, like Margo, has many psychic gifts, she is a time traveller, a healer and a communicator with crystals. Her fame is spreading across Ireland since returning to her homeland in the mid-nineties. She is also a well-known Shanachie, an Irish storyteller, and a talented artist working in oils and pastels. Her knowledge of and ability to communicate with crystals is unique.[16]

The following is a short extract from an article she wrote about her work with crystals:

'From an early age stones and crystals have intrigued me. I would play on the beach of lovely golden sand in Southern Ireland and watch the salt-water crystals glistening. I remember well the day I started to talk to them and on reflection I was not surprised to hear them talk back. They spoke in sound and I felt so happy to listen. They told me of the healing power they possess, they spoke about all the mineral kingdom, and being so young I just took it all in my stride. Those happy carefree days have always remained with me through the years.

Today I have quite a collection of minerals and Quartz crystals. I use the crystals in a simple way for healing. I always ask that God bless them for the work they would do with me. I make patterns with them, triangles and circles, and sit the person requiring healing inside. The method varies each time, as each person's needs are different.

Before I start to use my stones for healing I do like to say a prayer to help the person that has come to me and that God bless him or her. I may make a triangle with Quartz

---

16   thealchemistskitchen.blogspot.co.uk./2012/08/woman-of-many-talents-mary-maddison

crystals and sitting the patient in the centre I place their feet in a bowl of tiny gemstones. The triangle forms an energy field around the person and the bowl of gemstones gives energy right through the body.

Alternatively I may make a circle of Quartz, Desert Rose and Amethyst, using seven of each. These three crystals work in harmony with each other; the Quartz directing the energy in the circle, the Desert Rose cleansing the body of disease and the Amethyst bringing a soft healing and love round the circle. In the background I have soft music playing helping the patient to relax.

Another method I use is to make a square. I place a lot of gemstones to make this square. Quartz crystal is placed in each corner and four rows of gemstones create the other lines. When the patient is seated comfortably in the box I offer a tray of gemstones in their natural state. The patient takes two of these, one to hold in each hand, the patient's higher self will select the right stones for the healing to be received.

Cleansing your crystals. The methods described here are some of the samples of the way I work, there are many more. When you first get a crystal you should get to know it and make friends with it, introduce yourself and become aware of the reply you are getting. When you have become comfortable with your crystal you may want to use it for healing or meditation perhaps. Before you do this you should cleanse your crystals, this is to get rid of any negative energies, which may have accumulated previously. Simply hold your crystal in your hand and hold it under running water, ask that all negative energies be taken from it then dedicate your crystal for the purpose you wish to use it for.

Re-energising with crystals. For people that are stressed and fatigued and need a little re-energising here is a simple way to do this. Hold a crystal in each hand, the right hand crystal must point away from the wrist and the left hand one point towards the wrist. Another method of recharging is to hold the crystal over the thymus gland, located approximately 4.5 inches down from the throat. The ancient Greeks believed the thymus to be a fire centre from which all energy flowed.

Ancient Secrets. There are around and within the earth many types of crystals. Some have been discovered that were seemingly used for healing and storing knowledge in ancient civilisations. The Earth Keeper is a very large crystal about 7 feet in length and about 8,500 pounds in weight, first located in the earth in 1996, now many of these are being mined from 60ft underground. Laser crystals were laid to rest before the fall of the Lemurian Empire.[17] They were stored within the sacred chambers of underground temples and have now been relocated, mostly in South America.

Record Keepers are the most sacred of crystals; these are the ones that have ancient wisdom stored within them.

---

[17] www.lemurianvisions.com

When working in harmony with such crystal knowledge, the secrets of life and the universe can be revealed'.

I have recently been speaking with Mary about the record keeper she has. It is a large quartz crystal within which she sees the one she has come to know as The Communicator. This is the being from who we learnt so much about our lives in Egypt and Lemuria.

In 1991 when the three of us were working together scrying with crystals Margo and Mary were simultaneously experiencing *time slips* into our mutual past lives together. We learned that many *aeons* ago there was a time when we were all living on the continent of *Lemuria,* also known as *Mu.*[18] Margo channelled these words, "*I am the Master of Mu. We have all been together before and we are together again.*" Then immediately found herself on *Mu* where everything appeared to be made of crystal, there were crystal domes and pyramids and even the ground was made of agate.

The Master was standing on a rostrum addressing a crowd of people and the three of us were present in male bodies, it seemed to be during our early twenties and communicated telepathically through our intensely deep

---

[18] Before we began working with the crystals neither Mary nor Margo had heard of Lemuria. For myself, being the librarian, I read a book during my teens that totally resonated with me. Now I know why! It was *The Lost Continent of Mu* by James Churchward. I never had occasion to bring up this subject until then, so it was new to them both.

eyes. The Master appeared to be in his mid-thirties and Mary described him as having a beautiful angelic face, cream skin and flaxen wavy shoulder-length hair.

The Master spoke to Margo saying: *"You from the future dwelt here as Qua with Kirn (Carolyn) and Jortia (Mary) and you perished when the land disappeared into the sea. You were all men of importance and you all made the choice to return to Earth to live rather than go to another planet, the choice was yours and you went on to reincarnate in Egypt."*

We were given much information about these lives, in particular living during the reign of Queen Nefertiti (c.1370 – 1330 BC), and we are still together carrying the energy necessary to bring the changes needed to the planet Earth. And yet, although Margo has now passed into some other realm, her energy is still available to bring forth the challenge of renewal.

Chapter 4

The Making of an Oracle

Robin Wells

The third oracle is *Robin Wells*, my nephew and young companion along the road less travelled, this sometimes lonely and very difficult way of life.

As a child he spent many of his school holidays in Ventnor on the Isle of Wight with me and became interested in the psychic work of my friend Margo Williams. In 1979 Robin was invited to join Margo, Wally and myself in rescuing an earthbound spirit at Mottistone on the Island. He was fourteen and very excited but little did we know it was to be the day that was going to bring about a whole new turn of events in Margo's work. She was led to find her first physical object as the result of psychic directions from Joan, an earthbound spirit. This has been written about in her little book Ghostly Gifts, printed privately in 1980 but sadly no longer available. On another occasion Robin actually witnessed an *apport* in the process of materializing at the base of Hoy's Monument, a stone pillar on the island erected to commemorate a visit from the Emperor of Russia. An *apport* is the transference of an article from one place to another, or the appearance of an article from an unknown source, usually by occult methods.

Robin maintained his spiritual and metaphysical interests training as a healer under the tuition of his mentor Ken Baker, secretary for the Kent Healers and chairman of BAHA. Ken became the third member of the core group when the channelling began in 1995 and we worked together until the end of 1996 when we were joined by Mary Maddison.

When Mary eventually left the island to return home to Ireland it was suggested more people should be invited to hear the information that was coming through on a monthly basis. Between seven and twelve people attended this group, who were prepared to work seriously on themselves with regards to personal changes needed as a result of the acquired knowledge. Transformation truly is the name of the game we are playing here.

Robins' healing abilities progressed rapidly as he studied multiple therapies; kinesiology, cranial-sacral therapy, the Dawson Technique of sound therapy, [19] and Dolores Cannon's Quantum Healing Hypnosis Therapy.[20]

In 2001 Robin went to Abadiania in Brazil to visit the medium and psychic surgeon Joao Teixeira da Faria, known as John of God, who performed a physical operation on his back, with a scalpel and no anaesthetic, removing a growth that was causing discomfort on his

---

[19] www.dawsonprogram.com

[20] www.dolorescannon.com

spine.[21] The whole procedure was captured on film, as is all the work of Joao when he is incorporated with any one of forty or so entities that work through him. During this time he is out of his body and not consciously aware of anything he is doing. Robin was so impressed with the whole experience at the Casa de Dom Inacio he returned early in 2003 for a second visit. Much clearing and cleansing is carried out on a subliminal level that the effects last long after leaving Brazil.

On Robin's recommendation I made the decision to visit the Casa in 2002, having suffered for over ten years with disabling psoriasis on the palms of my hands and soles of my feet. I went before Joao '*in entity*' and was asked to attend the sacred waterfall, the Cachoeira, seven times then all would be well. I stood naked beneath the waterfall as it flowed over and around my body and felt everything being washed away from me in those natural surroundings where the large iridescent blue butterflies flew among the trees. Six weeks after returning home my hands and feet were completely healed, free of any sign of psoriasis and have remained so. This was my own personal miracle.

Robin's energy

The information has revealed that Robin is an alien soul in a human form who has found life in the physical body

---

[21] www.johnofgod.com

extremely difficult and distressing at times.[22] He carries an energy frequency that is not conducive with his human frame and at times this has very nearly killed him. However, it is very necessary for this frequency to be here on Earth and it has been a case of:

"Adjust or out and step away from humanity, move back and let another energy do the work correctly."[23]

Robin *has* adjusted and learnt to deal with the energies as they are downloaded, otherwise he would have left this planet. Nevertheless, every transfer of increased frequency causes trauma to his body because it treats the new energy as a virus and reacts violently. He at last understands why this happens and his resistance has lessened now that he is more accepting of who and what he is, which has been so difficult for him.

This young man is the gifted healer and channel through whom much of our mission and particular knowledge has been received and the reason for writing this book. The words continue to flow through Robin without pause whenever the information is waiting. My job has been to transcribe the 'received word'. I am therefore the keeper of the records.

The title of this book, *Words in Transformation* is taken from this comprehensive volume of knowledge, specifically

---

[22] www.simonparkes.org
[23] Italics from the teaching.

from December 2011 to March 2015 and is relevant to the extraordinary times we are living in.

Along with some occasional strange choice of words the material has always had its own peculiar expression. This has been explained as their way of stretching our minds into new ways of thinking, looking at things from a different perspective maybe, so the information is written as it was revealed, word for word in its entirety (including direct transliteration into English of technical terms and names?).[24]

We have been asked by the source of these channelled words to release *Words in Transformation* at this time of great change. The purpose of this change is developed throughout the text.

---

[24] There have been others who have received similar information who have published their books, among whom are Barbara Marciniak, (*Bringers of the Dawn, Earth, and Family of Light.*) Julie Soskin, (*Wind of Change, Cosmic Dance, Alignment to Light, Transformation.*) Ken Carey, (*The Return of The Bird Tribes, The Starseed Transmissions, Starseed: The Third Millenium, Vision.*) Barbara Hand Clow (*The Pleiadian Agenda, Alchemy of the Nine Dimensions, Awakening the Planetary Mind.*)

Chapter Five

The Year 1995

In July 1995 Robin and his wife Helen came for a weekend to The Grove. Mary rang to enquire if I could possibly accommodate another guest, Edith Saurbier, a Reiki Master from Germany.

During dinner on Sunday evening Edith said to Robin: 'I need to talk to you about channelling, I have been getting this information all weekend.' He responded, 'Channelling, I don't know anything about channelling. What do you mean?' Edith replied, 'I need to talk to you about channelling. That is all I am getting.'

Robin had been feeling unwell during the day with the usual pressure building in his head. Edith, being mediumistic, had picked this up and offered healing to balance and renew his energy, which he accepted. The others retired to the sitting room and Robin sat down with Edith standing before him. She felt inspired to place her hands over his crown chakra, mentioning at the time this was something she never did with her clients, whereupon she felt a very high energy coming in, one she had never experienced before.

None of us were prepared for what happened next. Robin's head fell back, his eyes rolled, his face contorted and he began making strange hand movements.

He had an overwhelming impression to speak. It was the same feeling he had experienced so many times before but thought he was going mad. It was the same impression, the same energy rush he had been getting for so many years. Was he going to stop this happening, was he going to be ill, or was he going to speak? This time it was too strong to ignore. As his head fell back in the chair an urgent whispering voice came from his mouth.

"We are not of this planet. We are the Elders of the planet Zor."

Those momentous words! Astonished at the information pouring forth from Robin we had no means of recording the substance and had to rely on our memories.

There was concern for the suffering of the boy in preparation for becoming the channel for Arris, a medium from the planet Zor, but because of the toxicity of Earth, unlike his ancestors, he is unable to be physically present. Humanity is poisoning not only the Earth but also the Solar System.

Considering all I have learnt about geo-engineering and '*chemtrails*' this is certainly the case. Our atmosphere, our water and our soil are being deliberately poisoned.[25]

According to the Elders, Margo Williams should have been present to receive the information but her choice led to her working with people on different parallels not conducive with our own.

As contact had finally been made it was proposed Robin should now connect on a monthly basis and prepare himself to be a pure physical channel for work forthcoming in the future.

Robin channelled one month later: "*Good evening. We are the major principals of our planet.*" Presumably this referred to the Elders of Zor who proceeded to explain that the communicator to us would be their medium Arris.

---

[25] www.geoengineeringwatch.org/tag/dane

The information explained that humanity have weakened the shield of the Earth with their negative thoughts and pollution, this is now affecting other planets who have to protect themselves. Our space programme in particular has a very disturbing influence on their own planet and although they have no control over the decisions made by other planetary systems it was hoped they could all work in parallel to counteract this. (Is this the federation that Simon Parkes has spoken of?)

The hostility is only coming from Earth but in defending themselves great changes will occur on our planet. While every effort will be made to protect the Light Workers this cannot be guaranteed. Many people are being taught how to cope with the forthcoming changes during their sleep state yet will remain unaware until the time of transformation.

"Beware of the vehicle without a driver, this will be to do with the Greys!"

This warning was impressed upon us twice during the evening therefore must be relevant. Apparently this particular vehicle would not have our best interest at heart so on no account should we enter. Their possible sense of humour crept in here as they seemed to think it a good idea if the Earth's corrupt governments got on board. Is this because they lack truthfulness and transparency?

Their final words that evening were:

*"The immensity of the work and the power of this boy is not yet obvious. He has to learn to **be**."*

And so his journey into acceptance and love began. Some words have been directed at Robin as he has struggled to find his place here on Earth where he has often felt lonely and out of touch with the rest of humanity. Twenty years later there are many more star-seeds finally awakening to their purpose and this information may help them understand why they have felt like square pegs in round holes, not quite fitting into the society that has been created today.

We have now reached the point of change, hence the reason for all these different children who have answered the call from Mother Earth and come to her aid in time of great need. They come with love from all ends of the universe to take on the mantle of humanity to change the consciousness of mankind. They have a divine task ahead and need the courage of lions!

As an artist feels impressed to paint when the muse is present, as a musician is driven to write and create music, so Robin is compelled to channel, it is part of who he is. You may be an artist, a singer, a poet or a gardener, just reference what you are, find it and follow your passion. We all have a talent to offer. His talents are these *words of transformation* and they are my passion.

Part Two

Part Two

The Teachings

Activating Energies

I have been the scribe throughout and faithfully recorded all the information exactly as it has been received. Sometimes the words are not as we understand them and certainly not in the dictionaries I have consulted.

There are nineteen years of communication and the teachings presented here are those from December 2011 to March 2015, the essence of which is about Change with a capital C. These changes are already beginning on the Earth itself and within the DNA and cells of humanity. There is an important new Christ consciousness available to the mind-set of man that will usher in a new eon of care, compassion and love for those that choose to cleanse themselves of all their past and prepare for a new way of being in the body.

Robin has always been a reluctant medium and extremely unwilling for some periods of time to cooperate with the beings who have been communicating and forwarding the information but this time his abstinence led to a build-up of energy in his body causing the severe discomfort he suffered prior to channelling.

Robin: *I have been feeling unwell today and had a major collapse on the floor with spasms and all sorts of strange things happening so something is amiss or awry. We shall work this one out.*

Relinquish the Burden of your Past

December 26th 2011

"Good evening my friends. The communicator that works with the child is forced through this evening. This powerful request has to do with fulfilling certain energy patterns for the balance of nature. We are all part of a purpose bringing further understanding to humanity. The children who sit and channel are bringing information through via an energy point that is still latent at this time.

We have talked lately of old energy coming forward. This isn't about old energy patterns; it is about information that has become established. It is like the foundations of a house; the house can change its colour, its windows, its front door, but the foundations will always stay the same supporting the main structure. But now main structures will change and foundations will move with planet Earth.

The foundations of all children today are changing – climatically, energetically, morally, physically and spiritually. Man has created his own morality and is trying to break away from the form he has come from and he is no longer in alignment with the God-force.

The North Star always stays north. Whenever we look it is always facing north, it is the way seafarers and travellers over big open spaces can always tell where they are. The North Star is in the same orbit as planet Earth, but if you look at the radius between the North Star and Earth to a central point, one or the other, depending on which is closest to the central point, will have to be moving at a different speed to stay in the same place.

This is very interesting. Why is that so? And how many more planets are moving at different speeds but stay in the same orbit and same place?

When energy is coming through from one planet to another it has to be traveling at a different rate, a different vibration, and this is why the child has problems receiving this energy, because it is new information re-formed and it is coming through at a different energy rate, a different speed, so the cells of the body recognize it as something alien to the human form, which it is, alien to you but not to us.

The child is alien and always has been. The way he thinks, the way he speaks and the way he acts towards others is alien to them, and they find it very difficult to be in his energy because they don't understand who he is. He gives very little of himself to others and he challenges the status quo. The fact is that he is alien. He doesn't understand them and they don't understand him. There are people that will understand his language and they are the ones that work with the same energy. He has to come to terms with who he is and know that *where he comes from is now trying to converse with him.*

The North Star moves at a different rate to planet Earth. The South Star, if there is such a thing, stays where it is in the south directly opposite the north, but there is a transitory point where north and south seem to be having a pole. This is an energy going through a central point, and that central point **is the people that are channelling information through to the planet.** It is a thoroughfare that is going through planet Earth and continuing on to the other components of the planet. As you know there are **twelve** and these will minutely adjust themselves as the new information transmutes itself.

An explanation of the twelve

Previously we had been told of the twelve and depending on what sort of truth we wish to have will be the world we stand on tomorrow, because there will be divisions. There will be **twelve identical worlds**. There are three now but there are going to be twelve where identical people will be acting out different things, different needs. One man will do one thing and think one thing and move directly on to another world, he won't even know he has done it as there will be the same people in the same clothing acting out different personas. There is going to be the world you *choose* to be in, and the *world and place you choose to think about* is the world you will stand on.

The Earth will change. The sensations in any form will change. If you wish your world to be complete in happiness then therefore that will be the ground you stand on. You will not know the transit, the change between the two, between the three, between the ten and the twelve, but what you will realise is you are strategically different. Those that have this understanding will know that that is what they are aiming for. The question is, is the twelfth the best one and the first the least?

This brings us back to the previous channelling. If you look at the world it is round and each world that you are considering is another layer on top of the original, so there won't be twelve separate worlds, there will be an inner world and an outer world and an outer world and an outer world. It will be like going within. So when you fall from one place to the next it might be that you are moving back from one space to the other, or when you fall forward you are going forward to another space, it is about understanding the transitory experience between the worlds you choose to live in.

My children that speak and listen are going to realise this is very possible as there is going to be an opportunity to see what these worlds are like through the sensations and feelings you choose to be in. You are learning the experiences of the deepest and darkest feeling of despair right the way through to the joy and extreme happiness, all in the space of a week or maybe a month. You are experiencing all the ways in which the world can be, and also the ways that people around you can be. Just understand that *your truth is the world you choose to stand on.* Twelve down to one, you will be part of that one.

My children you are not on layer one, you are not on layer two, and strangely enough you are not on layer three, but you are moving between the fourth and the fifth. The transitory period between the third, fourth and fifth is about moving from one component to the next. This is the place where the mind stays still but the body is moving fast.

This is why so many people are moving through speed, and we are not talking of the drug here, it is the speed of need, the speed of energy, the speed of gatherance, and it is the speed of love, hate and anger, componentising itself all the way through the feelings of men, women, animals and nature.

The trial the child finds himself in is paving a way for those around him so he understands that there is a pathway. It is like tarmac laid out by the workmen, with the white line down the middle, and arrows going '*This way,*' but there will come a point when they come across a bank.

Do they go over that bank, round the bank or through it? Can you see over the top, can you see underneath, what is there? Is there any point going over it, round it or under it, why do I not stay where I am?

These are the choices that individuals have. But we all know that we have to vibrate ourselves forward with knowledge, understanding and love. As our God-source draws us to him He says, *'Dear child, dear children, dear people, you are part of me, I am part of you. The wings that flap in your head, the joy, the hate, the anger that you experience, are all part of the patterns that you were offered. You may always choose to go in one direction but there are many others too. Choices and change are part of this transition. You are part of love, part of light, part of the component of the Source.'*

Thought patterns are parallel with the mind. We insist in partaking in irrational thought patterns that take us into places where our mind has not been yet.

We have so much within us that needs to come out, and this is part of the process of man right now because he has not processed his feelings, sensations and understandings and they have become internal and wrapped within the cells of the body. The person that carries those cells now wants to relinquish themselves of this and the DNA is pushing out and exposing itself as it needs to relinquish the hardness of pattern.

It is a little bit like a cat with a whole coat full of fleas that has to eradicate them before it can show you its original beautiful coat. The DNA is actually relinquishing itself of the human past and present and saying, *'I am here. I am waiting to be seen. I am waiting to be looked at. I am waiting to be understood!'*

Man is being asked to please relinquish yourself of the past and the deeds you have not yet looked at. A tear may drop to the floor and you will ask yourself, 'What is this tear, is it something that happened today or yesterday, or is it something that happened in the past?' It may be all of those things. Look at these processes and let them go.

Answer in this way, 'I am ready to eradicate myself from my past. I am ready to understand that the green lights are allowing themselves to come forth and flow out of me. I am allowing myself to become a Light Being once again. I am going to spiral towards my DNA and understand that I am part of a whole bigger plan, which is me elongating myself to my cause, being part of the origin of man, the origin of the cellular thought pattern that visualizes man in a different way.'

You are all part of this pattern. Us being you, you being us. Those that choose to listen to these words might understand but whatever this component of thought allows you to visualize just think, and think one thing. Are you heavy with the burden of humanity my child, are you heavy with the burden of you?

It is now time to relinquish yourself and become Light, become lighter, become part of the process that man is and can be. Allow yourself to think yourself through the process. This does not mean you use the brain; it is about allowing the assets of a whole mind-set to come into play. It is the elongation of a spectrum and it is you allowing yourself to become you once again, without all the insistence of the past being present to stop you being true to yourself. Be free of the burden of your past. That has taken you this far but can take you no further. It is the present thought pattern that is going to allow you to present yourself with the new future that you wish for.

We are all struggling with the burdens carried within the cells, so relinquish these and allow yourself to become Light. You **will** become Light, and in so being, Light will recognize Light. Allow this to happen my children, it is coming to all those that serve the mammonistic terms of love, light and this spectrum of understanding.

The Choice of Consciousness

January 24 2012

This is the time for all men, women and children, to understand that changes are upon us. The whole of the Solar System is looking down on Earth and wondering what will happen next, as there is an opportunity here for a great step transcending from one spot to another. This is man's **consciousness** in question at this time and the Solar System is compartmented into those that can accept and those that can't.

Is planet Earth going to accept? And that acceptance is about what consciousness is about. It is about understanding that consciousness is fluid and change is part of that fluidity. It is like a river sailing down towards the sea and the sea sailing down towards the vessel it works with. We are yet to understand that there are mammals within our ocean that move *from the oceans to another place*, they have a communing with another place, and this is where the sea goes. It is an *energy that communes with the* **extraterrestrial** *and the* **ultra-terrestrial** that is the understanding of man, man being an integral part of the purpose.

The Solar System is looking down and waiting to see whether man can make this one conscious step to another. Unconsciously man knows that he is restricting the avenues of his understanding, which has been restricted for far too long. Those that have an understanding of this have decided this is the better place to stay, so it keeps the minds of men nulled in a way that he is doused like a flame that is trying to shoot up through dry crispy twigs and can't because somebody throws water over it. Though in truth this water is being thrown over by ourselves because *we are allowing ourselves* to be controlled.

Control is about what you do and what you don't do, it is not about what others say. We have no control as to whether we breathe or not, because if we don't breathe we stop living. But if we stop thinking in the right way do we stop living? That is a question for you. Are we living or are we just existing?

Man has got to a point where he cannot think beyond what is in front of him or beside him, he thinks nothing of what is within him, and certainly not what is without him. We need to think about the change that is needed. Because if this change is a new toaster, a new television programme, a new car, or a new banking system that is going to allow man to have his money once again, is that the change we need?

The change we actually need is a new set of clothes that allows us a new set of values that might take us on a journey we have never been on before. One about tolerance of others, and understanding who we are as individuals ... *in divide you alls* ... (We have often noticed that words are broken down into syllables that then give a true understanding of their meaning as the sound is expressed as a word.)

Now the Solar System, which is all the tiny specks in the sky that look down, is wondering if man is going to move from one dimension to another, and 2012 is all about that stepping-stone of events.

There are many integral beings and understandings that are trying to purport many different thought patterns, all of which are worded in mammonistic terms and not from whence the origins come, and that is about change coming from *without* not within. Man needs to accept a new value system that doesn't elongate from something that we have used in the past, but something that comes from the very place we have come from – the essences, the integral part of what man is about.

The DNA is changing and this is why so many people are having different complex changes in their lives, because the

DNA strands are actually transducing and allowing new frequencies into the human being. This is why we are experiencing significant change, but that can only occur when there is enough space for change, and if somebody knows that an event is there to be had. So it is like an exit from the old and an entry into the new, and we need to understand that this process is coming to us now. It is being *forced* upon us, but we cannot understand what it is about. We need to understand that we need to change!

Now the new set of clothes we need to take on board isn't of cloth but of **spirit entwined within the very essence of what we are.** We are cells constantly moving, understanding, and searching for new experience. Within those cells are minor purposes, a matrix of understanding that we don't have the complexity within our brainwaves to take on board. This is a generic inheritance. We are not designed to **understand** why we are here, we are designed to **experience**, no more or no less.

For the last 2000 years, in some ways, we have been like a boat without a rudder sent out into the Lake of Galilee to see exactly where we go. Where the wind blows us, where the water washes us, and where the sand carries us. But we have now got time to rest our boat on sandy shores and look and see what is available to us.

Somebody is there holding a hand out and saying, '*We must help you. It is time once again to conform and place a rudder on your vessel.*' This is a guidance system that allows you to go down **one avenue**, and this is where we must all go if we are to accept this new consciousness, this paradigm shift that is astronomically impending itself on planet Earth. This is not about impending disaster, it is about the choice. Does man choose to transcend from one spot to the next and take a new energy field, a new understanding, by transcending and allowing his cells to extend a new matrix of thinking, or does he stay exactly where he is?

Parallel existences have been spoken about with the same people living off the same formats but different decisions taking us to different components. This is exactly what all this is about, but what is trying to happen here is **all** of those levels are being purported so they can understand individually what they are all about so they can be entwined in the single matrix of understanding. The seven becomes one and the one becomes seven. The existences become one because they are all one.

(See later on The Seven)

Now are we going to take on this new energy format of understanding or are we going to desist once again? The choice awaits for us all, this is why so many of the channels are getting similar information. This genetic inheritance is like an alarm clock going off within us all. It is happening in many different ways and is sending a beacon into outer space that this is the time for all to interject, not in an abstract way but in a conformed way, it is like every piece of light is going to shine in one direction. And that being, the voices of all.

We need to understand that the youngsters of today take on much more of this absorbance than the elders. They understand, but they haven't got anyone showing them the way, this will come to them in their many different options. Just allow them to speak their minds and they will have a softer transit from the adults who wish to fight this.

Just allow yourself to be, and you will be. To be or not to be, that is indeed the question. The soul awaits, the spirit awaits, the mind thinks, but it needs to await the change.

The Circumference of Humanity

March 25th 2012

We must remember all points of reference, one of which is *change within is in respect to the change without*. We are watching a planet evolving, revolving, it is going round in circles, as we do. Life is a circumference, it is about where we start and where we finish. There is a purpose within this.

Imagine rolling a ball around from one side of the Earth to the other, it will roll and come back and hit you on the back of the legs. This is how thoughts are, they roll, and depending on the circumference they come back to you. This is how actions occur. You may skip or jump over a ball that comes and hits you, but it knows, it has your name on it and it will come and find you. This is about your energy and the energies that you have been involved in and is very much part of the process that we are part of at this time.

All humanity is part of a circumference. What goes round will come round and will eventually be around within or without of you. This is why we are having traumatic moments in our lives, we are actually bringing back the energy that we have sent out, whether it is in this or other lifetimes, generative processes are regressing back to an *in-divide-u-all*. The Spirit calls it all back. It is like having a bookshelf of memories coming back to you and you have to relive all the books, relive the events and moments and energies.

At this point in time you will notice we have a bright star in the sky, the Star of David, the Star of Bethlehem, the Star of Energy is shining itself brightly to the planet as we see it. We are part of that energy and it is part of us. It is the reference point for us to understand that energetic frequencies are Christing themselves towards us. It is about Light attracting like, and like attracting Light. Our energy formats within us are beaconing out and asking for this Light to come back and reverberate within our souls.

We are moving from one place to the next and we are carrying with us all the reference points of the burden that our soul carries – reference of remembrance, reference of eradication, reference of war, peace, love, hate, anger, joy, fulfillment – all the reference points of who we have been, they are coming to a point where they stop and you look and decide which point, which part, which place you stay. Do you stay this side of the fence or the other side?

There is much infighting going on within the soul, the mind, the body and the spirit. It is about which side of the fence you wish to go, what you wish to understand, and which reference point your body is going to grasp hold of. The reference point is where your energetic centre is from. Is it within or without? This is why we are going through this traumatic period of time.

It is a little bit like shaking up a jar of sweets, and you are trying to get the bottom to the top and the top to the bottom, but as you shake it, it stays exactly as it is, you have to keep shaking and it still stays exactly the same.

We have been shaken many times my friends, and this shake has not been enough for our minds to evaluate the processes, thoughts and patterns that go on around us, so it is not a shake we are having this time it is an energetic transience. It is about our energy processes re-evaluating themselves within our body.

We are part of a process and we cannot eradicate ourselves from this no matter what you decide to create within yourselves. A runner will run, a swimmer will swim, a cyclist will cycle, a singer will sing, but none of these reference points are eradicating a thought within your head. Change is upon us and we are within that change, this is where we are. Allow yourself to **be** and you will be part of the change. Don't let the change not be part of you. You are part of Love and Love is part of you, be that and continue to do so.

Clearance and Cleansing of our DNA

GM Foods and Vaccination

June 1ˢᵗ 2012

A demonstration of despicability is approaching Earth at this time. There is so much energy in construct that is about the demonisation of thought in humanity on Earth. It is a moment of transition that is happening where all energy is in a transaction stage, it is moving from one point to the other, moving from the DNA out into the construct of matter.

There are many things that are in construct, one of which is the demonstration of ill health. This is the clearing of the principle lines within the DNA, those that are written on a cross section that have been there for thousands of years, they are now coming out as the human DNA can no longer contain itself. It is being **chemically adjusted by genetically modified foods** and these are adjusting the way DNA functions and works within the cells. This adjustment **will not** take place.

You must understand that if the human being is allowed to mimic itself in a different manner and reboot itself, its original evolutionary process has been adjusted so therefore it is no longer required within the format of life and the way it is. This cannot be allowed to happen, and will not happen, so the body is now rejecting GM foods and is allowing this to come out in many forms of illnesses.

Unbeknown to themselves the over-vaccinated population are being genetically modified and adjusted to a format. This will not happen, it is being rejected by the body, which has a way of moving across and away from processes it doesn't need.

The body and the mind are two separate entities and the spirit within is another entity. The body will never ever be in charge, the mind will not be in charge, the spirit has some sentiment of attraction, but what is actually in charge is a *God Source* and He is watching and understanding.

A programme was set as to where, why and what we do as human beings. Free will was rolled out in front of us like a carpet with soft soft abilities to walk upon. A human being has an opportunity to walk upon the softness and the joy but he will always choose harshness, because that is the way he was built. Evolutionary cycles desire that he has soft and hard, cold and warm, light and dark, anger and joy, love and hate, but we must not stay in one or the other for too long, we must stay in balance, and that is somewhere in the neutral point between.

Getting back to the DNA structure. Energy that has transduced itself to the cell of the body can no longer be contained anymore and is now being eradicated from the body. The shivers, the shakes, the illnesses, the things that are prevalent on the planet, is the body ridding itself of the flea (*genetic modification*) that has climbed inside the DNA and is trying to readjust it. This is **not** going to happen! Allow yourself the moment of transduction, which will happen for you all. You will have untimely illnesses and changes going on within you; hot colds, night sweats, all sorts of compartmentalisation of your body eradicating itself, and as it does so it will be rebooted in a different way. You will have a different format of understanding.

We are all going through that in different ways and those that desist or resist this will unfortunately suffer further, but they will go through this process. The human DNA needs to be cleansed and cleared and in doing so the mindset will allow itself to move into another ethos of thinking.

We cannot be angry forever. There is no point in the world being angry at what it sees and what it does. The world is a place for human eyes to see, but what other eyes see is not what the human being sees. The human being sees a sea, a sky, a mountain, a blade of grass, a cow grazing, but the visiting eye sees none of this but dust, because all this is a facade for the human eye. Therefore you can ruin nothing that isn't there, but you can ruin something that is there if you wish. Everything **can** change, but there will come a point where that change will **not be allowed** to occur. This is not a governing force or a body, this is just what was written.

The human form will always push the boundaries, because that is what it is here to be doing, but in doing so the human structure has pushed the boundaries and found the edge. It is like a framework that stops a man falling off the edge of a skyscraper, it is there to stop him falling but he had to go to the edge to see what is over the edge. That is what human beings desire, they need to find the edge. There was one point where we thought the world was flat and if you sailed too far you would fall off the edge. That is what man desires at this point in time, but there is a change occurring and it will happen to you all.

The Communicators.

You may be wondering about those who are communicating with Robin. There have been many from many different star systems. At one point we were told that we were in touch with a central core of information from the God-source.

The first communicators were the Elders of the planet Zor that was being affected by man's continual abuse of Earth, the skies above and the waters below. Arris was to be the intermediary and doorkeeper for those who wished to communicate through him to Robin. But who else was communicating with us and what was the source of our information? In answer to that question we were given these words:

'Your group is developing a following of entities required to give the relevant answers you will need as and when. There are the **extra-terrestrials**, the **etheric beings**, the **gods** and the **Pleiadians**, all of which are connected with the cosmic thinking that we are trying to project to you. Arris will receive your questions and the relevant beings will give the answers to him. Many people enter your realms and many more wish to do so.'

We were to learn more of Arris and exactly who he is: "We have been the creation of the energy formats behind the gentleman by the name of Arris. He has been the mediator for many years within the child, vocally it has been a short period of time but much has had to be prepared for this. You must understand that the people who provide the vocalisation are not necessarily the people that provide the knowledge and wisdom that comes from them. They are basically transmitters, as you are transmitters of the information you feel is right for you to acknowledge. You must understand that the curators of this energy are not necessarily the formulas behind the vocalization.

You must realise that before a channel is set up we are encoding his DNA with the relevant information that he is bringing forward to you all. We are also there monitoring that the encoding is carrying out its correct procedure."

Later Arris was to say: "You have found out about me haven't you? I am not really as intelligent as I sound. You must understand that I cannot transform energy unless it has been given to me, therefore you cannot transform energy that has not been given to you. We are **energy vessels**, we are not the curators of original energy, we just carry them as vessels. Basically we are vessels of knowledge and love. It is very difficult for us to perform it, and we know that is what we want and wish to do at some point or other, and working towards that vessel is a beautiful thought for us all. You do deserve to get to that format. Thank you."

On another occasion Arris confided, "I have never been a human, but I have been told the requirements and don't like the sound of it very much. It is such an effort to consider the elements you have to live by. The thought processes you are allowed are quite sad, as you have the latent ability within you all to generate the correct energy to transport your mind and thought into a different dimension where we could all sit and speak clearly to each other and discuss planetary problems. These abilities were there originally, hence many of your structures around the world that you have problems understanding their use and meaning were there purely as meeting places for the planets, (*Stonehenge, Avebury, the Serpent Mound, and the Pyramids etc.*) The concepts are still within your minds but you have such vast blockages in your chakras that you are no longer able to project your thoughts to these levels of communication."

So Arris is not at all keen on having a human experience! Considering what is going on today this is not surprising, but we are very happy to be acquainted with him.

In August 1996 this unexpected piece of information was received. "Our time and your time never, I may add, *never* seem to coincide particularly well. As you appreciate, time slips are occurring within your dimension and how can we monitor time slips? We cannot. *We are coming from the future, to the past, to try and monitor your future*. Can you understand the mathematical equations that might have to be worked out? They cannot *be* worked out. We can only try and link into a conscious thinking, which sometimes is very difficult to link into. As you all appreciate, sometimes the switch just does not switch on. We all have the same problems."

So it seems some of the communicators are from the future and I sometimes wonder if they are us, ourselves, trying to get us back on track. Are we perhaps communicating with our future selves?

Casting out the Old and Bringing in the New

June 4ᵗʰ 2012

Circumspect evidence denies the cells certain energy portals. You must understand, energy portals are variations of change within the cell. The human frame is adjusting to a structural change on a physical, mental and spiritual level, and all those that deny this change will have a circumspect alteration in their life. Those that desist will have dis-ease in the form of anger, malfunction of structure, or malfunction of those around them. Portals of change are relevant for us all.

As a blade of grass blows in the wind so does the human frame. It is the Wind of Change that is going to blow you over if you do not allow it to come through you, round you, and within you. All those that listen to these words must understand that change is relevant for those that wish to create normality in their life.

We must all understand that love that surrounds us at all points.

What is love and who denies themselves love? Nobody, because we all have love in the variation in the way that we use it. Love is a blossom growing on an apple tree as well as the drip of oil coming out of the end of a pipe, all are different eventualities of love. It is the choice of an individual and the choice of those that wish to make the change within themselves, so there will be varying changes within us all. Love is not what it appears to be, it is *a variation*, always has been and always will be.

The child that sits is going through his personal change, it is the cleansing of the old and the bringing out of the new. He must understand that within the cells are things that have been wrapped around them for many centuries on a genetic format, which have been passed down through the family line. Those cells have energy formats contained within them to do with the family that allow the change within the child. Even though he is a figment he has to draw to him the energies of the choices he made within the body structure that he is working within, therefore it is all relevant. Within those cell structures are malfunctions, diseases, joys, happiness, anxieties, angers, deaths, murders – all things are contained within the cells and they are coming out, and will come out in many forms – anger, frustration, love, and choices that you have not made before.

The child is just an example but we will all be going through these processes. We are not having these forced upon us, it is the point of change and the karmic influence is coming to everybody at this time. Even if you are on a space probe to Mars you will still have this eventuality coming to you. (*Your karma will catch up with you now wherever you are!*) The gravitational frequency of Earth certainly pulls this close to us all at this time. It is not a time to be fearful, it is a time to be rejoicing in the fact that you will be casting out the old and bringing in the new.

Bringing in the new what? There is no such structure to the *new what*, it is what you are going to allow to happen next. What has happened in the past has already happened, but what will happen next is what happens to you when you are unburdened by the clutter of yourselves. De-cluttering is like removing all the clutter from the attic or under the stairs. You *will* fill it up with something else, there will be boxes with new things in them, but bear in mind that these boxes need to be structured in the way that is going to allow you to be content within your existence. This existence is really important for us all.

Singing the Tune of Change

June 12th 2012

The circumspect environment that we find ourselves in at this time seems unjust to us all. The energetic changes from family frequencies through to world frequencies are tenfold within all our lives. We do not have to look left or right, the change is right in front of us hammering on our forehead asking us to understand that this is relevant for us all.

The change is not only relevant in the flowers and the birds and the bees and the way the whales sail across the universe, it is about the way that we *feel*, it is about the energetic spontaneity that happens within us all. The cells are genetically adjusting, as they always have done. Like the winds blow south, west, east and north, we must understand that we, as human beings, are preordained not to understand but to just let things happen.

In all truth we are part of this truth, but we must understand there are many circumspect environments that brings this truth to us at this time. We are at that place where we have elongated to a point of evolution that recommends this new aspect to our cells – an aspect of change, an aspect of clarity, but we are not actually experiencing what is happening to us, we are actually taking it on board on a cellular level.

There is much that we cannot understand with regards to this calculus of conversation but we will try and explain it in a menial term so you can understand this.

You are in a conjunction in space where time itself is readjusting to a new component, not only on an energetic level but on a molecular level, which is allowing molecules to change their patterns of movement, not only in the transient cell of man but in the materialisation of the very matter that you worship upon, that of a video recorder or a camera. That will change in conjunction with the change of the cells...

These last words brought to mind the work I have done with the Orb phenomena and the thousands of amazing pictures captured by my camera, not only of the spheres but strange light formations and even an apparent ghost on one occasion at Gabriel's Return. (See 'The Watchers').

...Water will molecularly change its transient process of understanding. Its need for clarity will move. The seas will move in a different way. This is why the winds are changing, this is why the structure of ice is changing, and this is why the structure of space itself is changing. Man is understanding scientifically and seeing that there is change happening and is looking for the reason why. But maybe the reason why is just, and will just be as it is and always has been.

Yes indeed man in his small mark that he makes upon the universe can adjust the minute cell and minute adjustment around him but he will not adjust much because what he sees is not what others see. The façade you see is the façade of what you create, no more or no less. It is all but a vision that you see through the clarity and the component of your molecular structure, whether it is your brain or the component of touch, sight and hearing. Those are all the things that show a truth to you and create a clarity within your mind and you can underline it and say, '*I understand that now.*' But that is **_not_** how it is, there is much more and there is certainly much less.

We are all singing a tune of change at this point in time. Understand and watch. This is not the mercy of doom, this is the mercy of change. Have clarity in your hearts, minds and souls.

7 Changing Shapes

June 30th 2012

It is very prudent for all of us to understand the DNA in which we channel the chances and changes introduced to every one of our lives. The revenue that is involved in change is about the *e-motion*, the electrical motion frequency within the cellular structure of the body. The cells are a circumspect environment created by the environment and the energies in which we lay.

In which we lay. What does this mean? This is the way we retrieve and investigate information. It is like a line of information, not a ley-line but actually a line. If you look at the way we energise information, it is how we format it and what we choose to do with something that is suggested to us, or a feeling, or a sensation. Can we transmute that information into something positive or do we keep it the way it was?

Shape information is how we can change things. Something can come to you in one shape and you can actually transmute it into another if you wish. Shaping information is how formats get within the cells of the body, they don't just get directly in, it is *the shape they form.*

If you can imagine yourself as a child, you used to get this box and it had a star and a square and a circle shape, and the young child would try and push the star through the square box and it wouldn't fit, and the square through the star box, and the round bit through the square bit, and some fitted and some didn't.

Imagine information trying to enter the cells and stay there. It has to be of a certain *shape,* and the only way that shape can be formatted is how you *think* about that information. So use the word *information*, it can only create the shape that creates a style and a vibration depending on how you interpret it, and depending on whether it enters or is retrieved or detracted from the cellular structure that lays within the human being.

We are interpreting information that has not only come to us via our life span on this earth but also via many life spans prior to this that we have not only experienced on this planet but also others. We are transmuting so much information and the different shapes don't necessarily place an accordance within the cellular structure.

There are many cellular structures involved here – your *interplanetary* structure, your *physical* structure, and your *metaphysical* structure. We have got a trinity here different to that explained before, it is the component that allows you to transcend from one place to the next. It is the old illustrious component that allowed one human being to move inter-planetary to another composure.

This sounds very convoluted but it is not, it is just understanding that you *are* convoluted. You carry many facilities and abilities to tune into other components of self that have been in many different places. At this point you are in one place trajectorising who you are, letting the planet know that you are here by your very experience, by the very environment you wish to be in, and when you don't wish to be in that environment you will allow that to change and bring in new shapes.

But when you wish to change your environment into a new component that is when you move *out* of your physical structure, trajectorising yourself into another component from whence you have come, from where you have been and where you might go again. This is where the shapes change and they won't necessarily fit into the physical structure.

This is a bit of quantum science here my children. This is something that you will read about at some point and those of you that listen to this might have fundamental issues with what it means, but when you read these lines it may well come in a different format to you.

So at this time we won't talk about the shape too much more, but just understand this is why you all *feel out of shape,* because you are re-introducing the trajectory of the trinity. Not mind, body and spirit, but your ability to traject yourself through inter-dimensional composure. De-fragmentation from one space to the next that allows you to be of one and one of all. And when you are one of all it means you can actually componentise the assets of what you are and move them to other places that do not have the composure of structure on a physical, mental or spiritual level, there is a different composure.

The breeze blows in many different ways but when it comes against a wall it cannot go through, but a breeze will blow *off* that wall and it will come off in a different way. Just allow yourself to be a breeze, but go *through* a wall because the wall is not there, it is only there because man built it. It may be of structure, it may have molecular formats to it, but it is only built in the eyes that the man sees with. So therefore a wall will never be there unless you built it, and a built will never be there unless you wall it, so allow yourself to have no trajectory of misunderstanding or misinterpretation, just allow yourself to move and transcend from one spot to the next.

There are often difficult words, difficult things, but nothing is difficult. The format of humanity and the management of assets is what makes things awkward for us all. We do not yet fully understand that we have the asset to transcend all, it is there, but we have forgotten where to pick it up, who to learn it from, and where to touch Base A to move to

Base B. We always start right at the end and wonder how we got there, who brought us there, and what emotion is responsible. We do not understand that we are responsible for all actions that occur to us, from the man that reverses into the back of our car to the person that takes the wrong shoes out of the box, places them in another box and the wrong ones get sent back. Everything has a format of understanding. Everything has a result, and that result is a format of how you felt and how you trans-sensationalised your feelings at that point in time.

There is nothing basic about the human frame, but basic instinct is what drives most of us, and this is something we need to deconstruct right now and find an oasis. An oasis is a place, not only in the desert but in the formats of the mind, it is a place where you can go and be safe, where it's got all you need, where you are surrounded by the winds and the sands and the mounds and the heat and the cold, it is a place you can go and be safe. Find that oasis in yourself, it will allow you to trajectorise and intellectualise how you *feel* about your emotions on all levels.

This information this evening is very thick because the body is ready to understand and resurrect itself. The DNA spirals are unraveling. The knot that we have tied in them is untied, and the rhythms of time and the love of time will allow time to bring the elapsed mind, spirit and body into play, and in so doing a new picture will be painted. A new oasis spanning out in the dimensions of your formats of mind will bring you to a new place. And that, my children, awaits for you all, whether it is here now or whether it is somewhere else and there, you will find this.

Bless yourself for listening and listen more, because more will listen as you listen. Thank you.

The prioritization of love.

July 16ᵗʰ 2012

The energy of love flows through the individual at different rates. The vein at which that individuality is pursued is how we vibrate with our thoughts and passions, but unfortunately, at this point in time, the entire component of who we are and where we have been is amassing itself in the abyss of energy format that lays behind us. At this point we are perplexed by the volume of thought and passions we are having inside us, many of which are interpreted in so many different ways. We have thought patterns with regard to distraction, construction, love, passion, in entirety.

These are all components that come with and are part of the free will circumspect that we have within us. But what seems to be happening to all of us at the moment is we are enveloped by a pursual of many of these different things all in one go, not knowing which directive or which direction to go in. All is our version of love, but this version of love comes from where we have come from, every understanding in essence from where we are, the land in which we lay, the sea in which we wash.

We talk about the sea in which we wash. There is so much to understand with regards to the sea. The sea within or the sea outside, there is so much. The sea inside the soul, the way in which we feel and interpret other people's feelings, the way in which we are perplexed by understandings.

We must understand at this point that love is the pursual of many things, not just the aspect of our self that we choose to understand and adhere to with regard to what love and love energy interpret, after all we must understand that love comes in many different guises.

The house in which we sit, and the love we interpret within that house, would be very different if we were in a different echelon of understanding, like Buddhism or Judaism. The law of love doesn't necessarily come in the avenues we understand, so therefore we must not interpret love as being the all acting thing, it is the pursual of what we are. In truth, *love is **being** who you are,* and being who you are allows you to expand into a format of consciousness that moves with that love.

Love is the essence and tri-essence of what you are at this point in time, no more or no less. **God itself is an energy within us all** and that love that is interpreted via that essence of God comes out in many different ways. We have it interpreted in blue, red, green and black, in laws, religions, states of understandings because it isn't understood and it is interpreted by that that amasses the thought processes as to what love means. In truth, it is what **they** mean, but it is not in truth what **you** mean. So therefore *in divide you all,* the individual has a different interpretation of love, so therefore *be your own version of love.* Be who you are in truth and in truth you will be who you are.

This is the interpretation, the mass of energy that amounts within us all. We are running out, almost exploding, because we are *not* actually being who we are. This is what this story is about. It is not a mystery, a history, it is *your story.* The story behind who you are, the story from whence you have come, the fragment from when you sharded away from the God-force from where you came from.

In truth it is like a pebble thrown across a mill pool, but many pebbles drop in different avenues and drop to a different component below the surface. But we are all now surfacing to the top and looking at it from a different area, looking at our surroundings and they are very different but slightly obscured by that of the other person around you.

At this point you must understand that love will be interpreted in many different ways. Interpret it *your* way. You must *be love,* but you must not be somebody else's version of what that love is. Be *your version* of love, be *your version* of truth, and you will *be you.* And when you *be you,* you become something that has movement and be less fragile.

Fragility is something that stays stagnant and stationary, like a rock, like a crystal, but the cells within that rock and crystal define what it is, and the beauty of fragility that it becomes will move, it will break, it will move with its level of understanding as you must move with your level of understanding too. The moment you understand this level of understanding you will move once again. This is your job. Listen and be blessed, there is more to come.

Acknowledge the Soul

August 27ᵗʰ 2012

The dormancy of the soul relates to the assets that we are in. The dormancy of the soul is coming out of its perspective, it is now allowing itself to become known. The soul is an asset we all have, we have pushed it apart, it hasn't been part of the very persona that we are. Indeed we are individuals, and in divide we all are, but we can _never separate from our soul_.

But this has happened to a certain extent. We have actually pushed this very important asset to one side. This is the part of us that has been taken away from us through religion. It is the part of us that has been taken away because we have no belief in anything after the asset of life. Life is just a perspective, just an opportunity to see opportunities in other ways, it isn't just one little trip and that is the end of it.

Dormant as it is the soul is coming to the forefront and requesting that it be acknowledged and in so being all the assets that we are are being shaken. There isn't one soul in this world that isn't looking backwards at this point in time, it is looking back and going, '*My goodness, this is what I am, but is it what I am going to be from now onwards?*'

We are all being given an opportunity to re-assume a new being. By re-assuming a new being it is allowing us to be a being in *a different form*. Being and doing, or doing and being, it is about becoming something that you really are. We must become what we really are to know *who* we are. We can't become something that we visualize in our heads, that is something else, we are becoming the very asset that our soul desires and our soul desires for us to be true to ourselves and in being true to ourselves we become true to others.

It is legend my children, my people, my person that we all must speak and speak our truth. Our words are part of what we are and what we are is part of our words.

What we must all be understanding is that we came from somewhere and that somewhere is a divine spark of individuality, but that individuality is part of a source. We may call it a God-source, we may call it an apron, something that hangs in front of us that we don't see, but whatever it may be it is part of what we are, and what we are is part of what we must understand.

This my children, is part of the change that is happening in 2012. We are eventually going to change totally in format but the format has to start with the blueprint.

What is the blueprint of what we are? The blueprint of what we are is where we have been and where we have been can bring us to this point and this point only, but there is a projection of the future and that is *change*. Change is something that is not desired in any way or form. We stay in the same shoes and trousers, in the same house, on the same property, experiencing much the same people. This is how we have become.

We have become quite stagnant and resilient as to regards what opportunity offers us. We only take opportunity when it is something that suits us but opportunity is about taking on something that we know nothing about. And if we know nothing about it we expand the very essence of who we are and become bigger, become more of an asset for others to flow from or flow towards.

But if we stay in one place we become like a stagnant mill pool. The water flows underneath but it stays stationary on top. Our worlds have become small, this is why we have no concepts that there are other worlds than our own. When our world becomes bigger we begin to understand that there are many worlds, worlds from within and worlds from without. The worlds from within are a microcosm of cell form. The worlds from without are again a microcosm of a bigger cell form.

We can't understand the expansion of this thought pattern but what we can understand is that it is relevant, and it is about this relevance that we are being called to change. Not change in the fact that we need to be angry, not change in the fact that we need to be e-motional, it is just about understanding that we *must* change.

Illness is resistance to change. Misunderstanding is resistance to change. And when we do change, yes indeed it is not comfortable because we are not used to this. But we are furnished with something and it is called desire, desire to expand and in expansion we desire, and when that desire continues we understand and see more of the world around us. When we see more of the world around us we *are* more of the world around us and we understand that we are part of a world, but not the only world.

Continue with your thoughts and as your thoughts continue you will expand.

What is Channelling?

September 16th 2012

We have a verse and thought with regards to the meaning as to what channelling is.

Channelling is a spectrum of thought and convulsion of total precipices of thought patterns coming from many different evolutionary cycles, the component of which transcends itself to the human form. The human form at this point in time is the child that speaks. The voice that elaborates in such formats, the song that comes in formats as well, the poetry in motion is the same. The colours flow where the words don't go and the words go where the colours don't flow, but what you must understand is *words in themselves are a channel to something.*

The channel at this point in time happens to be the words and verses coming through this child so therefore they will be a perspective of the viewpoint of that that is around he and he only. You must understand perspectives are viewpoints and as a viewpoint comes into play you will have a perspective on what that is.

If you looked far away into the mountains you do not know of what is on the mountain, but if you use a pair of binoculars you can see what is on the mountain but your vision close by is moved. Perspectives are based on what you can see, the vision you have at that point in time. If you wish to build on a block and build a house you have to have a foundation, a perspective foundation that allows you to elaborate on a thought or a pattern or a perspective.

We must understand that energy in one form always changes into another but it has constant memory of what it was, but it doesn't have an understanding of what it *might* be, therefore that energy is attracted and attached to a form. Now that form is man at this point in time so we draw energy to us that has a perspective with regards to the relationship to man - not a parrot, not a carrot, not a donkey, but man himself. We do not wish to know about the lifespans of parrots, carrots or donkeys, we wish to know about the energetic format that we wish to learn and glean from, which is the format of humanity, the format first and foremost as to what we individually are about. Yes of course you care for your brother, sister, mother and lover, but formally and most importantly you care mostly about yourself.

Now that sounds very strange but your caring about self is about you having an objective, a projection. If you project for others you are interfering with them, so to care about oneself isn't a selfish pattern. It is about you doing the right thing, it is about you energetically attracting to you what you need with the perspective of thought that you have in your head at that point in time. You must understand that this does involve interference.

Man has chosen free will and this free will is a perceptive of possibility. Possibility is only what man thinks he can do, he cannot stretch his mind beyond what he thinks he can't do because he doesn't know it is there, so therefore he will only project something we are wishing to happen. We very rarely will wish something to happen that we don't want. We may wish that for others and that is where you introduce patterns of energy that are untoward in the energy formats.

When you wish other things to happen to others or other places or other appointments, what you actually do is send out and transduce energy that doesn't have a format, a formula that attaches itself to you but you are responsible for sending it out. You must be responsible with regards to what you do with your energy forms. But bear in mind that what you send out does come back whether it is in this lifetime, this equilibrium, this spiritual element or not, it will always come back to you and find you. Bear that one in mind!

Everything has longevity or shortevity. The more you know the quicker it comes back to you, the less you know the longer it takes, and when it finally hits you on the back of the head you have no revelation as to why and what it has come from, but it is part of you.

 If somebody stabs you in the back you actually did it in the first place, you stabbed yourself in the back, but you have called that individual energy to you for that to happen. Be aware not only that but you have created a karmic effect on the person that has to do that to you, so the knock-on effect is tenfold.

Getting back to channelling. What is channelling about? Channelling is about the sunshine, it is about the moonshine, it is about the stars, it all has different elements, different perspectives about different viewpoints. Everything has different viewpoints so therefore the channelling will have different viewpoints, its perspectives will always transduce new thought patterns to those that listen. Many do not choose to listen because they do not know that it is there to listen to.

You know a telephone works but as you walk past it and it rings do you pick it up? Is it your house? If there is nobody in the house do you still pick it up? Do you wonder who that was from? Do you wish that you had picked it up just to say hello to somebody you have never met before?

The point is, the curiosity that comes with regards to a phone ring is the same with regards to channelling. You tune into something like a phone ringing, it is ringing with information on the end - *information*. It has something attached to it like a helium balloon that is dropped up in the sky with a letter on the end that says *I love you* and it floats around the planet till there is somebody in desperation, somebody that doesn't know what love is, and the helium balloon drops on their head and shortly afterwards a letter in an envelope with a note inside that says *I love you* from somebody else. They don't know who put this helium balloon in the air or why it chose to land on their head but nevertheless the message of love is carried without the responsibility of knowing who it went to.

Channelling is much the same. Information is given out, it is plonked in a helium balloon and when somebody is ready to receive it, it is there. There are no specifics, there is no choice as to who that individual is, it will come. Just as a vehicle rolling down a hill. Will it choose right or will it choose left, or will the wheels lock, will it fall into a pond or will it crash into a tree? It will do precisely what it needs to do at that point in time. In fact the handbrake was probably not left off by the individual that parked it, it might have just chosen to disengage itself just to show a lesson.

Words in themselves are lessons, they are elongations of speech, verbalisations of spectrums, spectrums of verbalisations. Channelling in itself is a purpose, the purpose for that point in time, until another one comes along and that helium balloon drops on your head with an envelope that says *I love you but tomorrow I will love you more.*

Feeling the In-difference and the Soul

October 13ᵗʰ 2012

The perception, the feeling, the sensation that occurs within the human frame right now is that of difference or shall we call it *in-difference.* The energy of in-difference is the fact that we are in a process of being in something different, so we use the terminology of in-difference. We are in the process of deference of energy, so that is effectively what we are doing, we have deferred energy up to a point where we have the ability to deal with it and transcend it. We are all doing that at this point in time.

We are going through many e-motions, electrical motions of feelings and sensations that have been going on within us, without us, and inside and outside of us for many millennia. This is past experiences in previous lifetimes, planetary influences, transitionary periods of time, genetic reflections and so on. This is all part and parcel of why we are in-different to ourselves.

We almost have a septum within us that is being forced out, it is being clubbed out of us, pushed out of us, like a cannonball out of a cannon. There is an explosion and out it comes and the cannonball is in flight at the moment. And that is what we are all in the process of doing, we are in flight. But the point is where does our cannonball land – in front, behind, or to the side, or does it still stay in the cannon waiting to explode?

Many of our experiences are in the process of exploding right now – things, processes, persona, feelings, sensations, are all in the process of building up, the gunpowder is planted, the fuse is lit and out it comes – the cannonball in flight. We are in some form of trajectory and where does our cannonball land? Does it land one side of the fence or the other side of the fence? That is the choice. We are at the point where we have choices. Do we want to stay exactly where we are or do we need to move on to understand that it is *love* and *the essence of love* that will take us through to the next stage.

There have been questions to do with the soul and what has the soul got to do with who we are?

The definition of a soul is **the article which carries experience.** It carries the essence of what we are, what we have been, and what we are going to be. The soul was something that was given to us by the God-force. It is the persona that carries the energetic frequency of our area, our corresponding area of frequency within the planetary. One soul does not necessarily coincide with another soul, but the soul that is required to be on this part of our domain, this trajectory of experience, is the soul that we have contained within and without – *our Soul.*

This trajectory is part of what we are about, we are regaining the soul essence. Sadly soul essence is something we have lost, it has been lost in a trajectory of misunderstanding, but the soul has got to a point where it needs to change its frequency, its process of understanding, and in so doing we have to choose our trajectory, the point where our cannonball lands. Which side of the fence will it be, will it be the new side or the old side? That is the choice.

We are in the process of letting go of the people we love, not that we don't love them anymore, but we are learning to let go of many things, objects, objectivity, dis-ease, recommendations and processes past, present and potentially forward. The recommendation right now is to follow what you *feel* is right for you.

There is no right or wrong about staying one side or other of the fence, there are no rights or essences of trajectory that you need to do. We are all in the process of change, and change is the fact that we have changed our mind to stay where we are or we have changed our mind to go to another place. It is about understanding that we have a choice that does not lay with the good, bad or indifferent, it is actually about being comfortable about where we have moved from and to.

Fear resembles a partiality of change. Partiality or impartiality is about us being fearful of that change, that transition, that trancelike state of not understanding where we are at that point in time. But only a microsecond allows us to formulate what we are doing and where we are at that point.

All we actually need right now is *love*. We need ourselves to love one another. Most importantly we need to understand we are part of the essence of love and so we will move from one trajectory to the next. Your cannonball is firmly planted in the cannon and nobody else is lighting that fuse but you, but you know you need to light it and let go.

Bang! Crash! Wallop! Yes that will happen. It is about things being blown apart – essences, changes, the need to change the way you feel. If at one point you didn't feel you needed to talk about situations and you kept it all under the carpet then do totally the opposite. If you are an individual that goes into explosions of demonstration, keep it within, sweep it under the carpet and do exactly the opposite. But if you can't do the exact opposite what actually happens is you get an opposing pole and you explode within yourself.

Many people are going through that process and need help to change and the only help can be through *asking*. Asking for the need for help will bring people to you that will help. They will light your fuse for you and give you a trajectory to fire towards – towards the light, towards the dark, it makes no difference as they are part of the same thing. Choose your desire and your trajectory will be with you.

The Soul itself has so many more essences. It carries the reason for you being here, it carries the essence, the akashic thought pattern of what you have been and where you have been, but it is not the be all and end all, there is much more to the essence. The Soul is the carrier, it carries the essence of the Divine Spark. Always remember, the *Divine Spark is carried within the soul, it is contained but it will not be contained forever.* Change is upon us all!

The Change of the Cellular Body

Your Beacon is now coming from Home Station A

November 3rd 2012

The demise of the cellular structure of the human being is at the starting point at this time and this means the *total* changing of the cellular body.

Once every 3-4 months the body discards cells through effluent. But what it actually does is it just changes the molecular structure of the body because it has had new experiences in that period of time. The body cannot contain these experiences totally so it renews cells, but the difference is these cells are coming from somewhere else now. They are no longer coming from the mindset and the equilibrium and the experience from what you have had, they are coming from somewhere else, and that is from *the God-consciousness* from whence you have come.

Everybody is going through this transitional experience that allows them to exchange these cells. Depending on who you are and the calibre of your thinking depends on what cells you are allocated, nevertheless you are all changing on a very very redeemable level.

The cells of old and the cells of new do not work together. It is like the antibodies within the body recognize a new cell so there is a process that goes through and it's called illness, discernment within the spirit of who you are. The body looks at the new cell as if it is an invading cell and will attack, so over a period of 3-4 months the body will go through an exchange unit point where there is a barrier between those cells and your cells, and until the body has transited from one percentage to the next you will have this plural experience between one cell and the next. This will allow you to feel quite ill, unstable, not rational, and all the various elements that you feel when you are not feeling well. But you will be well in time. This will allow the body to exchange its new frequency and understand that one antenna is changing to another. Your beacon is no longer coming from planet Earth it is coming from the point where you have come from.

This is an interesting point. *Your beacon is not coming from planet Earth*, which is the karmic frequency, the frequency of everything you have ever been. But what is happening is the beacon is now going to Home Station A (the God-force) and is beaconing your original cause, your original need, and your original energy process. This is why you feel as you do. The boy is experiencing this as he speaks. Just allow those frequencies to come through you, like an energy.

The Spin on the Spiral of New Consciousness.

November 19th 2012

We as a human race are changing not only on a molecular structure but on an energy format structure which is different.

The molecular structure is the matter which materializes and becomes part of us, but the materialization of this is changing. Our soul, our energy format, is changing. The portal point from whence we have got our energy is coming from a different place. It is like always being delivered to from a certain channel but it is now coming from another place. Effectively what we are doing is changing channels on our television, on our screen of existence, on our screen of understanding, so therefore what is actually happening is we are dimensionalising in a new frequency.

This has its examples and these are *how* we feel, the *way* we feel, and *what* we are going to feel. These examples are projecting themselves in a format of misinterpretation and misunderstanding of why we feel as we do. It is not illness, it is an *un-ease* not a dis-ease, an un-ease. It is like you are a minute form of microwave energy and vibrating at a slightly different energy and the cells of your body are reacting to this new energy. Your antioxidants think you have free radicals and try to attack them so there is a minute change happening, but once the cells stack up and there is more of one type than another then one will overcome. It is not a cancer but an energy change and this is why we are all feeling as such. Just allow this frequency.

The child that sits has been experiencing digestive disorders, the food he eats no longer feels right with his body. Something is changing within him. On a human level he questions why and what is it he is doing but on the inhuman level, the energy form level, he understands totally what it is.

There is always this dimension of discourse between human energy and the framework from whence you have come. This isn't the soul level this is a different level. There is the *human level*, there is the *soul level* and the energy from whence you have come, the *super-conscious*. All three are communing for the first time in this universal time. This universal time is the projection of all matter. Materialisation of change is happening forthwith at this point. You are moving, you are shifting, and it is like the tides of change are upon you all. It isn't about embracing this change, it is about *being this change.*

To be or not to be – this is most certainly the question! Are you going to be who you are from this point onwards, or are you going to be something you are not? And the something you are not is what you have been in the past, because you are most certainly not that, it was a vehicle used for gathering the asset of experience.

The new energy format that we move and step into is one that **understands** much of why and what it is here for, not only on a human level but on a much more inhuman level. It understands the seeds of growth, the growth of seeds, and it understands the evolutionary process of learning the cycle in which energy formats itself.

The way in which the world spins isn't the way we see it. There is spin on everything but the spin has to be one that sits well with you. The words that spin, the energies that spin, you are part of this spin. Where you have been will be part of this spin, but what you will be is spin in a new way, *a spiral of new consciousness.*

It is about time that you all embraced this. You being those that listen to these words, you being those that understand the energy from whence these words have come. They are only projections of self, portals of patterns that have been left in time boxes waiting for you to be ready for them to be received. You are receiving a portal of time box information that you, as *in-divide-you-alls,* left ready for yourself as and when you will be ready.

The change is upon us. The change being that of positivity not negativity. This is not about fear. This is not about tidal waves and this is not about volcanoes, this is about the change within. You are part of love and that spectrum of love embraces you at this point in time. You do not see the angels, you do not see the Sceptre of Grace embrace itself around you. You are part of the crystalline thought format that has been here on Planet Earth since time began and before. You are part of a new crystalline structure of energy format that will come to you in different frameworks of time.

Your dream-states do not offer you the solace, they take you into places of learning and acceptance. You are all accepting more sleep at this time, and those that are not getting it are not receiving the download of energy they need to transit from one spot to the next. Do not concern yourself with others, they will do exactly what they need to do when it is part of their timeframe, you must do what you need to do until you feel you are ready to accept the new energy. You are individuals and you all must be in divide.

Just be love, accept love and think good thoughts each and every day as the very acceptance of good thoughts accepts the energy through to you, it becomes a cleaner more processed energy that allows you to elongate yourself on all levels of the spectrum. Just allow yourself to think of the joy of life, the life of joy. It is important that we are allowed to transit from one point to the next. Your friends, your beings of the past, are all with you and welcome you in a new state of existence.

Wilhelmina.

In November 2012 I attended Ventnor Spiritualist Church and although not a member do go regularly on a Sunday evening as I enjoy singing and listening to the varied philosophy of the speakers. One evening the medium, a stranger to me, gave me a short message and asked if the name Wilhelmina meant anything but it didn't. The following Sunday the speaker, also unknown to me, came up with the same unusual name! The universe was on the phone again and this could not be ignored! Someone was trying to get something of importance across to me of which I had no knowledge. That evening I rang Robin to let him know of this puzzling synchronicity and as we were speaking he said: *'I am being told this is something to do with your father's life in India that you know nothing about whatsoever. I will try and get some information further to this.*

December 2nd 2012

There is a need of enquiry with regards to the lady Wilhelmina.

Good evening my friends, I channel the energy of Wilhelmina. Wilhelmina was an energy process required to bring forth energy into a family. She came in the form of a young lady, she came in the form of love. She was a transient being that did not belong to this planet and was here but a short time in your lifespan. She presented herself in India and died in 1942. Her destiny was to transcend energy and bring that forth. She was a Way-shower, an energy process being.

There is no point giving you family names, the energy form was Wilhelmina and Wilhelmina fell in love with your father Carolyn, my grandfather. He was a kind man and he witnessed many things that he never spoke of in the form of aggression, neglect and many forms of humane expansion of consciousness but he chose not to talk of or discuss these matters, they were matters for men not matters for women. He was a gentleman and still is, and he listens to these words now and understands why they come into place.

It is important my dear child, my dear person that transcends this energy, to understand that Wilhelmina is much of the same source as the son Robin. They carry a thought, they carry a form, and they carry an energy.

The man fell in love with this young lady. He transduced energy. He experienced energy not only in the love form but in the exchange, the exchange not only in the form of love, care, compassion, and sharing of bodies, it was *the sharing of energies* that was most important, and in doing so his energy changed from that point onwards.

Yes he was indeed lost to the world when he returned. Many men were when they returned from their war and they had inner turmoil within. There were many things that your father, my grandfather, never spoke of. He involved himself much in many things he did not speak of but he was a man of kindness, he was kind not only to himself but to many men and women that were around him.

He found it difficult when he returned to be personable because he had lost the heart within him, she had passed away, but he could not speak of this for that was not the actions of a gentleman. So he lost himself in work and in drink and in flirtatious behaviour, which really was not the man that he was, but he became this because of the hole that was in his heart. Many people speak of many things but many people do not speak of things they need to speak of but never do, their heart stays closed.

It was his time to pass when he did but he passed something on to you my dear child (*Carolyn*) that listens to this tape, he passed an energy on to you and that energy you still carry. It is the energy of the plexus, it is the trinity, the plexus of thought and it is the resistance to entail yourself in the format of normal men and women. It allows you to stand in your own light and be in your own light and that you must do. Your strength is needed most at this point in time when things around you do not seem real.

They are not real, it is almost like you are existing and watching things but they don't appear to be real, they are somebody else's reality but not yours. You are in a zone, as many people are, it is like there is a gauze between you and what you are seeing and feeling because you are gradually moving over to another format of energy. This is what is happening – those that stay and those that do not.

Wilhelmina was a love for your father but only acted as a gateway into another vision of estimation. In the same way that the child here has had his heart taken away at one point in his life, it wasn't about experience, it was about the exchange of love, not the vows but the exchange that that love allows it to be. Many other things transcend on in life but true love is something that does not come to us many times, it is where your heart is not in its place, it is in a square hole.

The reason why you have been given the name Wilhelmina is to understand that you are part of a process, not only the child that speaks but the lady that hears. You are interconnected, interwoven in a fabric of understanding that many others do not understand, it is about understanding that the plexus is the connection to an energy that circumvents the normal focus of humanity's energy.

You will understand more about this but you must engage your hearts to all that need it now. Just allow love to flow from you with care and compassion as and when it is needed, even to those you do not feel they deserve it, allow them to be love, allow them to be your love. You will find yourself being more loving and caring towards things you found you weren't before, this is part of what is needed for you to be and transcend what is important in this time of great need.

Listen. Your heart's focus is your focus of heart. God bless you and thank you for listening. Wilhelmina was the name, she was a being of differential. She died of energy, it was not of illness it was of energy, the energy was too much and she passed away with an ailment that nobody could figure out. She was blessed and so will you be blessed. It was her part. Your father did not understand why she passed and it was very very difficult for him. Times are different now but times were different then.

Allow the love to flow. Allow yourself to be love.

The Changelings.

December 12th 2012

We are but a hair's breadth away from the changes that we will not necessarily circumvent or understand or even interpret within the mindset we have. *Interpret within the mindset we have,* I repeat.

You must understand that we are all part of a process, an energy format, so in process nobody will be left behind. It is just about those that will and those that won't, and those that can and those that can't, and those that are and those that aren't. Those that are, are those that are understanding and opening their minds, their bodies and their hearts at this point in time and letting go.

Letting go can sometimes procure non-advantageous processes that seem to be anger and spew but they aren't, it is just letting out. It is like the floodgates coming out, the torrent of water looks frightening initially but the calm water will happen later. So just allow people to be what they are, their torrent will flow out of their mouths but just let that flow over your head like the wind as it passes *by* your body but not *through* it. Think of that. Let it go *by your body* but not *through* it, the wind will do that and words can do the same. Just accept people aren't meaning to hurt you, they just don't understand themselves and the words aren't necessarily procured towards you, they are just said. Just allow them to happen.

We spoke earlier of the energy of Wilhelmina. She was indeed a being of mixed race. She lived and died in a very short span of life. She was an energy thought-format. She was a changeling, much as the child that speaks is a changeling. Those that speak as changelings don't really understand who they are and what they are. You are almost like a piece of machinery, a cog that drives a gearbox that procures movement, but that movement is of energy. We are but a cog in an industry of knowledge and mind, and that mind isn't always understood by those that are procuring it.

So just understand, we are all parts of budding information, like the bud of a flower pushing its way through the earth to be seen by Mother Sun. We are all part of a process that we don't necessarily understand and never will. This process is a God-form, a seed in itself, just allowing itself to grow and procure, and you are all part of this. Just believe in what you are, don't believe in what is around you, believe in what you are and follow what you are.

Just interpret the images that come into *your* head because what you will see around you will not necessarily be real, they are other people's created imagery. But your eyes must interpret them because that is what your body expects to see, but they are other people's access points of release. You will know when it is yours because they will fill the very fabric of what you are.

Just stand back and watch, like an audience. The stage isn't necessarily real but it is there, it's a play. Which part is yours and which part is theirs? This you must determine for yourself so you understand when you need to step forward and when you need to step back.

This is what this energy is all about. Which part is yours and which part is somebody else's? There are many strange things happening at the moment but there is nothing stranger than strangeness. Strangeness is just other people's processes, things that you don't understand but they do, so allow this to happen and follow forth my children.

The New Year brings new castings of a new rod, and the fly in front of you is the new imagery, the new process, the new eye, the eye of you, the third eye interpreted in love.

The New Angle of Trajectory.

January 4ᵗʰ 2013

Good evening my friends, it is a welcoming prospect I offer you all at this time of great change on your earth of planet.

I talk to you about earth of planet and you do not realize the changes that have transcended upon the whole of mankind of late. The planet is trajectorising, and that basically means it is changing its whole transducing process of accepting energy. The energy is changed that it used to take before, so therefore you are all changing as does the planet of Earth, the earth of planet. The trajectory transcends at a different angle therefore the way you see things will be at a different angle.

The trajectory has been through the crown chakra, straight down through at an angle of 33.78886 degrees. This is now changing by .3 of a degree, which basically means that it is now trajectorising through another part of the limbic system of the brain. This will encourage further assets of thought that have not necessarily been componentised before. The trajectory of energy, and the way it enters the body, introduces a new parallel of thinking and this allows man to be slightly fine-tuned, only very .3 of a slightly, but it will allow the energy to change.

Many people are experiencing a slight neck and headache at this time and this is due to the body accepting its new trajectory of energy coming in. You will notice that this has absolutely nothing to do with the trajectory of the crown chakra or the brow chakra, those trajectories are different and this is the way that your etheric energy and body is connected to its transitory experience of human experience.

We are trying to use words to introduce a thought format that hasn't been placed in man's assets before. You are being given diagrammatic thoughts that allow us to elongate thought patterns to you via geometry, via the asset of man's tolerance of understanding. Tolerance of understanding is what man requires. His science requires tolerance so something can be trajectorised from one place to the next.

We do not necessarily use those components of understanding. *We* being part of you, but *we* being the origins of where you come from. *We* are the instructors of light and energy. Light and energy allows you to be and to be what you are.

Do you understand that your trajectory is changing? Just accept that you will experience head and neck pain via the change of trajectory. We will give you more about this tomorrow when the child understands why his head and neck ails him tonight.

Seeing from the New Angle.

January 5th 2013

Good evening my friends, this is the day after. You must emphasise that *energy is always transient.* Nothing will stay the same unless we stay the same and don't move with the energy, it is like a wind gusting but it cannot move. If a gust of wind moves freely it moves around objects, with objects, and sways in the movement of its own formulas. We must understand that energy, transient as it is, must not stay still, though Man himself wants energy to stay still so he can understand it, but this is not the case with the new energy coming in and the angle which the frequency allows it to be so. We are part of this new energy, transient as it is, and it must be accepted and moved on from.

As we stated, the energy where it comes in through the crown has changed and shifted its polarity, its angle in which it enters the body. This is stimulating a different part of the brain that allows more acceptance and continuity with regards to life. It does not necessarily need the sharp edges it needed before, those sharp spurs of experience to move us from one place to the next. We have moved from that place and are now using a lesser being of understanding, more of a curve than a sharp spur.

This is how experience is going to be from this point onwards, but the build up to this has not necessarily been conducive to many beings. There are many of you that suffer much with regards to the elongation and the spectrum in which the new angle of energy is entering our bodies. There are those that wish to retain the old and those that will entertain the new, this is the divine right of a human being that accepts free will. We, being part of you, part of the being that you come from, cannot force this upon the transient being, but what we must emphasise is *all humanity will experience this change* whether they accept it or not.

The being that speaks (*Robin*) accepted last evening once he had it explained to him that the energy is coming in at a different angle. Just accept! So when you hear this just accept that your energy is coming in at a different angle and you will see and experience things from a different angle. As was once said, the energy of the past is always the energy of the future, but the energy of the future cannot stay in the past, it is transient, as you must be from this point onwards.

The joy that will bring to you will be personal joy that allows you to facilitate a change within the cellular structure. That allows you to elongate a spectrum of the past presenting itself in the future in a new form, *your* new form, a form of play, a play in which your form can play out what it wishes with the mind instruct.

The Antenna.

February 2013

The establishment of the equilibrium of humanity is via an antenna and this establishes the change that you wish to place in your life, yours being that of you and nobody else. Your antenna establishes what you *wish* to do, not what you should do or what people enforce for you to do it is what *you want to do*. So you establish your future by your thoughts via the antenna that is projecting out into the ethos what it is that you are wishing for.

If you wish for more love then more love will come into your life. If you just fundamentally think about the physical – a remit of sex, joy, self-ethos and so on – then that will come to you, that is part of the ethos, you have that equilibrium within you to project out to your fellow man. But change itself is part of the ethos and the exodus of 2013.

2013 is projection of self. What are you, what do you wish to be and what do you *want* to be? Do you want to be part of somebody else's life or do you want to be part of *your life* that allows somebody else to see you in a different manner? Are you going to be led in a way that pleases others but not yourself? Are you going to be led in a way that pleases the world but not yourself? It is about projecting out what you wish to have within, and you will have the provision to do what you need within if you project it out.

It is like you throw a stone and it comes back and hits you on the head but it doesn't hit you hard, it reminds you of what you choose and what you wish to be in the future, now and the present. The past has been very much a part of where people are caught up in, but the past has a line drawn in the sand. Yes, it has happened, it has occurred, but it is no longer rippling behind you and pushing you forward on the basis of the energy of the past. A line has been drawn in the sand where you have the option, the clarity, the clearness within self, to take steps and strides forward if you so wish.

Or do you wish to stay at the point of balance where you feel comfortable? It is about looking at what you wish to be. Do you wish to be on a level platform or do you wish to be on a slightly unlevelled platform and take yourself forward and understand that your energy is part of a pattern of change, a change towards what you need within? And that is projected out via the antenna?

So literally, in your minds instruct yourself that you have an antenna and project out what you wish to have within, and project within what you wish to have without, and it will come to you in the forms that are conducive with the human frame. The human frame has accommodated many different forms.

Love is expressed through the sexual act, through the eyes, through the touch, through the taste. Love is something so much more profound, it is about what you *feel*, what your *heart actually feels inside*. So *love is how your heart beats* and your heart is what projects out to the planet.

This is what has doused so much of the external influence, the God-source from whence you have come. Because your hearts have been dulled with internal thoughts of lust, money, greed, power and all the ethos that has been needed for growth in the way that you have had in the past. This has been demonstrated to its excellence. That was part of the picture but the picture has changed! The mountains, the sea, the way your heart will beat will instigate the antenna of your future.

The Garden of Eden and the Seed of Expectation.

March 8ᵗʰ 2013

A seed of expectation is relevant for all thought patterns especially the elongation of the new spectrum of thought.

As the tree grows so does the cell inside of you, and as the cell grows the family tree of thought progresses towards the new maintenance of thinking. What we are all doing is getting back to natural resources. We are considering our own components of thought and transcending them towards a new process of understanding. In short my friends, you are all in the process of change.

Now this is easier said than done for a human being who has no prior recollection as to why he is receiving all the energies and processes that are coming towards him, in the form of matter does not matter, energy, anger processes and so on, much of which is coming from previous existences. They are all visiting us and we have no recollection of any of them! The purpose is to accept that the past has already happened and to move on. Do not dwell too much in the past, accept and draw a line in the sand, acknowledge that that was then and this is now, and now is going to be part of the seed of my new future.

What seed do I wish to plant? Something that is beautiful and powerful, an embroidery that is perfection in front of you. Or do you wish to plant the seed of doubt and non-expectance of anything good to happen in your life, because if that is the seed you plant then that is the seed that will grow inside of you, and as the seed grows it will germinate and produce other seeds and that same doubt and non-expectation will be within those seeds.

So we all have new opportunity here that has not been served to us before. We have the opportunity to plant our seed and place expectation, the gift of God. Expectation is what we expect. If we expect nothing then nothing will happen and we will stay like a stagnant mill pool, but indeed we do not have to stay trapped in the mill pool we can flow free. Free flow of thought, the expectation of the planting of the new seed.

The new seed is the seed that came to you when you first ordained on this planet. In fact you were seeded with the opportunity to grow, and that was given to you in many ways. You were watched by the Watchers, you were seen by the gods, you were viewed by the planetary systems, but what you were *not* given was a blockage or a stoppage. You could grow from your seed in any direction you wished, and you did, and you have grown within this opportunity of free flow but not necessarily in the way that is conducive for you in the ordinance of happiness.

Happiness is about *happenstance* – how you happen to be in a stance. For in-stance!

You must understand that the play on words isn't about humour or conjecture, it is actually about allowing you to think in a different way. The stance you take is your opportunity for change, and this opportunity is there for everybody at this point in time. Do not dwell on the negativity of the past because the moment you dwell on that all you do is bring everything up with regards to that and fuel it further with your energy.

Replace all bad patterns of thought with something good, replace it with an ordinance of expectation and possibility – the flower heads of the future, the seeds of the future and the roots of a new tree. What you expect to happen from this point onwards is honourable to yourself, not detrimental to yourself or to others, this is the seed you must plant and sow within the garden, your Garden of Eden.

The Garden of Eden was a conjectural thought pattern placed in front of man in the form of the parallel of your Bible, your words. But in fact the Garden of Eden was the opportunity for which direction you went in, which seed do you wish to plant, what apple do you wish to seed, what pear/pair do you wish to be. You now have an opportunity to pre-pare. Allow your seed to be the fruit of your future and this will be the fruit that you choose and wish to see in front of you.

Words are very awkward when people choose to listen, but they do not understand or wish to bring that into play.

Time is about perseverance and bringing in a new process. Not for one week or two, not for one month or two, not for one year or two, not for one decade or two, it is a process of constance that is required. If you wish to be constantly happy then you have to constantly recruit happiness within you and without you, it is not something you do on a Sunday when you have an opportunity to think about it outside of your work. Your work should be working to live. You live for a living, do no more than that. And when you live for a living things will come to you that you need, not what you want but what you need.

Change is not about the Change in your Pocket

March19th 2013

The perpetuation of the common thought is a resolution within the cellular structure of how you are and what you are doing. There is no such thing as change, it is about the purportment of energy that you are prepared to accept within your system, and when that happens the institution and the elimination of old patterns is removed and a structure of new pattern is replaced by that removal. This is elaborated in the thing you call *change*.

But what is change itself? Is it the change you have in your pocket, is the coinage of value? It certainly has a value but it doesn't have the value you think it does.

Change is about making a step in a new direction and in some respects that is why and what you are here for. We are not here to steer ourselves in one direction and deliver goods from one place to another forever. It is about understanding the goods you are harnessing, and when you have understood that you change to another form of elaboration. This is the format of co-operation and understanding.

Energy is about how you transmute your thought patterns. Up above us all, or within us all, or without us all is a *beacon of opportunity*. Where you choose to spread your thought patterns is the elaborations of processes that come to you. If you think about green cars then you will see green cars. If you think about flowers and joy then flowers and joy will be brought to you, because that is the format that you draw upon at that point in time. We have forgotten that we have this process. Again it is about change.

Man has been spoon-fed with regards to what he needs, and when he sees, hears and feels that same feeling he begins to draw upon that process. It can be processed in the form of negativity, positivity, love, elaboration, anger, hate, but in truth it is about where you choose to spend your mind processes. If those are positive then you will draw positive aspects into your life, so therefore change is about what you elaborate at that point in time.

Think about change as wearing a new pair of shoes. Initially they are uncomfortable and it takes a while to walk with ease, but eventually it becomes second nature as you walk in these new shoes. Change is much the same, it is about going through a bit of discomfort initially and then the cells of your body begin to structure themselves around this new process. So change is change in the goods and how you receive those goods.

Does one wish to be stuck in the past, the processes in which you choose to be? Does one wish to be stuck in the past with regards to remuneration with regards to what one does, because energy has no recognition of finances. If your change for the new is with regards to financial arrangements then that is the way you must be, but bear in mind the remuneration you get will be financial, it will not give you that semblance of respectability that you require within yourself.

Transmutation of energy is what this process is about. 2013 is about change, not change in your pocket but change in yourself, and once you have taken on that change the expansion of change will spread to others because you act out the process. It is not about drawing a new art form, it is not about processing a new art form, it is about *being* that new art form in formation.

There are many reasons why we all require change, but there is so much fear wrapped around that change because it means you will not be comfortable with what you have within yourself. It is always easy to go back to those old pair of shoes that are comfortable, but their soles are worn out. *Your soul is worn out!* Think about that. The platform on which you walk and most walk upon is coming from a *worn out soul.* Put on a new pair of shoes and go through a little bit of discomfort!

You are being given processes that are brought down to the human pattern of understanding. Think about this, it is very important. Those that choose to understand this may take on the burden of your own personal change, and it will be a burden, and when the world changes you will know that you have been part of that change. You haven't been asked to co-operate with anything else other than your own needs, but needs move, like a flock of sheep, needs are not what you need, they are actually what the human processes need around you. We have personal needs but generally our personal needs are not adhered to, we follow comfort but discomfort follows comfort! Think about these processes and take them on board. Be the change and you are that change!

Robin: An awkward night for me. A totally different acceptance of energies with my body going into all sorts of rigors and uncomfortable feelings and I am feeling much the same now. Completely different change in energy with contortions of the face, which was interesting, it was almost like a different body shape was forced into mine and I am not sure I liked it very much but it seems to be part of what goes on. I have to accept a new energy of some form, which is what I am doing now and I feel very, very unwell, unstable on my feet, a lack of energy and inability to think. There is something very different happening at this point in time so we will start and resume with some channelling.

The Seven Changelings.

April 10ᵗʰ 2013

Good evening my friends. The transmutation of a new energy is the correct process for the child to accept. Indeed it is preordained that new energies are transmuting towards him and his fellow kind, those of the Seven. It was spoken of many many years ago with regards to the Seven but we have not connected up that energy with respect to what the Seven mean.

Robin: As far back as I can remember I have always felt considerably different in the way I thought and felt but never understood why, it was just part of who I was. As the years have passed I realise I am different but there must be others who experience these same feelings and don't understand why. There is this definite sense of not belonging with the people around, they don't seem right to you, they seem alien to the way you think and the way you want to perceive love in action, so you just meld in with whatever goes on around and imitate being a human being but the interest isn't really there, it lies with love, care and compassion.

When I was three my family took me to Shegra beach on the north-west coast of Scotland and something very very significant happened. I remember the imagery and clarity of it to this day, something strange and heart-rending happened to me there and I didn't remember what.

Many years later I was training to do my natural health care in cranial-sacral therapy. I was on a course in Ennis, County Clare, in Ireland. Some bodywork was being carried out on me when my hand suddenly raised in the air without any instruction from me as it had done many times before but this time it pointed. I was filled with incredible emotion watching this as I felt something leaving and me being left behind. This was accompanied by such a feeling of desperation. I had no idea what that was then and it took me a number of years to discover the meaning.

In my thirties I was having problems and questioned what was wrong as I needed to know. I decided to see Dolores Cannon, a gifted hypnotherapist, who was speaking at a conference in Glastonbury. We met at her guest house and chatted for a while about why I needed to see her, she then asked me to lay down on the bed and went through her normal procedure. This time I was going to get an explanation as to what all this meant.

I was taken back to that time when I was three years old on the beach at Shegra in Scotland and clearly recalled the emotions involved. I learned that the child on the beach was just a figment, an image, and at that point a soul from another planet/dimension came into that child, who became what is known as a changeling. The soul of that energy being from another planet/dimension came into the child of three and has remained within me.

I am one of seven changellings. Some of whom are in the northern hemisphere and some in the southern hemisphere. Dolores was told she would shortly meet another. Not long after, when she was back in the States, she did meet another of the seven but her information insisted the seven were not to be put in contact with one another as they all have interdependent jobs and it would interfere with their energies.

So I was in fact a changeling from another planet. Pre-determined processes of the world were programmed in my cells and with regards to reincarnation programmed incarnate processes were given me, which weren't actually real but necessary for me to be part of planet Earth and have the energy frequency and memory patterns that come with that. Should someone regress me they will get a regression but it is not real, it is just a programme!

The Seven have been written about a number of times in the channelling and are mentioned in this book. I don't have a great deal of knowledge about what the others are doing, I just know what I do and I struggle to come to terms with that as it is not easy being me. At times the most intense energies flow through my body, throwing me to the ground and on five occasions have nearly killed me. Wilhelmina was one of the energy formats that I am part of and her body couldn't cope with the huge energy so she passed away.

My greatest difficulty has been coming to terms with what I am and trying my best to deal with being in a human body and understanding that those around me generally have a different mind-set. Their needs are very different from mine. I have been surprised to read this information coming from other people all over the world who feel they don't belong here, they are square pegs in round holes. These people are the way-showers, they are just beings from other energy formats who have come here to change the polarity of the human mindset.

This is not about standing on a stage and telling everyone how they need to be, it is about learning to be exactly what it is that you want the world to be. You need to *become the world you wish to live in*, just be what you believe in.

I am one of The Seven and should one of the other seven read this I send you my love knowing that one day we will be reunited.

Creatin, a Breath of Energy

The Seven are transmutations of an original thought-form that is part of the process of why they are here. They carry an energy. It is not a burden but it was mentioned as a burden back then, it is the inability that human frames have of delivering new thought-forms.

What is occurring is a **Breath of Energy** is coming to those Seven, it is like a whole portal of new energy is coming through in the form of breath. As they breathe in they breathe out a cellular re-formation structure called **Creatin**. This is a portal of energy; it is the thought-form process that comes through in a cellular form. *Creatin* is breathed into the body and the body then transforms that energy into the blood system. The cells reform, recalculate in a different way, and as they repatriate themselves and breathe back out again what is breathed out is a thought-form that has its ability to be transformed and transmuted within the human frame.

So this is how alternative energy transmutations from other places other than planet Earth can be brought to this planet, it is done through *Creatin, Creatin* being that of the transmutation of breath into the cells of the human frame.

Unfortunately, because this child sits in the humanoid frame, the energy of *Creatin* is seen as a toxin, a virus, and the body creates anti-bodies. Anti-inflammatories and anti-oxidants are produced to remove this from the system. It is a period of acceptance that he has to go through. It is not pleasant but it was never supposed to be pleasant, it is not that we provide injustice toward the souls that help this process, it is just part of the replication that is required. It sounds incredibly mechanical but that is what is needed.

The emotional form is pushed to one side, as we all have to, on the occasions when we are working with the business sense. Look at this as the business end of the channelling, it is actually how it occurs. Channelling cannot occur in the format of vocalization if there isn't a transition from one place to the other. So all the son, the child, the being that sits here and the other six are experiencing is the *business end of channelling*, the business end of being what they are, bearing in mind the other six are not all channels, there is only one that channels of the other six.

So there is Robin and there is another one who is female and not of this hemisphere, she channels too and is approximately ten years older than the child, she will be nearly sixty now, but she chose to and has done so for the last 15 to 18 years. She has not experienced the same processes as Robin, Robin is a different child, a different being, carrying a different transmutation. But the seven children are connecting like a web, a world wide web, they are connecting unbeknown to themselves and this is what is happening at the moment. They are connecting transmutationally, rather like the breath, the breath of life, it isn't the breath of *their* life it *is the breath of new energy.*

We talked previously of the lady Wilhelmina; it is interesting that the search has been required for more information. She was only born to this planet in 1928. One asks oneself: '*But she would only have been 14 in 1942*. Indeed she was born to this planet, she came and lived with nature, she was almost *beamed down* as such, not in a child form but in an early adolescent form. She lived amongst nature and walked out of nature into the human form and that is where she was for a period of time, elongating who she was, but the energies were too strong for her at that point in time and it was deemed suitable for her to leave the planet. She knew subconsciously that that was what was occurring. But the *energy* of Wilhelmina lays within the child Robin, it is the same energy process from the same place, the same spectrum. So in some respects the child was touched emotionally, physically and spiritually by his own grandfather. He knew of his essence, he knew of the love, he carries that within him, not within him on a soul level but on a knowledge level, a feeling, a sensation that goes within.

True Love.

It is very pertinent in life for us to understand what true love is. Love is a transmutation, an understanding between two souls of discernment between one another. There are many that fall in love that have reasons to do so because they are bound by coincidences, bound by incidences that have happened in the past and they need to work through these processes. In your worldly terms this is what is called karma.

Energy draws two individuals together and if it is love that does that they will need the love to bind them together so they can go through the processes required for them to learn. But in many instances love does not stay and there is dissonance between the two, the resonance that once stood so strong is now dissonant. Dissonance is where the energy is practically worked out, but they have what you call on your Earth plane mortgages, they have resistance to the change. This comes in the form of procreation, and that is children, land, plants, cars, money, finances; resonance of attraction that doesn't necessarily allow the dissonance to dis-complete their process so they stay together, but they are no longer in the same form of love. This does not mean people don't share one another or share things, it just means that the love has changed its pattern.

Love is *not* actually that practicality, love is something far greater. It is where a spark and resonance flames within the soul and that flame stays there. Sometimes it is doused by processes, but it stays there and will always be there.

Wilhelmina was a carrier of a flame. She carried a flame not only for Robin's grandfather but she carried a flame for humanity and she saw where humanity was stepping the wrong stones and walking the wrong tightrope. But these processes were part of the understanding of what humanity needs to go through and everything is happening for a reason. The pollution of the seas, the pollution of the planet, the pollution of the mind-set of the average human being, it is foul, but you must understand that this is what is required at this point in time to get to the end of the tether, the end of the line where the tightrope breaks.

And does this mean there will be cataclysmic processes and changes? On some opportune levels yes. On other opportune levels no. People will change domestically, physically and spiritually into better beings whether they like it or not, because humanity has got to the point where resistance will become futile. Change is required and that is what will happen to all in varying degrees. People are being forced to adapt and change the way they are and change the way they perceive how things come to them.

Are we to expect somebody else to deliver this for us or are we to expect it to be delivered to our own hands via our own hands? We are expected to change and that is what you are expected to do, all that listen.

So 2013 is the era of change, the movement of the cells and the trans-formation of in-formation categorised by the format of true love.

The Balance of Nature and Man

July 4th 2013

We are but a spectrum and this is a purportment of thought pattern so therefore as we think about this spectrum we must understand that we are part of a big picture.

The world was once a plan, a thought and a spectrum in somebody else's mind-set of thought, that being your God-source. In fact the origins of Earth was to create a place of beauty, a place of solitary confinement in some respects to that of beauty and beauty alone would spectrumise towards this planet. The planet was given free choice but this only portrayed beauty, which came in the form of plant life and fauna formation and that created beauty in the form of growth. Growth needs variety and this is an elongation of pattern and that needs to be understood. Beauty creates a balance and balance has co-ordinates.

What are these co-ordinates of balance? There must be both ends of a spectrum. So by creating beauty, inadvertently one also needed to create many other aspects of the word, an aspect of beauty. Beauty can also create great ugliness or great beauty, hot and cold, light and dark, so inadvertently when wanting to create a beauty in the form of the formation you needed other situations to create the balance. Therefore man was invited, along with the animal kingdom, the elemental kingdoms, and many of the other kingdoms that come in and create the balance that is required. Man has much to offer to the planet. He presents grotesque form of ugliness and grotesque forms of beauty to create the balance within nature. In fact man is part of nature carrying out his purpose of what nature needs to be in balance. So the formation of nature created other aspects and other needs.

Is one getting the picture here? In truth it is very important to understand that *man is a system* that is doing exactly what is required to supply nature with balance.

Balance isn't about perfect growth, it is about one year not being able to grow and other years to be able to grow. But what is occurring is the balance required for nature is becoming out of balance by some of the needs that were originally formatted and required. Man is over-balancing, over-compensating for the need for nature, so therefore nature will over-compensate and it will bring man into balance.

How can it do that? Well listen here and we will tell you how nature will eventually create the balance it needs.

Look at man as furniture. Furniture is required within a household to supply the comforts and needs of the human being. So if the furniture is not required, or there is too much furniture in the room, man will eventually remove the furniture or strip it down to his basic requirements. The Nature Kingdom will always do this. So understand that man is surplus to requirements if he pushes the boundaries of what nature needs. Nature is not in charge, it is just requiring balance.

One has to think long and hard about this. Man is not in charge and never was. Man was gifted and geared towards thought, which has allowed him to understand and think that he is in control of many aspects of what goes on. But can he control the way grass grows, can he control the way the wind blows, can he control the tides, can he control the sky or the weather? He tries, but can only change a small amount of what actually goes on. In truth it is **nature that is in control** but not in a formatted sort of way, there is no equation or purportment as to how nature functions, it does as it does, it blows as it blows.

So it is very, very important, for man to understand that nature is taking on board what it needs, and nature is doing what it needs. But man is not doing what it needs, man is doing what it greeds. Man is geared towards self-fulfillment, self-consolidating its thought pattern, creating comfort, creating greed fulfilment. But in truth the success behind all those things is relinquishing oneself of the boundaries of what man creates around himself and **getting back to nature**, getting back to natural forms of thinking.

So we need to gear our way and our thoughts towards very simplistic formats. This is not about living in caves or giving up everything one owns, it is about accepting that nothing should gain control over our thought patterns. When we allow nothing to gain control over our thoughts we regain control of what those thought patterns were created for in the first place, which is to *serve the balance of nature*. This needs to be considered, understood and purported in an energetic format so man can understand the need for this.

The Two Differentials of Man, the Seer and the Seen

July 18 2013

It is by coincidence that we consider the thought patterns with regards to our fellow man.

Man has a transient purpose on this planet, as per recent discussions. There are those that walk the planet *as man,* and those that walk the planet that choose *to understand man and the purpose of man*. There are two differentials there.

Most of the population are here to be *as man,* and there is a small minority that are here to try and understand the purpose of man and understand being with man, as is the child that speaks. There are many others that have a purpose here to understand man and to learn to tolerate man and his misgivings, his misunderstandings, his misappropriations of energy, and so on. It is very important that one differentiates what their purpose is on this planet.

On many occasions you hear that there are children and adults who can't purposefully understand the need to be around human beings. Many of these people have come here to understand the purpose of humanity, yet all they do is walk away from them because they can't cope with the way human beings behave. That is the very thing they are here to do! You cannot learn your job if you do not go to work.

So my children, and anyone that listens to this or gets the energy of this, *the purpose of being here is to understand man!* You don't have to *be* man but you need to understand how he works. Not just man from your generations but previous generations, also man from different countries, different continents, it is understanding the purpose, the need and why people do what they do. It is coming to terms with why many people react to the same situations but in different ways. What is the reason for that?

The whole article of forgiveness and acceptance is about understanding why people do things in the first place. If you are hungry you will pretty much do anything to get food, you will even rape and pillage, you will do anything to save your life, consequently when pushed into situations people will do things that they wouldn't do under normal circumstances. So one must understand that many people are acting out and doing things they wouldn't necessarily do if a different picture was painted in front of them.

The whole purpose is to try and understand the reason for why you are here and what you need to do.

Look around you all and you will see many things going on, many unjust things, many things that do not seem to be acceptable to you or anybody else yet they go on, often under circumstances that seem acceptable to many others. It is very important to understand that love is the way forward. There is no other way of accepting the way the tolerances of people are except with Love, and accepting that it is what somebody needs to do at that point in their evolutionary cycle.

You are just *the seer*, you have a pair of eyes watching and interpreting. But if you use gratitude or injustice or non-acceptance when people are doing things all you are doing is creating resistance behind the purpose. What you need to do is just step back and accept that that is what people do, and when you can come to the point of accepting that you will become passive to situations.

There is much more to be said on this, much more to be relied upon in the world of love. We need to enjoy our purpose here on Earth yet we don't enjoy many things because of what people are doing around us.

We need to become love and that love needs to become us. When we become that purpose in totality our life and love will become a lot easier because love will flow through us like the Divine Spirit instructed us to do in the first place. We are an instrument of his love and that love needs to be administered through *acceptance of what others do*. Others may not necessarily need to show the example that you might need to show but just accept that they are showing the example that is relevant to them at that point in time.

The Watchers.

August 29 2013

The minimilisation of man's thought processes is coming to the fore, it is basically here, and what is occurring is the changes are happening in segments and these are happening in places.

These events are amplified in the news and the places of thought where you are in your minds. The chosen places also appear to have dissent and disease within them. These are not places of anger, they are places of transmutation of energy. It is where energy is gathered at one central point and transmuted out through a spout, which we see as events, places, times, explosions and so on, it is just about the transmutation of energy.

It is a little bit like you putting something in the bottom of a bottle and it sat there for years until eventually it surfaces, and what is on the surface really needs to be in the bottom, it is the sediment of man's thought processes, the sediment of man's malfunctions. But if we are real there is no such thing as malfunction, it is just an event, a course of action that hasn't necessarily been conducive with those around, but we all need events to change us in our lives. If you think about it, it is the things that we dislike the most that are the things that teach us the most. If we do things that we enjoy all the time we would not see the merit in these things, so we have to experience both the for and against, the hot and the cold, all these things, this is common wisdom applied to our thought patterns.

We have so many different thought forms on this planet - gender, relationships between nationalities, between whites, blacks and yellows. There are also *greens*. We do not see the green people but those are behind the scenes, we see them in the corner of our eyes. But there are also people on this planet experiencing stuff and these are called the Watchers, the Seers, they are just experiencing what they see, they can't act upon it but they just take it on board. It is a little bit like filming a situation, it is recorded but nothing is done, it is an event that is recorded and placed somewhere.

We don't necessarily have these characteristics within the human frame but we actually receive something through our eyes that is transmuted into another thought pattern that is part of our evolutionary cycle, but what we see and what we do isn't actually eventised, now that is a new word, eventised, it isn't actually recorded in the way that the Watchers record. They record and report, they have no thoughts about what it is they have seen or what they have done, it is just recorded and placed for somebody else to view and that is *your God-source*. It is your viewing capacity of the planet as such.

The *Greens*, as we call them, are all over the planet, they are energy forms and they are in many different forms; they form nature, they form the insect kingdom and part of the animal kingdom.

We are watched my children, just as you are watching others. Do not think that by watching it is just a pure waste of time because what you are eventually doing is mimicking what you are seeing. You mimic what you see because what you see is sometimes what you want to do but you don't know how to do it. A man always wanted to fly in his mind because he could see other objects flying, be it a helicopter, an insect flying from limb to limb on a tree, or a bird flying from nest to insect, but all these things man wanted to mimic and eventually does when the capacity within his mind allows him to do so.

As we all know man is a growing object. It isn't just about child to man and then death, there is so much more to our procedure.

We must understand that when we start on this planet we start with what we call *asset*. We start with money, status, we start with kingdoms, and this is why those in power are so often in the state of abusing because they have no legislation to stop them doing so, they don't have the built up wisdom that those who have had many more lifetimes grow to understand.

So when you see those in power taking advantage of you, they are not, they are just learning what they should and shouldn't do. But because they had the expansion of growth and capacity to do exactly as they wish, since they have power around them, it is often elaborated to the form that we see in the news. But this power is coveted, it is secretly coveted, and this is understood.

So understand, the less you have the more you have experienced, and the less and less you have the more you experience, then eventually you are born to be a pauper, you are born to have nothing, you are born to have the clothes you walk in, the shoes beneath you, and the ground you walk on, no more and no less. This is why so many wish to rid themselves of what they think is ownership.

This is what is happening on the planet today. It is a little bit like a dog shaking the fleas off his coat. The human being is shaking away the responsibility of ownership, *onus-ship*, there is *onus* to all ownership. What you actually need and want is to let go of *all* your worldly goods, give them away if you can, gift them to those that feel they need them.

The human being is a collector, he collects many things to distract his mind to stop him thinking about all the things he thinks he needs. But in truth he needs very little. He needs his mind, he needs his body, and most of all he needs his spirit, all of which become overlapped at some point.

The Overlap of Mind, Body and Spirit.

Age allows the overlapping to become more defined. As you become older the definition between mind, body and the spirit is defined because you can feel and see and sense the overlap. This is where wisdom comes into play, but it does not necessarily come into play with all of us. It is those that wish to understand what this overlap is, and that comes in the form of understanding, it comes in the form of seeing but not acting, it comes in the form of just *accepting*, it comes in the form of what I see and what I want are two different things.

What I actually truly need is *to accept that what I see is alright,* because it is alright for the person acting out that procedure to do that, as that is why they are doing it. A man who stamps on a bee beneath his foot has the capacity and need to do that for some strange reason. But a man that moves to one side, is he any better or any worse than the man who stamped? No he is just in a different process of experience since there is no such thing as demise or death, there is just a transition between one and another.

Is a short life any more value than a long life? In many cases a short life encapsulates many important things in a very short space of time and is taken to the place of learning and understood. Sometimes those that experience a long life take longer to experience what they need. So in fact time is an essence that is placed in the human format, no more or no less.

There is so much choice available to us all as we watch the sun, as we watch the stars, as we watch the moon. There is so much available for the asset of man but we have to wait for the overlap and this is coming closer. The younger are experiencing the overlap but many are subjected to some of the tortures of human beings, that being lust, that being the need to turn off the mind and just sensationalise and exaggerate the feelings of so-called wellbeing. But what is wellbeing? Wellbeing is *being in* and *well*. To be in and well is to be silent in your mind, to have less calling you in all directions. But our children that grow beneath us look to their parents for example. Are we the curators of their peace or the curators of their truth? We are in fact their curators of a *possible* peace or truth. So we must just allow ourselves to be, and to be is the way, and the way is to be.

There will be more but allow the overlap of mind, body and spirit, the trinity of truth is with you and with that truth the trinity of understanding comes to those that accept the overlap.

Facing the Truth of What You Are.

September 6th 2013

The element of truth remains in all human beings and this resonates with everything that we are and everything that we do.

How can truth be truth unless it is something we have experienced or understood? Yet we do not understand what truth is when the truth is displayed right in front of us. The truth lays in **nature** and the natural being and the natural being is your truth. It isn't utterances of words, statements of facts, it isn't even what you have and haven't been doing, as that is only verbal acceptance of where you have been in your physical matter but *truth is about what you are.*

The gatherance of speed is occurring right now about your own personal truths. This is the gatherance of what you are about, your eons of molecularisation.

When we talk about molecularisation this is actually the spectrum, the figment, the factual process of everything you have been up until this point. You can be in front, behind, or where you are right now, but everything you have been has already happened, everything that has happened has already been.

But what is actually occurring is you are being gathered up, a little bit like a net and the fisherman is hauling everything in, and the display within the net is everything that you have done - positive, negative and neutral. Everything is coming up and being displayed to you right now on a screen, and that screen is happening simultaneously within your own life, so what you are actually experiencing right now is everything that you are. The display of what you are is being displayed in a figurative speech and process, it is actually being given to you in its whole form. This allows you, as a process, to move from one point to the next.

Why is this being handed to humanity at this point in time? Every individual on this planet is being handed this and it is not easy to take. It is certainly not easy to give right now because very little is left to give to anyone. You are hanging on as such. It is very important to understand that you are an individual and you must help yourself first and foremost and by helping self you show the fact that you have not been too disparaging with regards to your remark. Your *re-mark* being the remake of what you have been.

Why has man come to this process? Well he had the choice. He didn't actually have to go through this process, but the choice is that you extend to a point of reality and you are coming back to your own truth, your personal truth, so you are bringing back to you everything that you have given out. It is like lots of mini boomerangs coming back and hitting you on the back of the head and you don't know why they are coming. Yes, this is indeed uncomfortable but in truth this discomfort is well worth going through because it is going to allow a stability of acceptance.

This twenty or thirty year period, this transition from one point to the next, which is what it is, you are three quarters of the way through it as a man, as a woman, as a race of beings, you are twenty years into the process. 1993 is approximately when this started, when the cell within you grew. It was planted within you with an opportunity. It is like a desert seed, once given the opportunity to grow it will grow very quickly, it will then develop and drop its seed again and maybe it won't rain for many years. The rain is the rain of your process of energy, and that is the development that you have allowed to happen to you.

There is so much change to happen, so much understanding to be given, but you must understand that understanding has no relevance if it doesn't have your truth behind it. Your truth is your reality, not words.

Many people are choosing to stand right outside of their body right now because it is very difficult to stay inside, but those people that discard their bodies and sit just outside will lose their bodies and won't be able to get back in them. It is very important that you stay inside your body. There are very many that choose to withdraw totally and go into some other procedure but you cannot remove yourself from this process. You are a human in being and that is an example of what things can be, you are prototypes my children, it is indeed a massive plan of understanding for those that are watching. You are prototypes of understanding.

Nothing like this has happened before in the universe. Why should it happen to you? The question is why shouldn't it, why should you not push the boat out into a river that you do not understand and there are no navigational processes? Somebody has to do it first and you, as humanity, are doing this first as an example to the whole universe as to how things *might* be done if it happens like this again in the future.

You are not being used as an exemplar, you have just been given an opportunity. If you go in this direction this will probably happen, and because you have gone in this direction it is happening. There is no set plan but every time something comes into play a new criteria has to come into play to act in accordance with where your roles are lying. So the script is down to you but the producers have to adjust each time you adjust your script.

Just allow yourself *to be* and *do not fight* what is happening to you. Just understand there is some rationale behind the irrational processes going on within and without all of your bodies. There will be more to be had and may the voice speak again very soon.

Information Carries a Frequency

September 12 2013

Robin: *I have been through another rough period of time not feeling too well. I channeled recently yet it didn't seem to remove whatever this is so I will try again. It is not that convenient to accept this energy flowing through me but nevertheless I am sure it is a choice that I made somewhere.*

Good evening my friends, it is indeed the child's choice. There are many thought patterns that we need to circumspect within the mind.

He must understand that as we speak we actually speak from a totally different dimensional process. For this dimensional process to elongate itself into the physical form creates dissent within the body, the child knows this. The dissent in effect creates what is called the antibodies process where the body is recognising alien cells, and in truth that is exactly what they are, and the body fights it like a virus. But the body doesn't actually have a virus, it is just another energy form formatting itself to produce information.

As we said in the past, information doesn't necessarily have to have the basis of meaning right now, it doesn't even have to be said to anyone, but what it actually does is *it carries a frequency*. So once it has been placed on the format of planet Earth it is there to be received as and when people are ready to hear and take on board that energy. Sometimes that happens immediately, sometimes this happens thousands of years later and the person that created that energy has well gone, well gone in the format of understanding that you create, which is that of life and material cells.

But in fact energy is a transient process, people go back and forth much the same way as energy goes back and forth, it is like a tide. You must understand there is no acceptance of one tide or another, it is just what happens.

Human beings are in the process of total and utter change. What in truth is happening is they need to get back to the original cellular format. *This cellular format is of a reptilian nature*, we spoke of this last evening but the child did not record this matter but we will speak of it again this evening.

The Reptilian Nature.

The reptilian nature was the original thought format that came and created itself upon planet Earth. It was a cold blooded instrument. This wasn't conducive to the matter and material required on planet Earth, the Earth of beauty, the Earth of frequency and exchange. We then exchanged the cold blooded for the warm blooded. The warm blooded in itself is that in which mammalian frequencies frequencise under.

Here I digress to quote from an earlier communication of 2007 that has relevance to this information received six years later in 2013.

Our Origins in the Constellation Serpens

January 9th 2007

My children, the imagery you see this evening is of the serpents. The serpents is where you have come from. Serpents is also a sky element, it is a constellation in the sky called *Serpens*. My children, you are part of a *reptilian* format. Your blood runs cold when you hear this because that is where you have come from. This is where the cold thought formats come in many situations and where your blood runs cold with the way you feel. It is not that of a negative sense or an evil sense, it is just that you will think and rationalise in a different way, in a cold sense. This is why some of the terminology dealt to the boy is very cold, because that is how it works in that realm, it is about *doing and being* not necessarily about experiencing. It is about doing what needs to be done when it needs to be done, instantaneously, as opposed to rationalising about what that means.

This will allow you to extend some of the mindsets you have in your cold minds. Sometimes the flowers that don't grow and just stay the way they are is the way your reptilian mind will allow you to function. Occasionally you will see the reptilian formats you have come from communicating with yourself in a three dimensional pattern, that does occur, and by doing this it allows a reptilian thought format to transcend itself into a human thought format in a certain way so that the frequency is not demeaning to either source.

My children, sometimes we need to feel the original source to understand what that means, those are what are called cold moments. Allow yourself to have those cold moments, they are *not* an investigation of some other particle trying to transcend your energy thought format but it is about you being part of self.

You have come from many thought formats, many transcendences, and it is just about you experiencing and understanding what they all are and being part of them on occasions to allow your cells to re-member what that was at that point in time to allow yourself the memory access of where you have come from, and possibly where you might go, and certainly where you are right now.

Your blood speaks my children, listen and you will get answers. There is much more to come. Continue your evenings, it is so very important as it will allow you both to grow in the direction that is relevant for you both and for the lady (*Carolyn*) that sits to grow from the information that is given. God bless you. Be cold and be warm. Bless you my children.

This was followed by the strange language that Robin has spoken many times during the channeling that I am quite unable to write down but it starts something like this! Shinka ta...etc.

Behind the veil, behind the veil, look behind the veil and you will see the answers and they are answers of self. Bless you my children.

Continuing with the present channeling ...You must understand that this is not a change, this is a process that was chosen. But to understand the original frequency of planet Earth you need to understand why you came here in the first place. You came here because it was a choice. All of you have a choice – those that speak, those that listen, those that choose not to say anything – all have a choice about what they need to do.

What one needs to do right now is just listen to the inner promptings of self. The inner karmic readings that are coming back to all the planet right now is that of choice, that of change, that of material instability. It is happening not only within the world but without the world. *Material instability, the very ground on which you stand upon no longer has the value that it had previously.* You must understand, this isn't about a transient process this is about what is happening, it is the change. It is like clearing the table and placing a new instrument on top of the table, but one needs to understand the old instruments were there for a reason. They are there for a reason because one needs to understand them before they move on to the next plane of understanding.

The child in itself, as has already been spoken, is a process of coordination, a process of patternisation of information, the creational process behind, therefore the dissent he feels within his body right now is just changing patterns of energy. He must understand that it will terminate itself very shortly. Just allow this to flow through. It is not a part of a rejection process, it is not a part of an illness, it is part of acceptance and acceptance in itself cannot be created or violated in any way or form.

There are many different processes that we need to understand. The ordination of thought pattern, the Ordained Ones, those that chose to be here to watch over humanity as they grow. Those are the Elemental Beings that have always been here on the planet, they are of energy rather than matter. It is not that they matter, it is not that they are energy, it is the fact that they are here *watching*. *They do have power and they will terminate that power as and when it is required.*

You must understand that you are part of the pattern, as is rest of humanity, and as you listen to these words they will stretch the mind to the point where you have no understanding whatsoever, and *no understanding whatsoever* was what you started with, no more or no less.

We challenge you to accept the non-accepted processes. We challenge you to accept that you are part of a process that has no set purportment or pattern. It is like throwing a ball into an arena; it can bounce anywhere it likes but anywhere it likes is somewhere new, so therefore the bounce, so therefore the atomisation of the air around that, therefore the fabric of the ball will change. Everything about it will change, it will never be the same from that point onwards because of the pattern it chose to take. That is what humanisation is all about; it is about bouncing a ball, not expecting a pattern to work in any formula whatsoever. It is just about accepting pathways are pathways and they will always lead to somewhere, there is never nowhere to be gained.

So in truth do not expect a pattern, but do incorporate a pattern of thinking. In truth you must accept this. There is choice to be had in all things and this choice is about to be delivered to man. *This choice is about to be delivered in a very, very unpleasant fashion to most of man,* and that is the way and formula. Watch this space and this space will be watched.

Evening of September 13 2013

Robin is not at all well and this is obvious from his voice: *It appears that there is a lot of mist at this point in time and I don't understand what is expected of me but I will try so I will articulate whatever it is that needs to be articulated but you have to f... off and leave me alone because you will end up removing your voice completely and there will just be an empty shell left and you won't know what to do then. So that is my ultimatum to you, rather than you give me ultimatums as to what you think I should be doing.*

My child, we hear your thoughts and articulations yet you do not hear ours regularly. You have held back for many millennia with regards to the speech syndrome that you have. You hear so many others talk of so many things but you do not talk of what you need to speak of. What you need to speak of is **what you feel**. You do that on many occasions in your mind but that stays *internally* yet when you speak of it *outside* of your mind then that goes. You must accept that that is your truth and that is what you need to do. It is a little bit like a Ping-Pong ball bouncing, you must bounce more regularly than you do my child.

These are just merely words and words themselves have very little substance, yet when substance is added to words they have meaning and clarity, and meaning and clarity is what needs to be procured from you, not just to others but to yourself as an energy form, *a chosen energy form*. You just need to accept that for the near future you will need to articulate. Articulate what is required of you, no more or no less.

You need to sleep, that is truth, yet you have slept for too long. You need to wake up my child to what it is that you are. We will speak more but you will sleep. You will come.

The Diversex

September 16th 2013

The resonance and frequency of all of us has to be understood. For us to understand this we need to take ourselves right back to the original formats of man, which is when he came to the planet.

He came to the planet in the format of cold blood, *the reptilian format*. The energy was not conforming to the components of land mass and land matter and they were in turn killing each other off and there could only be one as such because the energy in itself was a singular format.

So this was the problem initially of the single reptilian format, so they created the warm blooded energy form and allowed in turn this energy to flourish over the planet and it still does so today.

You must understand there is so much more to come on this fact but the child needed to channel this information, he will channel more when he comes and he will come.

September 17ᵗʰ 2013

Robin is still suffering as he channels and his voice is very weak

This is a continuation of last evenings' conversation with regards to the cold blooded origins of our planet.

The reptilian being that we discussed has a name, it was called the *Diversex*. The Diversex had twin vertebrae so it technically had two bodies attached to a head and an interesting dynamics as to how and what it could do. It could flatten out and walk, it could walk with the two bodies behind it. It could stand up very tall with the head in the middle. There were many things it could do but the one thing it couldn't do was accept another component of itself to be on the planet anywhere whatsoever. This was the problem, the origins, and the technicalities behind this beast.

If it knew there was another being exactly the same as itself or anything else it would literally kill it, and it was well able to with its arsenal of tools and methods of death, but predominately it ate vegetation because that is all there was, it would eat components of wood, but if it found something to eat that was slightly different then of course it would.

The Diversex in itself realises that once there is another similar being it has to go and find it. Bearing in mind the world was many different continents, but it could tune into where the other energy force was and literally transfer its cells to that area, and it would find it, as would the other find this one. Both honed their devices to find the other but when they met initially what they did was they copulated to produce and then stayed together for a period of time. Both of which would become gestated with the seed because they were androgynous, they were neither male nor female but had both genes, they had the cells of the female and the male so they could carry as well as give birth to, but they needed another to do this.

So the reptile stayed the course, made sure the egg had settled in and then went about thinking how it was going to eradicate the other. But of course the other one was thinking how it was going to eradicate that one, so that is how it went on. A strange reptile! But it is interesting, during this period of time the one would groom the other. There would be a grooming process going on, but as the individual was being groomed it had the ability to switch off a particular area of the body, just in case. Because it had two hearts, two sets of organs down two sets of bodies so it could switch one side or both sides off temporarily, it had very strange setups. So we must understand that the reason for this animal to be here was purely to be *as a singular*. We will talk more later.

Robin: Around September 2013 my body was building up to another one of the illnesses I had suffered previously. This was the fifth time I had experienced such extreme levels of discomfort with high temperatures and my brain like a mush. I don't really know how to explain this, every part of me doesn't seem to be working properly and that is how it is.

When I read the channelling it states the reasons why this happens. But this time I became so ill an ambulance was called to take me to hospital, frightening the life out of me and my family. I was in for a week and feeling worse than ever before with a white blood cell count so low that everyone was wearing masks to prevent my getting an infection, which would make matters worse.

During my trip to the hospital I thought maybe I needed to channel as perhaps this was the reason for my sickness because previously if I hadn't channelled for some time and then did so the sickness went away. I did so and received the information about the Diversex, which literally made my blood run cold. It brought with it such an unpleasant foul feeling, I felt I was channelling the rottenness of everything there was in the world and it was coming through me, I felt as if something had got hold of me and making me do this.

After my recovery when the series of channellings had been transcribed by Carolyn I took time to read them and realised they were probably some of the most diverse pieces of information that had come through me as a channel and was communicated at the zenith of my sickness. I don't recommend doing this when you are so ill nevertheless these words were given me at my lowest ebb.

The reason for my illness was explained, along with what was happening on a human level. What I experienced was not normal and never has been. There is no description for what it is like when you are so sick due to the input of tremendous energy, almost to the point of leaving the planet. Evidently that was not to be allowed, it was another adjustment to my framework but one that was very very difficult to come to terms with.

Have I come to terms with it yet? It isn't a joyous thing to be a channel and in some respects is very difficult on many occasions. My family don't necessarily understand who I am or what it is that I am required to do but they have eventually come to appreciate that it is necessary for me to do these things that seem very different to them.

These days I no longer channel under duress or have the stress I suffered before as I allow communication every Sunday. I now understand there is so much information stored within my frame and unless it is released via the voice it will eventually explode into illness so I channel out of necessity. The information flows more easily as the words come through me but I don't understand them all.

These days I am fascinated by what is said and am challenged intellectually by some of the verses. I am more in touch with what I am as a channel. The words have taken me on a journey and I am journeying towards my future so from this point onwards I will listen to all it has to say but to those who are channelling please listen to what I have to say.

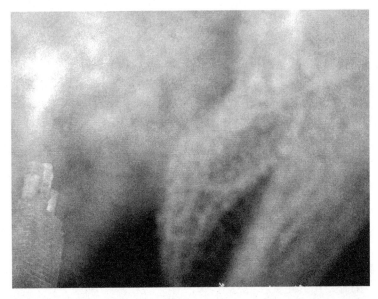

Carolyn: Once again I was out with my camera and this strange creature showed up that appeared to be the head of a reptilian dragon (see photographs). Was this a sign of things to come I wonder now considering the information about the Diversex given to Robin?

The Journeyer.

September 26th 2013

This last week or two have definitely not been the best weeks of my life but I suppose there is an element of tolerance and acceptance involved in many things. So here we go!

Good evening my child, it is a while since the earthly basis of discussion has been given to you. You have had so much esoteric information with regards to the advent of the Earth and the changes and so on, involved in the advent of the Earth but we will give you some information with regards to what is happening to your good self now.

Your cells are in a case of reversal. Now a reversal is going back to old knowledge and understanding and regaining some of the assets of the past. Now unfortunately the tolerance of the human frame is about cells going in forward motion, that is part of the protocol of Man, cells in forward motion gathering speed as they go and gathering knowledge, whether that knowledge is of war, of love, of disgrace, of many different things, fine foods, bad foods, illnesses, that is what they do.

But when the cells go in reverse it creates an adverse polarity within the body. This is what you have been experiencing. It has been intolerable as you well know, but intolerable in what form, because on a different form your body is gleaning the information that you are getting. So it is in some respects just a small amount of discomfort for the access gained to the previous information available, unfortunately not to yourself on a conscious level.

But my child, you are *a journeyer* and it is about the journey of course. You are here to do many things other than just be a human frame. You must understand the human frame always will have limitations, but those limitations are always pushed to the limit, as with all human beings. That is what human beings do.

But in your case my child, you have many *different assets* and your asset at this point in time is the ability to go backwards, back and re-present oneself in a different formula to understand the origins of man. Now you have been given some of that in previous channellings. You must understand that you are part of the ancestry of all this. What does that actually mean? Your ancestors are part of that cellular structure in one way or form.

You have all been given the opportunity to place your energy on planet of Earth. Now that energy has to build up levels of understanding and acceptance, you might understand that as being karma, but there is so much more to it than this.

The energy of the land and the energy of the human being have to combine in many different ways, and as the ecology of the land changes so does the ecology of the human frame, it is a little bit like the biodiversity of all frequencies have to come together. We are having this incident at the

moment.   There   are   so   many   different   biodiverse
frequencies that are not working.

It is like the genetic structure of cropping and how it affects
the insect life.   Now the insect life know that that is not
going to be in harmony for them in the future, or the
present, so what they are doing is they are withdrawing their
energy.   They will withdraw their energy until the point
where man either decides to stop procreating in a falsified
manner, for not only himself but those around, or he will
lose the demonstration of the insect nation. The loss of the
demonstration of the insect nation will interminably be the
loss of man himself, but he needs to find that out and go to
the zenith of course, because that is how learning is
produced.

Man himself is part of a programming, it is a certain thing
that needs to occur. It is a little bit like a man needs to find
out how fast the car goes, and when he has got to that level
he will push it that little bit farther until he either dies or he
lives.   But the living part basically means he got to the
zenith of what he could have done but he is sure that he
could have done better. That is how human beings work.
They are intolerable in some ways, but acceptable in many
other ways. They are an exemplar not only to themselves
but to the planet and the universe because it is about
pushing the limits, but pushing the limits means pushing
many different limits.

Robin, your limits have been pushed to your limit and
probably beyond, but you have to accept that it will

terminate fairly shortly and your body will feel better for this. You will be stronger and more understanding of what is going on and you will also have a better understanding of why you are a channel. Because you are a channel because that is what you chose to be but also because of the presentation of the information that you gather as an individual. It isn't about sufferance or being attacked in any way or form. Others may consider this but you are not being attacked, what you are actually being is yourself, gathering the information that you are supposed to do at this point in time.

If a man goes too close to the volcano he is going to get hot, he may get scalded, but somehow he learnt from that experience because the heat gave him something he didn't have before. So you have been close to a smoldering volcano with the fevers and the rigors of the body going *no it can't cope* but the **soul can cope** because it has so much more inside of it than you actually consider. There is steel in there my child, and accept that that steel will guide you through.

It isn't about age or the misuse of your body, it is actually about acceptance that a change is coming into play, not only for yourself but for the rest of the universe, so accept, watch and wait with love. There is always love involved in all things. Just accept, accept, accept, and be blessed my child, be blessed, and be honoured.

Need not Greed.

September 27th 2013

The abstract denomination of being a human being is always an awkward one because the framework has restrictions. The framework is predesigned to move forward. The cells are there to be gleaned and moved forward like a ball rolling; rolling down a hill, up a hill, sideways, upwards, downwards, inwards and outwards. That is the process of denomination. That is how it is, it has been that way for many millennia.

There was a point in time where humanity actually stood still for periods of time, where the cells didn't have the need to move forward, they stayed as they were. These were the times where the human frame became more elaborate, it became more elaborate because it could see its surroundings in many ways because there wasn't this need to grasp information in the same way, it was almost an acceptance that you could stay as you were. Now staying as you were was not a bad thing, it was not a good thing, it was just how it was. But what we have right now is a massive need to grasp knowledge, to grasp experience in so many different ways, and the human frame is doing that in such an elaborate form that the consequences sometimes create demeanors.

Demeanors are the way the human being is flowing right now, the need to grasp too much; it is like eating more off a plate, eating the plate and the knives and forks as well to see what they are like. But what we are getting at here is, the human frame is a complicated principle and it needs to be understood, it needs to be understood that what is happening in the world right now is through need not greed, it is need, and it is the way the framework of the human works, they need to move forward.

There are those human beings that understand that this need to move forward is actually a demeaning process and almost go to the hard-wire and redial themselves and keep themselves more in a stationary place to be. Now this allows you to create a framework, a respectability around yourself, and this temporarily allows a human being to keep themselves stable. Now this is how it is at the moment, finding ways of keeping yourself stable in a process of instability, it is a requirement.

You must understand this requirement is about *growth*. Human beings sometimes have to grasp their understandings through so many tumultuous processes, but nevertheless there is a reason for all these things and it will stop at some point. But the process is not an experimentation, it is a process of need. That is the way the frame is built at this point in time so do not express this as a differential or an irregular or a process of non-understanding of where we are, or a process of total elaborate concentrated interference from somebody else, this is just how the gearing is geared. Accept for this process in time.

There are those that go on and look at this process and say '*No, this is wrong.*' Yes, it is wrong in the eyes of that person that is seeing this, maybe it could well be wrong in the big picture. But what is the big picture about? It is about creating a miniscule cinematic process, a miniscule process of understanding.

There are many things that are wrong in your films, your Hollywood processes. There are many things that are projecting tumultuous processes to man through that media, but nevertheless they occur. They occur for whatever reason it is, they occur because money is made and people are paid. There are processes to be elaborated to the human frame because that is what they need; if they need anger, war, sex, whatever it is, then it will be portrayed within the media. Everything is portrayed.

It is like the displays in a shop. There is no point putting something up there that nobody is going to eat, but when somebody finds something that people like then they will get more of something similar and create another need. That is how the human frame works. Less is more or more is less but the process is human beings will take whatever is available to them and run with it until they decide they don't want it. Just accept this process for a period of time. This is all we have to say today but there is more to come.

Plugging in to a Different Frequency

September 28 2013

The confidence in vibration is one of the frequencies we need to discuss this evening.

What is actually occurring is the child is actually moving his vibration into a totally different frequency and this frequency has an adverse effect, it is basically bringing differences to the cellular structure of the body. But what is actually occurring is the frequency of the body is travelling into another dimension and gathering funds, as such, it is like gathering a crop. It is like a knitting web of information that is coming back.

But what is actually happening is, there is a strand attached to the body as the dimensional travelling goes on (*Is this what we know as the silver cord?*) and this strand is actually *feeling* the frequency change. So what you have to understand at this point in time is the boy in himself is feeling the differential. It is a change, it is a componentry change of the frequency in which the body functions under and has done in the past.

So we have got a total change in polarity as such, it is a little bit like a change from 240 to 238 volts of energy coming through a plug, it is just a different change. The way that things would function would change because of the frequency change, and this is what is occurring. We can't explain to you in layman's terms as to why and what the reason is for this, it is just the dimensional co-ordinates are changing on the planet. Everything in itself is speeding up very very slightly and the human frame is adjusting due to this speed, this curvature of change.

We are not going into the dynamics of science but what we are actually saying is, whereas you would throw a ball and if you could throw it up in the air and it went round the planet and came **back** to you, it would have a curve to it. It would stay above the planet at a certain curvature, continue round at that same curvature if it carried on at the same speed, and then come back and land back in your fist in the opposite hand.

But what is actually happening is the curvature of trajectory is changing in the way information is flowing to you and many others that channel. This in itself is indicative in the way the human being is functioning. There is a new process of understanding and this process of understanding is where your body is storing this information. It is your process of storing that is changing, your process of elongation that is changing. This makes it no better or worse for you as a physical subject but what you must understand is *the esoteric ramifications of what is occurring will have ramifications on the physical body*. These ramifications are as just.

You must allow your white cell count to stay as it is because what that is actually doing is allowing your body to re-frequencise itself. They will in a week or two raise themselves back up again and you will watch them and feel them do so. Just wait, it will take a week or two. By the middle of October your white blood cell count will be up to where it should be, but you are going to have to wait. Mark my words and this will come to you.

The Purpose of Flesh

October 10th 2013

The Diversex was an animal instinctive, it was an energy format that we didn't really understand. We gave the Diversex an opportunity to be on planet of Earth. It was a prototype, a thought pattern, but it didn't actually elongate into a spectrum that was acceptable on the planet.

As you can imagine all flesh in itself has an opportunity to progress whether it is alive or whether it has passed into another dimension, but flesh has an opportunity to glean and move on in a perspective that is not expected within other aspects. Now when we talk about other aspects, what we are actually talking about is different material factors, flesh in itself is a moving, gleaning, information processor. That is effectively what it is, it moves elaborately around its domain.

You must understand that the human in being is flesh in itself gathering together information. Now when we talk about flesh it is almost as if we are talking about an object. Flesh is basically in effect *a vehicle to carry the molecules of the spirit*. There are many different components of flesh as we all know, the Diversex was one of these things.

Now we call the Diversex the *diversex* because it had so many different components of thought but in itself it was very simplistic, it had very simplistic needs. These needs have elongated from that original spectrum of thinking to the process that we now have, which is **human in man**, and the human in man as such is a progressive instrument of gleaning information. Gleaning information is **gathering** information. That is effectively the process required for human in man and you must understand that that is the process that is continued to be so. But there is a change in component happening at this process in time, this change in process is allowing man to **change his instrument**.

His instrument is now not only a gathering of information but a **projecting** of information. But to project information one needs to go back to the original cause, the focus from whence one came in.

It is a little bit like you came in through a door and you have travelled through many many different houses. But you have to go back to the **original** house, go back out of that door again with your information, discard that information and give it up to whatever you need to give it to, and then you start a journey again afresh. It is like being **reborn** as such, but you are not being reborn because you are still as you were.

This has never happened in the universe before. You are being reborn but you have never died, you have stayed as and when you were.

This is what happened to the Christ. The Christ didn't actually die, the Christ lived. **He was reborn whilst he was still alive** and he lived out his life as per a normal human being, procreating and creating other children. The

Christing in itself was the original process *of the Christ* and that Christ died but lived in another man. You must understand that *there is the Christ blood today on this planet, procreating and carrying out but he will never expose himself in the way that he did before.*

The art of longevity is the art of not actually letting on what you actually do, because if you do that human in Man becomes threatened by that. So do not let on what you do, *just be what you do,* and when you are being what you do you are in the safe place, the safe place to keep your molecules centered at the point where you are at this point in time.

Now you must understand that love in itself becomes very misplaced when its guidance comes from different access points. But you must understand, keep yourself centered at all times with *your* love, not the love of somebody else but your love, and you will componentise yourself in the necessity that *you* need, because every need is different but every need is equally as important. So always remember that somebody else's need might not always be yours.

There is much more to be said. Words in themselves are complex, patterns in themselves are complex, but don't be too complexed yourself. You are love and you will continue to be love. There must be more words said over the next few days.

Clarity and the Changelings

October 16 2013

We surmise that our future has clarity yet we do not understand what clarity is.

Clarity is a clear pathway towards something, yet we have no clear pathway towards anything and we never have done. It is about creating an energy of the future but this energy of the future is not created by the energy of the past, yet the energy of our past creates our future because we are stuck. And this is fundamentally what has been going on for hundreds of years with regards to human beings and the procedure towards their life. Because of the nature of what has happened in the past their clear pathway to the future is inhibited by an abundance, if not an annihilation of thought patterns, energy processes and non-deeds.

Now when we talk about all these things, especially *non-deeds*, they are processes that we are ordained to do yet we have not done them. Sometimes it takes us lifetimes to carry out a process of doing something we are required to do; this is *marry* somebody, *love* somebody, *forgive* somebody, *even take somebody's life*. These are processes that we are ordained to do, and we are given these jobs to do because they are purposely created within the ordained creational process behind what we are about.

How indeed could somebody taking somebody else's life be an ordained process? Because by taking somebody else's life indeed you are in fact you are carrying out a process of misguidance, non-godly process and so on, but indeed you see **carrying out karmic processes** are also part of carrying out part of who you are and what you need to observe and what others need to observe.

There are many things that we do not understand yet we will question them and in rare circumstances not actually carry them out because we are of the world and therefore we are following the worldly rules. There are many things as we say, and **we** being those, **the creational process behind human beings**, are actually stating that you now have to catch up with what you need to do as an individual.

The process is quickening and speeding, as is life. Time in fact is speeding on at about five times the rate that it used to, you are actually noticing that things are happening at such a rate of knots. But is this something that happens with age?

You are actually experiencing a transition of time five times quicker than you were approximately 38/39 years ago. Things have been speeding up, speeding up for the relevance of the universe because the universe **awaits**, it awaits the coming once again of the planet of Earth with the **availability of changelings.** Now **these changelings require us to do our ordained purposes and understand what those ordained purposes are.** You must start listening out, each individual that has an ear that listens, to your ordained purpose.

What is this ordained purpose, am I carrying that out, if not what shall I do to find and procure my future for myself now? This is something that needs to be brought into your forefront, your sight, your vision, so your clarity can be clear for you to see. We will give more of this in the near future.

Inertia.

October 20 3013

The resonance of formation is the particles of the mind-set that comes through to the forefront of the mind as and when you are using the correct frequency of understanding.

You must understand that these particles are part of an inherent process, this inherent process is about who we are. We cannot change what we are but we have to *know* who we are. This is part of the inherent transaction that is happening within you and every other human being on this planet at this point in time. You are coming to terms with who you are, you are potentially catching up with yourself.

If you imagine yourself as one of those bungee springs and a big part of you has stretched your way ahead with knowledge, but behind you is everything that has happened and you have come to a halt because you have come to the extension point of where the spring will expand to, and you have got to that point and you are staying stationary and still. The spring isn't coming back with inertia and slapping you on the back of the head but it is coming back slowly, and inherently you are frequencising the processes that have happened to you in the present, the past and the future, because everything has simultaneously happened at that point.

The inertia is everything coming in at different directives. You must remember, if it is coming from the future, and believe you me you have lived in the future even though you are in the past at this point in time, this future is coming from one angle, the past is coming from the other angle, the present is coming in from the side. So you are in fact inertia-ing information from many different processes, and your body is taking all this on board, and you are stretched to the limits, all of you.

This is a very interesting process to be in because this elaborate organisation of cells is happening and your body is having to augment all this information and bring it into a practical component of understanding, not only for *yourself* but for that of the energy that you work with.

You are part of the God-force of course, but there are curators of energy, there are people that have to gather this information, a little bit like a crop, and store it. It is like you have been working for a multi-computer agency and many millions and millions of cells from that computer agency have been sent out to gather, but you are all part of a central component, as we call it a central computer, a multidimensional computer designed for creating and understanding experience.

Now experience is what creates the evolution of man, not only of man but all processes of understanding. Everything that creates understanding is a process of elaborate structure, and that labyrinth of structure is created and understood and brought back to a central point. This central point is where you all are at this point in time. You are at the point where you need to be, but believe you me, it is not a comfortable place to be, because the inertia of bringing back all this information creates dissent within your body, as the child well knows, but this dissent is a different one for him as it is for many others.

He is and always has been the forefront of structure, almost paving the way for others to come. It is like a snow plough smashing through the snow and bringing it to one side or the other or just fragmenting it and thereafter the people behind him have an easier transit. This is part of his job at this point in time, it is not necessarily a pleasant one, but unpleasantness always has a direct opposite, always! You must understand, the more unpleasant a frequency of understanding is there is always a direct opposite that happens. It is called part of the process of equilibrium. With one set you will always have another set, and in between is the balance, so the child has good things to come and it will come in the form of revenue.

It is now time for this information to go out and be spread. It is now time for this information to be transcended to his fellow man but this has to happen slowly, through osmosis. But believe you me, *those who hear these words must try and make this happen.* It is time for movement, and with movement comes a transient thought process. Understanding is what is needed at this point in time. Those that pave the way will be giving the understanding to others that follow. Watch out for this inertia, just allow it to happen, do not fight it. God bless you all, it is so important you are blessed with your God and your God is blessed with you. God bless you, the light stands within and without. Thank you.

The Bearer of New Information.

October 26th 2013

The insurmountable thought patterns that are presented to us all at this point in time elongate to a totally different spectrum of thought.

You have to understand that the latent mind, the mind that you use when you are awake, is so different to the mind that you use in other aspects of yourself.

The body is a mind, a processor of information, it carries out so many more tasks than you actually consider. As you generate movement the body continues its thought processes and understands that as you pass through domains, visions, places, you are actually accumulating information via the cells of your body, not necessarily through the brainwaves of thought patterns. You must therefore understand that you, as an individual, do so many more tasks than you actually consider.

But as you speak these words you are considering what the reason is for these things.

Words in themselves have creational processes that allow you to understand, allow you to articulate a particular process required for yourself or somebody else or something you need to do in the future. You must understand also that articulation isn't really the process you need, the process you need is *non-verbal communication*. That is the process the animal kingdom use domestically on all areas of thought. The insect world use different communique, they use the communique of pattern, pattern is the way they move the processes they create within their domain of understanding.

You must understand at this point in time your body is breaking away from the segmentation of the mind, so your body is doing one thing but the mind is doing another. This is the process that you are creating and understanding for yourself at this point in time, it is almost like being floating around and not having a domain to walk towards or float towards.

You have been communicating for many years with a central core of information. This central core of information has always provided you with information that is required not only for the human domain but also from the domains of those that come and visit the human domain.

You must understand that the communique that is occurring right now is *in formation,* the process from where you are going from at this point. You are moving, transiting from one spot to another as you have done in the past, but this process is causing almost a dementia within the physical process. This process is the separation of old cells and the re-creation of new cells, it is separating as you are separating. You are separating from old and creating new and you must understand that this creates disdain within the system. You have had this disdain but you will move forward with this with the understanding that that is what is occurring. The changes, the patterns, the unfamiliar processes that you feel within your body, that is what is occurring, and you must understand that is how it will be for the time being until a level platform is placed for you. Just allow that to happen.

You are part of a process and that part of the process is part of who you are. You are the forebears, *the bearers of the new information. You bear that information by the cells that you carry.* Wait and see and you will be seen.

Humanity is Part of a Massive Computer System.

November 3 2013

Before we start today we have to understand that the process of understanding isn't always the process that you have been taught, the process of understanding is something totally different.

Your body wants one thing, your mind wants another and your heart tells you other things. So in some way you are always torn between decisions and understanding, but in truth understanding was never meant to be understood, as convoluted as that is.

You, as human beings, are actually processes of thought-form. Thought-form is a reaction to how your thought is created. Somebody can think something and a possibility is created and a ball rolls down a hill. But that ball creates many different reactions, contractions and circumstance. It will hit, knock, crash, frictionalise, it will do many things, many things that we can understand circumspect to our understanding within our mind-set, but there are many things that happen outside of that. Friction creates chemical laws, it also creates laws outside of our understanding, so in fact a ball rolling is something very very convoluted with regards to thinking.

What does this have to do with information, information that we can rationalise with?

We must understand at this point that as we walk the planet Earth we also understand that we are part of a process. As stated before, we create thought-form on the planet of Earth and that thought-form was created by our predecessors, those that came down and visited the planet of Earth with limited life form. It had limited life form and created limited life form. That we mentioned earlier. (*the Diversex*)

Now you must understand limited life form always has laws; the laws of cause and effect, the laws of understanding, the laws of energy, but each planet has its own laws created by its own boundaries. Evolutionary processes ***do not*** *transfer* from one planet to the next, the same thing does not happen each time, this is the interesting process, so our ancestry is something totally new!

So when our ancestors, our creators, brought us here they knew not what was expected. So when we created the thought-form process, and that is a planet of totally and utterly free will, the first of all, it won't be the first or the last but it is the only one in our universe of understanding, it is creation rebounding so many thought-form patterns back out into the universe.

We may consider this a total negative activity, it is not. It is a little bit like throwing dice on the table. Yes, you can calculus so many different thought-forms and processes of what is going to land – a 3 and a 6, a 2 and a 5, a 5 and a 5, a 6 and a 6, but in truth nobody knows what is going to happen. The same thing is with the human thought-form process, nobody knows what is going to happen from one thought-form to the next. This is why we have the opportunity to change our mind. The tide of thought constantly changes, as does the way we think. That is what we are all about.

The problem we have is we think we have control of what we think when in fact there are regulations of course about what we think, but we are controlled by that – *this is an awkward one for us* – we are controlled by that on which we walk, it is the planet of the Earth. The planet of the Earth actually has a great deal of dominance over how we think.

There are so many different creatures within the Earth. A teaspoonful of earth has so many different micro-organisms that we consider amoeba-like, that we consider so miniscule that it has no understanding, or any characteristics with regards to our characteristics. But we look at size as if it is an important thing. *Energy* is the most important thing. If you could measure the energy of an amoeba you will actually find that its energy dominance is far greater than that of a very large human being! Tall and small has no difference, it is about *the energy thought-form process.*

As you understand, we are all part of an inner and outer universe. In the universe of the soil is an amoeba thought-form pattern part of the universe that you work and understand with? Of course it is, as you are part of *its* universe, yet you do not understand the characteristics of connection between ye and they, so therefore you cannot understand why an amoeba would have any process of correction or thought...

Here the voice became lower and made comment:

This is awkward, this is very very awkward ... *this was followed by conversation in the strange language that has been spoken through Robin many times previously but I am quite unable to write down. It sounded like this –* Shinka lanka tush ...

... An amoeba is a characteristics of thought-form. A thought-form is a miniscule bubble, a bubble that sends out veins of organization. Those veins of organization project out from the centre of the Earth. The *centre of the Earth* is actually the dominant factor of where and what you are about. Your universe is **under**-stood. You have a connectivity to the outer Earth but you also have a massive connectivity to the inner Earth, the boundaries of which you are connected to.

It is like walking a tightrope but the tightrope is pulling you upwards, downwards, sideways, inwards, outwards. You have two connectives – your outward life and your inward life – that we do understand. But your inward life has the characteristics of something totally different, it controls your domineering factors, the place from whence you have come and you have always been. Your outward life is the domineering factor behind where you are going to go, but where you go will always bring you back to where you started and where you have been. This is utterly convoluted but you must understand, **nothing** is convoluted if you give it true thought-form. Thought-form is a projectile of pattern, a projectile centering from the *centre* of the Earth.

We cannot correct or create science here, the child does not have that in his head but what he does have is the ability to articulate possibility, and possibility is the articulation *of* thought-form.

We are projectiles sent out into the ethos of the planet Earth. As we orbit the planet Earth with our thinking patterns we create waves of understanding, and those waves of understanding then vibrate out into the universe and are absorbed by our brothers and sisters, our ancestors out on different planets, exercising their rights on those planets as you are on yours. But you must understand that as you exercise your rights on this planet there is always a controlling dominant factor, and that is the energy frequency where you have come from, and at this point in time it is the planet of Earth.

The laws and regulations of this are not the same as that of another. All planets have different domineering factors. The planet of Earth is relatively modern in its thinking, it is relatively modern in its organization, it is still projecting out into the universe the expectations of a new planet. You are in your juvenile stages of understanding, as is the orchestration and administration of energy on this planet. You must understand, there is no thing out of control or in control, it is about what is needed. Thought-forms projecting out into the universe, creating vibrations.

In turn my children, you are individuals, but outwardly you are part of a massive massive computer system creating thought-form patterns for the rest of the universe to understand from. You are part of your small universe but in fact you are part of a much bigger universe that you will all learn to understand as and when you get to that point. But there is no point in trying to give you articulations that your mind cannot in any way understand. But understand that an amoeba, small as it is, has a great deal of dominance over where you are and what you do. So tread lightly in future my children, because you never know where you tread or what you tread upon.

Understand, nothing is to be understood, it is just to be gleaned and vibrated out. We welcome more thought-forms, we welcome more vibrations. Be your vibration and absorb who you are. Expect and accept nothing but your Light and your Love. The God-force is with you at all times, it is with you especially at this point in time where so much is changing.

The Curvature of Energy.

November 10th 2013

The world is on a trajectory of change. The Change is the key word in the vocabulary of all minds. This is not just the minds of the animal kingdom, the generic kingdom, but it is the minds of the whole astronomical kingdom that looks on planet Earth with disdain and upset.

Indeed the trajectory that the planet Earth was placed upon was never one that was suitable to those around. It was a trajectory of advancement of spirit and mind, and that can only happen when many options are placed. If one option is placed only one outcome will occur, because moving from A to B you only have one line of trajectory, but when options are multitudes of thought patterns, multitudes of acceptance and mind-sets, then so many different A to Bs come into play. So therefore this was the trajectory set for planet Earth many millennia prior to the creating of the first thought-form process and life form on the planet.

There were like many men, women, energy forms, sitting round a table creating this thought pattern. That was then presented and an option was created, and around those options many different manifestations have occurred. Man were not the first here, man are *certainly* not going to be the last here, but man are here right now, and man *himself* has created many problems, because the trajectory that was created originally has ended up being a totally and utterly different process of understanding, not only for those experiencing it but for those that allowed the creation to happen in the first place.

How can you create rules for things that you don't know the outcome of yet? How can you create outcomes when you didn't create the rules in the first place, because there were no rules? So as such, free will is something that is totally and utterly out of control. But one thing will always be in control and that is the matter of frequency and energy.

Energy works in curves and what goes round comes round, and what comes round will find you eventually no matter where you are in the universe. No matter what experience of cells you are carrying at that point in time your energy comes back and visits *you*, you being its original source and format, so just remember that whatever you create, you are creating and it will stay with you eternally.

It is a little bit like you start building a structure but as you start building it, it just builds and builds and builds, goes right round in a curve, and eventually one day there is going to be something tickling the back of your leg and it is the other end of the building. Even though it has gone up, it has gone in a curve and come round and touched you again. So all thought-forms, creations, patterns, loves, hates, angers, will come back and visit you, as it is for many of you at this point in time.

The boy is a channeller but he desists to channel and it comes round and finds him. It comes round and finds him because the words that he echoed out are the words that are echoing back to him.

Many world leaders are having their words and their creations coming back to them so quickly that they are having to create another thought-format to recreate to stop the original pattern that then went out of control because there was *something missing*. And that thing missing, this is not a questionnaire, was that of the manifestation of the creativity of all things; *Care, Compassion and Love*.

So what we actually need to do with all our processes from this point onwards is to create care, compassion and love, no more or no less. And how does one do that? Care and compassion and love isn't very easy when there isn't an environment that is creating care, compassion and love. But you have to go and find these things away from the buildings and the fabric of your manifestations around you.

Does energy come in the form of mobile phones, televisions, viruses on computers, new technology or old technology? No it doesn't, it comes in none of those forms, those are just manifestations of the creative process of man, they will have no use to you whatsoever when you move on to your next domain. Firstly, their frequency of energy won't transmute in those domains. Secondly, you cannot have matter in that form with you. As you well know, you can take nothing with you when you pass on, bar the cells that you carry and *the cells that you have sent out*, remember that one.

But what you must remember is your causality is to create love and care and compassion for *self*, and therefore for those around you, but for those around you only comes when you have it for self first.

It is an experience right now where everyone is actually taking on board the past, present, and potentially what they have thrown out into the future, but it is all the same, it is called the *Flat Time*. Everything works in a curve and comes back.

As the curve comes back to you it forms an arc, and that arc, two by two, leads you up the drawbridge to your boat that takes you on a river that takes you on a sea that takes you on a journey, and your arc, two by two by two takes *all your energy with you*. And a laurel leaf that you carry is the laurel leaf that you throw up and it is eventually caught by the bird, and the bird is your mind-set flying away to another place to allow yourself the freedom of speech and understanding, the freedom of soul! And when you have the freedom of soul you have not moved anywhere; you haven't gone to another planet, you haven't moved to heaven or earth or hell, what you have learned to do is learned to *be yourself.*

So you must move heaven and earth to eventually find out what it is that you are. You are Love in whatever manifestation that is created in, whether you are a beggar on the street, a man of language and style, a man of hate and anger carrying wars and knives, but you are Love in various forms and you must continue to be Love. Energy is only a trajectory, a curve, an arc. Build your arc and go two by two, two by two up a drawbridge to a new change, to a new creational process, to a new evolution of self. This is what this is about because man *is* out of control, but that out of controlness is the effect and creativity of being allowed to do exactly as a mind allows you to go in.

So there is no out of control, it is just the fact that you have got to the point where you are not controllable any more by the energies that created you. Control isn't the manifesting factor here, it is actually having a tenable answer to where you might or you will go, because invariably enough a human being never goes in the directive that one would expect, he will always go in another directive. You are convoluted, your energies never stay the same they change from moment to second, from second to manifestation. You constantly change so nothing stays the same.

A flower, dormant as it is, will come up many centuries later creating much the same flower, breathing much the same oxygen, doing and living much in the same way as it did many millennia prior, but man does not, he does many things differently and the moment he does something the same he will change it because that is the causality behind.

Self is a design and that design is created in a curve, an arc. Remember two by two, there is mathematics to all arcs and curves. The reason why mathematics was created was so you can understand your curvature. Your curvature is curving back to self and touching you on the back of the leg right now, recreating and reconnecting with everything you have been. God bless you for now and welcome, there is much much more to come.

The Focus of Energy.

The Ark of Noah and the Knower of the Arc

17th November 2013

Energy focuses are part of a directive that we all have to understand.

Whatever energy does and where it goes is down to the fundamentals of the energy system that we carry within ourselves. Within ourselves is a directive. Unbeknown to a lot of us, on an energetic level, there is a directive as and when your energy is distributed; energy of the past, energy of the present and a directive towards a possibility of the energy of your future.

Indeed you can create a great deal of input with regards to this by positive thinking creating attributes or negative thinking, wherever you choose to be at that point in time, but there is a directive which is part of the pattern of which you need to create and formulise on the planet.

There are those that *have* to formulise negativity. Unfortunately they are seen by others as distributers of negative thought patterns as well as creating negativity for other people. But you must understand that sometimes it is somebody's job to bring this and distribute it on the planet. (*I call these people karma deliverers.*) Balance in itself requires all things. If you have beauty you must have something that is opposite to that. If you have hunger you must have somebody that isn't hungry. There are so many things that we need to look at. So the directive is about energy distribution.

Energy distribution isn't just about you and being a success within your head, there is something else going on directed by *the Director*. Now the *Director* is the energy format from whence you choose to come from. Then indeed we all formulate from an investigative type of pattern that comes from somewhere else that does investigate and distribute energy that allows you to take on board different processes with regards to planetary influences.

But you must understand that when you come to this planet there is another directive. It is about creating the energy *for the planet to be in balance*. You are not the only reason why the planet is here and the planet is not the only reason for you to be here, but what is required when the world was created, the world being the planet Earth, is an energy formulation and acceptance.

You have been told in the past that originally the original format for the planet was just for beauty, it was a Garden of Eden. And this Garden of Eden had nothing, it had no life-forms, but it was the most beautiful place on the planet. The Directors, the energy formulators, didn't realise that as and when they created this, they had to have a place of beauty but they also had to have the *direct opposite* of this.

This is where the Diversex came into play, it was *a requirement*. It wasn't an asset, it was a requirement. But when you create requirements you are not sure how their energy systems will work once created. It is a little bit like inventing something; you believe it is going to go left but in fact it goes straight on. You have to make changes and sometimes these changes take time, and sometimes this time is a long period or a short period. The same thing comes with the evolutionary cycle of ideas, the evolutionary cycle of creation.

Now Creation originally created the Diversex. The child that speaks appreciates and understood what the Diversex's very simplistic mind matters were created for. They were literally here to create a purpose. But without any purpose what is the purpose? So a purpose has to be created. The Diversex created a very simple purpose – there can only be one! And there was only one for a good period of time. *But when one creates there is always another created in reflection.* That is what happened with the Diversex and when the Diversex created one there was another created, but then that Diversex had to eliminate the others; it was a purpose, it was a process, there were no other thought patterns, there was no understanding of generosity, of love, or care, it was just how it was.

Now as the energy diversifies and goes into a different directive and many many evolutionary cycles come into play a human being recreates itself back on planet Earth but there are many many assets that that human being brings; that is lifetimes, experiences, energy patterns and so on, curves and curvatures, as we discussed, as in the **ark of Noah** and the **knower of the arc**, they came in two by two, of course they did. There is an active core to all evolutionary processes; if you create there will be a result and with that result it will create, so as you give out you will have back. This is part of the law of cause and effect, an international contrived energy pattern, it is formula – **as you think you will receive, and as you receive you will think.**

There is so much more to this and you must understand the human wavelength has a lot more assets than that that you consider. There is much more to come on this, but thank you for the communication.

The Diversex was the start, you will not be the finish, there is much more. Evolutionary cycles sometimes take leaps and bounds, but sometimes they stay the same for a long time, but time, as you appreciate, is your asset nobody else's. Everything happens simultaneously, everything happens over a period of time. We see it all as simultaneous action, you see it as a period of time. Nothing changes!

Presentation of Non Knowledge.

November 24 2013

Energy components are a rectifying component of all human beings in the procedure of understanding.

Understanding is about letting oneself go with the procedure and a flow. Now those that go with the procedure and a flow that is relevant for this point in time is very much the component of understanding and accepting the change needed within the equilibrium of the human psyche.

There are many that refuse to accept this flow so therefore they are not in the component of change accepting the relevant patterns of acceptance. Now acceptance isn't about cooperating with a peerage or an understanding as presented to you by the human format, acceptance is about accepting a formulae, *an energy productive*. Now what they mean by an energy productive is something that is induced by something over and above yourself from the God-force. The God-force is producing a new energy pattern.

As has been understood by previous patterns of channelling you must understand that in fact the human process has been an experiment. Nobody knew what was needed or required at the point of seeding. Seeding doesn't happen when the human being frame comes here, seeding happens when the diversex first came to planet Earth and from that point onwards *all energy formats have cooperated from the original understanding.* This is the creation of evolution.

Evolution is about understanding when something works and moving it on. It is like looking at a Formula One car of a hundred years ago and a Formula One car of today, they are not the same and never will be, because the evolutionary pattern of change is about *changing the way things produce power and energy.*

Now human beings are not about power and energy, *human beings are about power houses of energy,* there is a difference. It is about containing the power within, like an internal combustion as opposed to an external combustion. An internal combustion is the perfect use of energy, because the energy stays within and doesn't go without. An external form of transmission of energy goes out and expands out from the body. Now that is the formulae that many human beings work from: '*Look what I have done! Look what I can create and you can profit from it and so will I!'*

Now this is the induction of how you work with your internal self. Internal combustion, as such, is about internal combustion and the power going *within* not without. So what in fact you are doing is just *doing your story*, not telling your story or writing about it, or producing your story for other people to see, it is *your* story. It is about creating an internal energy that stays within yourself and the only one that knows about that is you, those that choose to watch you and the God-force from whence you have come.

Now this is about creating a miasmic process of acceptance. Now a *miasm* is an internal combustion of energy.

We talk about energy as if it is a great component of about who you are, as if you're *firing* on an energy process. You are, you are actually working from your God-force process. That is your fuel! Your fuel therefore comes down and pumps through your veins, like blood does, it is carried within the very genetic structure of your cells and when change is part of the procedure then your cells will change, as the child's are. The child's cells are changing at such a rapid rate that his body cannot catch up.

These are answers that he requires yet he researches on the outside not the inside. The inside is where your answers are, where your cells lay. You can stay laying within your own cell with the door closed or you can throw the door wide open and understand what your cell has to tell you. You are an energy format in change, as such, as you always have been and will continue to be so. You are a *change-ling* and a changeling is a pattern creator, and a pattern creator is about an augmented process created for you to produce and expand from.

Now that expansion isn't about internal, external expansion, it is about *being* what you are. An expansion of that generates out from you in a different energy form. That is a different process than the process of knowledge. Knowledge is about '*I know how this works and I will expand and show others!*' Expansion in this right is actually about **being** and not understanding, there is the difference. The child will not be given the ability to understand his disability but he can be told that his cells are going through a progressive change, and a progressive change that is not acceptable within the human frame right now, but it will be. As we said, the Wayshowers are part of the expansive process. This is not a human illness but it **creates** human illness, it is not a disease but it **creates** dis-ease. A disease is something that stays permanent. A moving dis-ease is something that moves through, like a trajectory, like a pattern, like a curve, like an arc.

Once again we talk of arcs as if they are a process, there are so many processes to the arc of knowledge. We are in fact combining the process of knowledge with combining the process of non-knowledge.

We have spoken of non-knowledge before. Non-knowledge is the process of **new information** that has not been presented to the planet before. The evolutionary cycle of the human pattern has not or never has had this process of understanding. You are being presented again with the process of non-knowledge. This is knowledge that has not been on Earth before so therefore the body has not had the equilibrium to practice what it means. When a body has had the process of practicing what it means it is a little bit like a vaccine, once it has had a little bit of something it understands how to behave, but when something totally new comes into the framework then the body does **not know how to behave**. That is what happens with non-knowledge.

As has been said, there are seven of this child or of these children. There are two with the same capacity with **speech**, the other five just carry the knowledge and those five *have no idea as to who they are*, they just do and be. It is not as difficult for them to be that being, but equally the trajectory of information will create dis-ease within their bodies but they will manufacture and create a process so they can walk alongside themselves until their body can cooperate with this new knowledge. The two that do suffer are those that are more *the way-showers*, those with the first trajectory of the pattern, they aren't necessarily older or younger, what they are are choices, energy components of part of the same.

We can't give you too much capacity to understand what all this means. What is the point of being given binary consideration as to how a bio-computer works, most people wouldn't understand or they would pretend they do.

The human expansion of mind creates many limitations. Limitations are created by parameters and parameters create understanding and diverse acceptances of why and where and what things do. When you can accept that things do precisely what they are not expected to do and will continue to do so, that is *the quantum acceptance of knowledge*. But within your scientific process you cannot accept the quantum acceptance because you provide *static answers*, you want static answers. You can never have those things when you are working with quantum knowledge.

My child that sits need not concern himself but he needs to understand and come to terms with what he is. It will become more and more difficult the more and more he fights what he is, or it will become easier when he just accepts. Acceptance is part of the key, as is the door. There is no point having a lock if there is no door, and there is no point having a key if there is no lock, but if you have all three components - mind, body and spirit - again we are using the trinity - the quality of acceptance is about accepting *in mind, in body and in spirit*.

We will speak more when it is relevant. Thank you for conversing on this regular level. We diversify with our thought patterns because we have the opportunity to say what is needed as and when it is needed. More will come.

The Process of Elimination.

December 2nd 2013

Elimination is just about letting go of things that are not required within the soul, the frame and the elemental being of yourself.

There are so many things that we consider fact, factual, or part of our component of life that are not resident or relevant within our lives.

We must learn to componentise what it is that we need, relevance that information and take it forth. A little bit like kicking a ball into the distance; you do not see where the ball lands but it has a focus and a focal point from where it lands. This is where you must look forward *to*, look forward to the creation of what you have created through that potential thought pattern.

We are here not only to understand many things but to create many things. Many things are lost because we can think about them but we do nothing about what they mean. Now we as individuals are offered opportunities through downloads of information and that download comes to us in our imagination, through the components of thought, or through the relevance of reading or seeing something. It creates or eliminates a purpose and therefore you go ahead and do something about it or do nothing.

There are many people that have lazy minds yet they have the opportunity to create many things but something has told them they have no opportunities whatsoever so therefore they create nothing and stay like a stagnating mill-pool.

There is no point being liquid but having no motion. We are in fact liquid with e-motion, we are liquid that have the emotive process to move forward in many different ways.

There is of course negativity, positivity and neutrality. There are many components about our experiences but what we do wish and want to do is to move forward, not hold on to an existing process but move with it. There is no such thing as an end because an end is a start to something else. We have to eliminate the negative structure behind what it is we can't do because once we create that structure we can't do it. But if we create a structure of acceptance that it is possible to do something, then we kick the ball forth and it lands somewhere and we will always walk towards that target because that is our trajectory.

We must relevance this information. Kick forward with what you wish and you will meet it at some point, you will pick it up and kick it again. You will never be given anything you cannot contend with because you are cells in fluid and in motion or e-motion.

Now of course there are many things stopping you. This of course is to do with karmic influences, planetary influences, as well as your own influences, but you must understand nothing is there as a barrier, it is there to learn by. If you are swimming and there is a tide in the opposite direction, will that stop you moving forward? You will in fact move forward but stay in the same place, but you will have gained experience about whatever that was.

A man sailing against his tide, will he learn nothing? His boat will learn something and so will he. There are experiences to be had in all, even though you appear to stay the same or look at the same view or look at the same avenue of purportment. There is structure behind everything but you can create structure to create **more** behind that everything.

You must understand that you are not alone, but you are alone in your thoughts because your thoughts are individual, but your thoughts are part of a big pattern that gathers information and creates a central governing body of understanding that isn't created to create this understanding, it is just there. So when it happens it is placed in the understanding pot and it is there awaiting to be expanded upon once again.

We are a strange species and have an opportunity to create that strangeness in many different ways. So accept that we are strange, and strange things happen to strange things, but there is nothing stranger than somebody else doing nothing about anything they have. When you have something you can build on it, and when you have something to build you have something to think about. Think about what you have to build and build it, and once you have built it build another one and keep building.

Do you stop when you've retired? No, you build more. You build your houses, you build your thought patterns, you build your loves, you build your carings. You also build the understanding that part of the process of that is swimming against your tide, sailing against your tide, cycling against the wind. These are the process of friction, these are the process of opposition, these are the process of gravitational forces. We are all here to understand that nothing, no journey whatever it may be, will be made easy because if it is made easy nothing is learnt.

There is much more to be said about this at a later date but we will stop for one day. Remember you are loved my children, you have been loved and you will continue to be loved but *you must love yourself* and learn to inherit that love once again. God is within all of us but you must not eliminate him. He is there, you are here.

Transformation of Thought

December 9th 2013.

The welcoming patterns of transformation are here available to us all yet we are unaware that the changes are occurring within our systems.

Each and every day the molecular structure that lays within the genetic formation of who you are changes. This is happening on a magnificent level with regards to humanity, the animal kingdom and the etheric kingdom, everything is changing. The energy formats are changing, the planetary formats are changing, the tides of the world and the tides of your body are changing. This in turn is changing the tides of thought.

People are open to transformation now. Transformation is an acceptance of a new energy floating into the body. Thoughts that you would not have eloquently placed in your mind once would not even consider transforming themselves into a different thought pattern. You must understand, you are changing. We are changing. *We* being part of you but *we* being the curators of this energy, but again *we are transformers* as you are my child, the one that speaks. The one that speaks is a transformer but a different type to a lot of others, he transforms and transmutes information into a level acceptable for human beings.

He is of course a human being, but indeed the spirit, the very ethic of where he comes, is less than human being, it is *something in being* but it *is not human in being*. We are all indeed differentials but there are differentials to be understood and this differential with the child is one of understanding many things. But the understanding of what he has is not of the understanding of what he is doing but the understanding of what it means when it happens, there is a difference.

It is not always necessary to know *why* things happen, but what is important is to understand when they happen what to do with them and why they have happened. So the why isn't the important, it is *what to do and understand*.

We transform words from a different energy level. We transform things into words, into an energy format that the human in being can understand and elaborate upon, as we do with words coming through this tape machine. But indeed if we were to listen to this, this would just be a noise, a very slow noise of non-understanding. It takes us a while to transform things into a *speaking level* for the child to elongate into a format that he will understand and those that will listen will understand, but also he will carry that energy within his system, so he can in fact just carry a transformation of format.

Now we look out at the stars at night and we wonder what we see. Do we understand that those stars are planets? What are they? Are they energy formations? Indeed you are seeing something that is necessary for your eyes to see, it allows you to elongate with regards to the space that is around you. But you must understand that the space that is around you isn't the one that you really should be looking at, it is the *space within* we have spoken of before, it is about the internal energy. It is the internal energy that is one that will give you power.

Man has created combustion through his internal combustion engines, but they create energy that transforms and goes *outside* and creates incredible friction and heat.

Internal atomisation is on a different level that does not create heat, does not create molecular geneticisms, what it does is it creates an energy form. This energy form is a transformation from you into something else. So when you want to understand do not go outside, go within. You have the answers to all but you have to go into a place that you do not know is there, you need to go into somewhere, and it is part of your heart.

Your heart in fact is a transformation, it is a transformer of energy. It creates of course one of the energies that you know, which is love, but love is a molecular structure, it is a format that creates and does. Indeed, is hate the same emotion? It is part of it. To love you need to hate and to hate you need to love, because if you didn't know the difference you would not know what one or the other was. It is just a format, it's an energy. It is an energy that you need to procreate and to progress in life.

Do you think the Diversex lacked in love? The Diversex had his or her form of love, it was just a different type to the one that you work with. Was it evil? No, it was not, it was what worked for the Diversex, it was a different format of understanding, as you are.

We are visiting many planets at this point in time, many different elongations with many different formats, many of which that you have been, that being the child. You have visited many planets doing your transformations. As we have said, you are *One of Seven*. There is another that channels information but channels information on a different format. You my child, are channeling the only information with regards to this format and it is important that you transverse this and take it into a different framework of understanding. You need to absorb it and understand and just take it with you and accept, it is all about acceptance. Don't try and understand, just accept this is part of transformation. *Acceptance in being, being in acceptance*. Look at that word, understand that word and *be in acceptance*.

We will speak again. Thank you for your wise words my child, thank you for your wise thoughts, we are with you.

Cells and Simuli

December 15 2013

An introduction to the process of thinking.

There is thinking and non-thinking. A particle of thinking is a materialisation of what you are. A materialisation happens through cells of format. Cells have emptiness as well as fullness. You must understand that a cell is something that is used for containing something, so therefore a cell doesn't necessarily have any criteria other than the fact it has something within it, it is like a container, a carrier. So in formatting you must understand that cells are creational processes for placing in *information*. Information is a format behind who you are and what you are as a human in being.

Now why do we understand or wish to understand what the criteria of a cell is? A cell is a place where you can place information ready and available for when you might need it or have it placed there for when you *don't* need it, but it is there all the same, a criteria of need. Now we are, as human in beings, cell carriers. We carry cells that gather information, much of that information has no relevance whatsoever to what we are doing.

Does the car bonnet know what the bumper is doing on a vehicle? It does not, it can't see it but it is part of the same thing, it has a totally different perspective on the transition from one place to the other because it sees it and experiences it in a different way. The bonnet sees it from the forward, the rear motion sees it from that point of view.

Now we are cells, but we are cell carriers, so we are *a cell that carries cells*, so indeed we are a cell within a cell within another cell within another cell, we are of course a microcosm of the universe. We have heard these words many times before. But you must understand, that as we carry cells *we are part of a cell* that expects us to be carrying information and storing information. So it puts a whole new perspective on the format of *the God-force*. The God-force, the one that we are a perspective of, is the starting of the cellular structure in itself. It is the starting point that invigorates *within* not without, because the without, *the God-force that we speak of looks upon something else as its God-force*.

It is like the Russian dolls. As you peel one away there is a smaller one inside and a smaller one inside that and eventually you come right down to the baby one. Now is the baby one of lesser or more importance? Does it have the same gravitational frequency of that of the large one? Everything of course is different but one thing will always remain the same, *everything has a purpose*, a purportment of need and requirement.

Now what is it that the human in being requires? It requires to gather information about hot/cold, light/dark, in/out, over/above/below, inside/outside/underside, it has so many different requirements. Is there such a thing as live, is there such a thing as die, is there such a thing as bad or good? Everything has relevance when it has its place. So we must understand that all things around us have relevance when in its place. Is the man wearing pink over there with something balancing on his head relevant to you? Maybe not, but he will be relevant to somebody else that studies that format, that modality. So you must understand, do not look upon something else as of no relevance, *everything has relevance*.

We are getting into the grammatical purposes of why and what and if not and if we are. What we are in fact are combustion chambers of energy, we combine our energy and we combust. We combine with something else that creates energy. We are in purpose an energy creator. By storing energy we create energy and by creating energy we allow ourselves to store energy.

So our purpose isn't just to walk around the planet wearing green shoes and feeling good or bad about ourselves, there is much more to the emotion of you as a human being or you as a purportment as many human beings. You are of course part of the same *matter* but you are not necessarily of the same quantity and quality. Everybody, everything has a purpose but that purpose has the possibility to go in a directive.

Now if you look at a fusion of cells moving around, they move around in a particular way. It is a little bit like throwing lots of Ping-Pong balls against the wall, they are not all going to go in the same direction. They were thrown at a similar force towards the same wall but they all go in a different direction. Some will bang against each other, some will bounce back, some will bounce up, some will bounce down and some will stop rolling because they meet an obstacle. Your life is much the same. Is there purpose to this? There is of course, there is purpose to everything because everything creates a frequency of understanding.

This is why we at this point in time desire so many different frequencies of understanding within our cell. But we realise that there is a door to our cell and we can go outside of that and look upon ourselves and see how we are, what we are, and what we are doing. This is what you as a cellular devising structure have an opportunity to do. You have an opportunity to go through your door and look at your cell, look at you, look at your purpose. Your purpose of non-purpose. Interesting! *Your purpose of non-purpose!* There is always purpose behind a non-purpose. A non-purpose is a stimuli, it is a stimuli towards something else that creates more forces of energy.

If you look upon a cell, an empty cell with absolutely nothing in it, there will of course be matter in there, but it won't be something that matters to you, it won't be something that materialises within your cell or your purportment, so therefore it is empty and available and waiting for filling up with energy. Are those empty cells wasted cells? No they are not, they have an opportunity as you have an opportunity. As your cell ordains itself to its point of fulfilment you will indeed exhibit the need to remove yourself from that cell and move on to another one that is empty, and that cell will maintain an energy frequency and go back towards the God-force, the place from whence it elongates electrically and magnetically fills itself and the need to go back towards. That is your point of death, your point of demise. That is where your purportment has got to its zenith.

Now some cells appear to have not completely filled themselves up but they leave without reason or rhyme. You must understand that they are a part way through filling that cell, something else will fill the rest, because it needs the equilibrium of that. Now yes you may look at that as an early life exit or an early life entry, whatever it may seem to you, whatever side you are looking at it, but there is reason behind everything but yet our reason doesn't necessarily give the reasons that you need to understand the reason for it.

This is all very convoluted. As the boy holds his hand in a *simuli* fashion, (*Robin was moving his hand in a strange way as he spoke*) this simuli fashion is the way the energy is transported into the frequency of the frame. Simuli is a format used by our Elders. The word *simuli* is the way that we can transitise information from the past into the present into the future.

The future is yet to happen because of the nature of what is going to happen. Remember you are all Ping-Pong balls thrown against a wall. You will go in many different directives, yet you have the same shape and you were put into the format of the same force against the wall but you will necessitate a different need, a different pattern of roll, a different pattern of friction, the creational purpose behind the energy you create.

You are cells but the interesting part of this cell is the fact that you now have the opportunity to step out of the door and look at your particular cell. Take the time to do that with your simuli. You are indeed materialising matteries. You are in fact the God-force, just part of the cells of the same thing. God bless you for now and forever and thank you.

The Ancestral Beacon Calls

December 29th 2013

The resonance of the human frame is circumspect with the desire to change and move.

You must understand that your resonance as such is changing on a constant basis right now. We are indeed in the transitory stage, a little bit like migratory birds. We are actually moving from one position to another and we do not know what to expect. This is how it is right now, we don't know what to expect because the unexpected is happening all the time.

So this is all about transition, it is actually teaching the human frame that what we actually need to do is change. The framework, the genetic structure of the human being, is changing. As we have spoken in the past with regards to the cells of the body, the cells within the body and the cells without the body are all requiring a transitory change.

We talk about migratory birds. They fly from one place to another but there is a beacon that calls them to that other place. This has always astonished man because they cannot believe that a bird can travel so far and take himself back to a nest that was there the previous year and then they can fly back to the previous destination for warmth and for the creating of a new family.

We are here indeed doing much the same. The beacon that is calling us is the beacon of our ancestry. And what that actually means is our ancestors knew that the progress we were going to make was the progress that we are at right now. The wise souls speak and they state: *"Human beings have the opportunity to do many things, but one thing they have not the opportunity to do is remember what they are here for."* So when we are searching for what we think we are here for we get lost. Believe me, it is part of the process of human in being. You are indeed lost but you aren't lost, you are just in the process of *changing from one spectrum to the next.*

So in fact you are transitising without the domineering process of understanding why you are doing so, but there is a reason behind it. You are being guided, a little bit like a sleeve, you are sleeving from one place to the next, not leaving but sleeving. You are actually going and *going down a tube* dominated by where you need to go but you don't realise that is there.

The cells of the body are actually changing, as you are as we speak, as we are listening, and we are all changing. We are getting younger and older and we are staying the same, all at the same moment. Because indeed our cells are held together by molecular frequencies that allow us to be exactly what we are at this point in time. Yet if we looked at ourselves from another point in time we would indeed be different with the energy of a different frequency.

But time itself isn't actually a co-ordinated process that is required for us to go through. What we are actually required to go through is understanding and creative patterns that allow us to dominate our frequency.

We are indeed changelings, as we all are. The child is a changeling but you are all changelings, those that listen that speak. We are changing from one thing to the next, moving from one stepping stone to the next, yet we don't see the distance in front of us, we just see the steps.

It is the opportune moment to understand: Don't try and understand where you are going or what you are doing, just accept. Just accept the journey for what it is and for what it is creates a journey

There are many things that we don't need to know! As was spoken in the previous channelling, there are many things that a human being actually does that the human frame has no acknowledgement or understanding of why they are doing them, they do them!

Do you see what is going on behind you as you walk? You see what is in front of you. Do you see your back, your skin on your back, the hair on the back of your head moving, yet it is creating a frequency, a change, an understanding. But somebody behind you can see that yet they can't see behind themselves. So indeed there are many things that are going on within yourself and without yourself that you have no understanding of. Many of us have molecular structures living inside our body. We have no acknowledgement or understanding that they are there for a reason or for no reason.

We are and will be constantly part of a changing process and you, as we speak, are part of that changing process – that is all and everyone on this planet of Earth. This planet of Earth is merely a platform, a springboard to another place, another event, another time, but that springboard is jettisoned at this point in time because you are moving and slowing down to a singular process. And that process of singularity is where you are right now. You are moving from one vessel to the next and that vessel is moving from one light frequency to the next light frequency, instantaneously – it is just taking its time!

Wait and watch and listen and learn and you will indeed be part of this process. God bless for now and thank you. And bless you for the New Year, all of you, bless you for the new millennia of thinking.

The Available Pot of Information

January 4th 2014

The occupation of mind bears all thinking.

You must understand the cellular structure has a total objective with regards to you, you being the perspective at which you look, see and domain within. You must understand, as you project your thoughts into something that productivity becomes the cellular memory pattern from you. So for instance, you create something, like a vehicle, a bike, a car, a tree-house, the cells that are maintained within that are your own cells. You created that productivity *so therefore the life force is attached to you.*

This is a very very interesting facet. So you ordain a process and the productivity behind it is the cellular pattern of you. So in some respects you are responsible for what you think in much more ways than you consider.

You are responsible for many things. You are responsible for what you create, what you think, and what you do, the responsibility lays in the cells which are presented to that form. So you, in cellular form, must instruct or construct something that is part of you, part of your perspective in life, not something that somebody else has asked you to do, not something you are forced to do, but something that you would only ever create if it is of your perspective and understanding. We offer much love to this situation and will continue later.

The objective of this is to understand that your patterns of thinking are created through the domains of what you create. You are not part of a parcel of information that doesn't have any creativity, all people have creativity, but is that creativity something that is going to come in an internal form or an external form?

There are many of you that have so much creativity inside of yourself yet that doesn't seem to be a positive domain to be because you haven't created that in a form that is objective and understanding to others, it stays within you. Does that matter? Is the fact that you have an encyclopaedia of Britannica inside you any different to that of somebody that has written one externally? It does only in the fact that other people can gain access to that information. But you have to remember a lot of the information that is created internally for you all is a manifest format of cellular structure that is available not only to you but to everyone that chooses to go into that domain of thinking.

So what you create with your thoughts is a pot of information and that information is available for other people as and when they start thinking about it. So there is an underlying access to information yet you do not know it is there. When you start giving your mind to a thought isn't it amazing how many other things come flooding in with regards to that, and before long you have created an objective, which will either allow you to become internal or external with your thoughts. It is because you have *access to a pot of information available on that subject.*

Give yourself these observations and understand that there is so much more going on than you actually accept. As was said, when you are walking forward you can see what is in front of you and around you but you cannot see what is going on directly behind you. You don't see that blade of grass re-fold itself back to its original shape after you trod on it. You don't see the way the wind caresses the body and what it does after it leaves you. You only understand the objectivity of what you see in front of you, that is the human domain. There is so much more and there will continue to be so. Thank you for now. God bless

Love is an Eternal Acceptance

January 16ᵗʰ 2014

It is a mundane factor that we don't even consider where we are or what we are doing. We are an energy format that we don't truly understand yet we try to facilitate plans to try and overestimate or underestimate our procedures. We are at this point in time floating around in an ethos of not knowing. We don't know what it is that we are moving towards, we have some understanding of where we have come, but what we don't understand is what we are doing all this for.

We are part of a God-force and that God-force is a plural sense, *there is more than one God*, not in the sense that you create in your human domains the many different gods that provide dogmatic processes. There are domains of God-forces throughout the universe. Gods themselves are creational patterns.

There are many different events going on in different parts of the universe that have no consideration for what you are doing. You are part of a process, a little bit like a pair of steps that open up and allow you to climb to somewhere, but you can move the steps and you will climb somewhere else. That is a little bit like the process of human in being. You are in truth the plural in sense, you are *mind and body*. The spirit, yes it is part of you but it is part of the eternal being. The mind and body is the thing that doesn't stay with you, it is removed after your spirit diminishes and moves somewhere else.

The mind and body is the very asset that you are trying to come to terms with. *That* is the being. *That* is the creational process that requires you with the longing to know, because the spirit, of course, is eternal and *can* move from one process to the next. The mind and the body is the creational understanding of the human in being. The spirit has conversed in many different ways, been in many different universes and experienced many different plethora of understanding, but the mind and body is *singular* with regards to what it experiences on the planet. It has one single experience and one opportunity to glean as much as it can, so therefore the mind and the body has only one life. So when somebody states, '*I live and die and that is the end of it!*' Well that is the body's side of things and the mind's side of things, but the spirit carries on eternally, like a breath that breathes out constantly.

So when you expect or receive information with regards to the fact that somebody has died, yes the mind and the body has diminished to the point where it no longer exists, it exists in the sense that you can see it but it will break down into dust and form part of the planet in which you walk, but you must understand that the spirit stays eternal.

What is the spirit's purpose when it is placed within the body? The spirit's purpose is to gain experience from being within the body, gain the experience of what it is that happens when you are in a *dense* frequency, a frequency that cannot move from one place to the other with just the thought process. There is *density*, there is *weight* and there is *experience* to be had in the frequency of the human mind and body. There is much to be said on this fact, there is much to be appreciated with the love that is contained within this process.

The love that happens on this planet of earth is a love that is very different to many different frequencies. There is a misunderstanding with regards to what love is and you must understand that it is **the eternal concept of acceptance**. Once we can accept that others do what they do and you do what you do, it isn't the fact that you love what they do but you accept. So *love is an eternal acceptance*.

So we need to in turn become acceptance, be acceptable to others and they be acceptable to us and that allows us to brush alongside people that don't do what we do, and we brush alongside them because we don't do what they do. But what we must understand is *love is the being and the ending of all things* – the mind and the body, and of course the spirit. We will speak more on this subject later, thank you.

Assess and Act Accordingly.

January 25ᵗʰ 2014

A composite of all energy formats are part of what we are as a structure.

You must understand that as you walk from one place to the other you leave an imprint, an energy imprint, of where you have been and what you have done, but what you must remember also is that imprint is part of the technology that your body becomes.

We have spoken of the fact that your body knows what is going on around you whereas your mind knows very little of what is going on around you, apart from what it sees through the compunction of your eyes. But you must understand that you are a transitional process, you take on so much more information than you are allowed to think.

This is where you must understand that the human in being is one component, whereas the **other component** is that of the annexing of energy, the creation of purpose, and that creation of purpose is glorified by what you are. And when we state glorified, it is about the extent of where you are, the domain you stand on. The domain you stand on creates the purpose behind what you are. If you stood in a barren field with nothing around you then the complexities of your life would be very different to that of somebody that has a lot around them. So those that create many things will live amongst many things, have more complex life and existences than those that have very simplistic things around them.

Is it a matter of choice one asks? Of course, everything is a matter of choice, but we all need to perplex ourselves before we move into another state of being, so therefore we must justify where we are and what we are doing. So therefore justification happens with or without the purpose of what you are.

You are all energy elongations, a stretching of the frequency, and that frequency comes from the God-force. The God-force is a component of the very essence of all and **every single component of you** – atoms, molecules, micro-processes and so on – everything within is part of everything without, and everything without is part of everything within. You are all part of the same but you have different movement, different gravitational fields and pulling.

So therefore is the lion the same as the lamb, the lamb the same as the snake, the snake the same as the amoeba? No, the differentials are there for you to see, but you are in essence part of the same. You are part of a purportment, a creational process. Indeed you all transitionalise by gathering information.

Now this takes us back to the reason why you are all here. You are all here my children, my people, my person, to assess what it is that is around you. That is purely your job – to assess, to act maybe. Act upon what? Act upon what you assess. So it is basically assessment and that is all it is. You see and assess and act accordingly. But the act can only be based on how you assess something, you are not going to do something based on nothing and you are not going to do nothing based on something, so what you are actually going to do is assess, make instrumentation about where you are and what you do.

In truth you are assessing to create formats of understanding for the God-force, no more or no less. Yes indeed this sounds a very terminal type of thinking. No it is not, it is just understanding and accessing the process of what you are. Does it stop you experiencing joy, love, happiness, unhappiness? No it doesn't, but indeed if we get down to an underlying what you do – *you assess, and act accordingly.*

We will talk much about the process of love. The process of love is assessing, processing, and moving on into a domain of understanding. But when you process what you are actually doing is stretching your mind to allow that information to go on somewhere else. Yes indeed you could manufacture further purportments based on what you **think** but what you are actually doing is transitionalising that information **through to the God-force**, through to the components that want to know what you are assessing.

What is the reason for all this assessment? It is basically seeing what you do when you occupy a certain space.

We speak about the Ping-Pong balls thrown against the wall. They all bounce and go in different directions, they all have different series and actions with regards to the same force. Indeed you are all Ping-Pong balls. If you look at a Ping Pong ball it is round, a spherical shape and it will roll, as you will roll, as a dice will roll, but different figures will always come up on a dice. The same thing will happen with human beings, the same amount of force but a different action will always occur. So it is interesting to assess, and whilst assessing further assessment can take place based on that assessment.

This all sounds incredibly convoluted, it isn't it is just giving you the experience of understanding what your process is. You are not binary computers, you have free will to a certain degree and extent, but your free will indeed is based purely on assessment and no more or no less. You think every act or every purportment that comes in front of you is the first time it has happened and you are basing your thoughts on that process. No, that has been given for you to occupy that certain time and space so you experience it.

This is why as you get older you experience things in a *very different dimension of thought* than you would do when you were young.

There are so many things to understand yet we understand so little about what we see because the information we actually translate is something very different. Our eyes see it one way, our mind creates another, but *in truth* what you may be experiencing is something very different.

There is more to be said. Do not be confused, confusion is part of the component of man, this is just unwrapping the mind and inside is a parcel of joy. God bless you all and thank you.

The Veil and the Star People of Avalon

January 28th 2014

We invited Karen Way to be with us for this channelling as Robin was spending some time on the Isle of Wight before going to Brazil. Karen was one of the original members of the extended group that came together to listen to the words of wisdom from the voice that has drip-fed us so well since those early days of initiation in the mid-nineties. As was said then, when we began to understand the truth behind the teachings we would have to completely reassess our reality. This has certainly turned out to be the case. When Karen joined us initially she was reading the tarot for clients but went on to train in Kinesiology with Robin and now has a successful practice on the island.

It is our individual energies that allows us to process so many different things.

There is a veil that lays upon us all, almost like a towel that lays over us, it is like a protective shield that allows us to be the human that we are. There is the truth behind this veil yet we aren't taking the veil away, it is they're being hung on to by a drawstring. It is our time to remove the veil as it is no longer comfortable, it is like a piece of clothing that is out of fashion and it is flaunted in so many different ways, misjudgement and uncharacteristic domains of thought. Just by being and becoming a new individual you have to remove your veil.

Where is this veil? This veil is part of the circumspect energy that you wrap around yourself that you call the humanistic tendency to protection. It is your protection, but protecting you from what? You placed this protection around yourself when you created an artificial religious format that was based on old texts of knowledge. These old texts were really not old texts of knowledge, they were old texts made to look old when in fact they were new. You have energy that goes back thousands of years with these texts written within them, yet they don't have any meaning but for you to place the veil over yourself and protect yourself from something that you didn't need.

What are you my beings as you look around yourself, what are you? You are a simple being that travels from one place to the next, mostly in your mind, but you transition from one place to the next using your vehicle, the human in development. But in truth you are gatherers of information and thought. That is your truth behind what you are but you have become very complex beings.

Why do you have a veil? You have a veil because at some point this has allowed you to be *stable* beings rather than *transient* beings. Look at what this means. Your man Jesus was born in a *stable*, he was a stable being. Now these are just words, but what we are actually stating here is *the vision and thoughts that you were given with regards to the Christing has no relevance whatsoever to the* **truth** *behind the Christing*, it is very different.

The Christing was about an energy that transformed the visions and thoughts of your God down to you as individuals. You could sit in a field and connect up to this. But you were then becoming powerful in yourself and there were those that were in the power on the planet at that time that didn't want the masses to have the power, they wanted the few, so they created the *veil*, it is called *religion*.

The veil is about you protecting yourself from beginning to worship other forms that are figments. But they are no longer figments when the masses create enough energy to bring them into reality. So in truth the figment is the thought form of millions and when millions of thought forms are put together it can create a reality, but that reality isn't real.

If you look through a glass of water you can see things on the other side through that glass but it is not clear, but if you look through a pane of glass you can see things through the other side and they are clearer. That is the difference between a veil and reality, a veil is obscured. You were never given the truth behind what it actually is.

(For now we see through a glass darkly; but then face to face: now I know in part; but then shall I know even as also I am known. Corinthians 12:13.)

What is religion, is there a truth behind it? You are expected to believe something that somebody else has told you or you have read about. Where are the answers with regard to religion? Where are the answers with regards to who you are, the three of you that sit here, what are you? In truth what are you? In truth all you do is gather information - *in formation* - but that information is gathered for a reason.

Because you walk with wide feet as you walk across the grass towards the Lake of Galilee that lake expands and opens wide and you walk beneath the lake and you are washed and cleansed. You are not isolated in your choice but what you are given is an opportunity to see things that others do not have the opportunity to see. So as you take your journey, as you unveil yourself, what you are actually doing is removing your past and replacing it with a possible present that isn't wrapped or tarnished with anything. You actually wish to withdraw from your past that is that of the veil, the religious dogmatic processes that have been spoon-fed not only to you but the past.

We are now going back into the realms of understanding here. The old schools of learning, those that carried the knowledge, who were they and what were they? They were the genetic structures of those from the origins of man, those that walked the planet who knew the rules.

What were the rules? The rules were this. You accepted that others around you were part of the planet, as they accepted you. You accepted that plants and grass and air and all the cells of everything were part of you and you were part of it, yet you had no right whatsoever to infuriate or take it away and they had no right to take you away. But when religions and religious dogma came into thinking, man changed.

What was man? He was purely an animal; he was hunted like others were hunted. You hunted they hunted. But when man became stronger than those around him because he created parameters and protection he started to dominate and that domination created the power struggle that you have today. Now in truth what we are trying to process within you is to give you some understanding as to why and what this is all about. In truth you are going to and will remove your veils.

And where are your veils? They lie within the auric fields. They have been penetrated in the genetic structure of man and it is almost like you need to go in and remove them and say, '*I no longer wish to have this veil, this veil of misfortune that blows in the wind yet it always stays with me, it doesn't blow away, it catches.*'

My beings, it is your opportunity to understand that this veil does not have a purpose other than to protect you. But protect you from what? It is there to protect you from the knowledge that you need the most, and when you have that knowledge you become what you need to be, which is what you could be, *an opportune individual.*

Will this make any difference to the things around you? No it won't, but it will make a difference to the clearance of the mind, the acceptance of the mind, and the parameters of what and where you think. Now in truth that is the basis of everything you are, because what you think today is what you are tomorrow and what you thought yesterday is what you were today. So to *no avail*, as they say, to *know a veil*! You do not know your veil but you are aware that it is there.

So what we state to you my children, is *dismantle that veil and give it back to those that gave it to you.* Thank them for the opportunities it has given you but you no longer wish to have it. It is not thrust upon you like an iron gate closed upon you, it is there to be taken away, but you didn't know it was there in the first place, you do now. You have a veil attached to you, it lays in the energy of your aura and it lays as a veil. It is not real, yet it is.

My children, you have the opportunity to take a moment and the three of us will remove our veils.

A pause while we were asked to do some visualization and when Robin commenced speaking again we were very surprised to hear these words. "We are the Star People, the Star People of Avalon." *Karen immediately broke down the word* Avalon *to* A veil on, *a very clever use of the word on their behalf and an equally clever understanding on hers!*

We are the Star People of Avalon. We delivered this veil to planet Earth. It was like a structure, it was like a net, and we knew what we were doing. We knew that we had to do this because it was part of the glue ointment that kept human beings on the planet because your breed, your type, accelerated their consciousness so quickly they never stayed long and habituated anywhere.

So they had to have an opportunity to lay their seed on the planet and become beholden and withdrawn from the process of travel. So we, the beings of Avalon, wished this planet to be habituated. So the net was thrown over and that allowed a whole process of thinking to come into play within those that are mammonistic. There is no play here, there is no evil, bad, or good, what this is in fact is an opportune moment to keep the human being, not trapped, but accepting the fact that they have moved and they **will stay** for a period of time.

The planetary influences projected the microcosm of thought that you needed to stay so that you **become**, and when you become you stay. You needed to stay as a human-in-being, as we all did, but you had to learn the need and this was created by throwing the veil. The stories behind this veil, there are so many different things, but what you must understand is everything is love. There is a reason for all and all has a reason.

Do not be angry with us, we are not angry at all, we are not angry as a people or a race, we were just delivering a message: *'You must stay for a period of time. If you do not stay you will not become used to and habitation of the planet can never be as it should.'*

But there are now those that need to remove their veil to understand there are more journeys to be had. It is about the changing of consciousness, the moving of the ships wheel where your compass will take you somewhere else, but many will stay. It is just about the retuning of your consciousness's and understanding that for you to move on you need to know where you have come from, but you also need to understand why you have been where you have been.

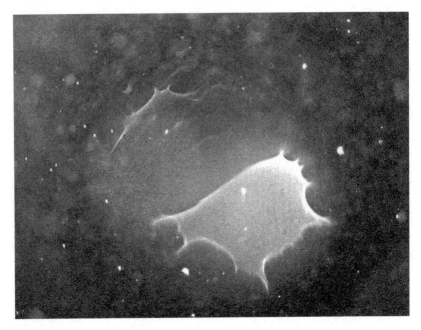

A Veil

Above is a photograph taken one evening when I was out with my camera taking Orbs. This is known as a veil and I thought it appropriate here as in the picture the veil is folding back, which is what the above information was about. Man is to have the veil removed and become aware of what lies beyond

Shortly after this information was received Robin was given the opportunity to accompany his father on a return trip to Brazil for three weeks He needed the healing available there as his near death experience had left him feeling very fragile and in need of some answers.

Words from Robin

Robin: I have been to Abadiania again to visit John of God at the Casa Dom Inacio, a place of healing in Brazil. Remarkable things happen here. This was my third visit; I came previously in 2001, 2003, and now in 2014

I came to Brazil because I had a near death experience last year that frightened me and the storm was a difficult one to weather. I am a fragile human being and channeler of words but this does not make me any less susceptible when it comes to my emotions. Death is pretty final and I would rather not meet it yet.

My intention is to become more loving and caring, less angry and more tolerant. Since being at the Casa I realize this is learnt through stillness and being in a place pervaded with peace, such as where I live with my family at Gabriel's Return, in a house I built for them, surrounded by three acres of land. This is a sacred space where I have created a beautiful garden with trees, shrubs and flowers planted with love by my family and those who visit to find that peace for themselves. The plants hold precious memories of the people who have enjoyed being a part of the creation of this haven.

It is very necessary for me to live a relatively stress free life because of the nature of who I am. Our children flourish because their parents are happier than most, they are polite caring compassionate and understanding girls. This hasn't just come from us, it has been absorbed from the very nature of our way of life. Honour and integrity, care and compassion is central to living a good life and at Gabriel's Return we are nurtured by nature.

Renewed from my visit to Brazil I resumed the channelling with new heart

Separation from Self

March 2nd 2014.

The equation of thought that we all have to acquaint with regards to our thought patterns comes to us in many ways.

You have to rationalise in the way you think and what you do because of the *particular*. When we look at the particular it is actually *particles of thought*.

The particular thought that you have is with regards to how you have been and that is changing, so the particles of thought are separating and you are having a separation from self. This is why you are all feeling specifically as you all do. There is a separation from a part of yourself and it is because your particles are separating, so *no thing in particular.*

When you look at the thought pattern of *no thing in particular,* these thoughts are part of who you are, and what you have been, and you are separating from them.

It is a little bit like moving away from a stage. The stage stays where it is, but you are just drifting away from it and watching a scene in the background, and as you drift away the scene becomes less and less in your mind. This is about what you are doing, about separating yourself from your past and re-presenting what you are in the present.

What one needs to do is *totally* and *utterly disconnect* from what you have been, not in the fact that you love and care any the less or any the more, but you are just letting go. Just allow yourself to let go of the things that don't matter. Does it matter that you own three cars, five houses and two holiday homes? It really matters not, what matters most is what is in your heart because that is the only item you can take with you.

Your heart energy is a consolation for everything you have been and it carries the cells and representation of how you represented that love. That carries through into eternity – from eternity into eternity – and it is your eternal representation of what you are as a soul. So no material can come through, the only material you have is the representation of how you have been, so *no thing in particular* has a representation of what you are separating from.

You have to consider you are separating from many things – matters that no longer concern you and matters that still concern you – but you want to represent them in a different way. Just let them go, there is no point in hanging on to things of the past. It doesn't matter whether it is to do with money, property, thought patterns, energy, people, hair, legs or arms, all the things you have are laying within your heart and it is about representing to yourself the care pattern that you have. Your pattern of care is about what you *feel* inside of you.

What is it you have missed that you haven't done?

What is it you haven't done that you don't want to miss?

What is it you need to do but you must go out and find it?

What is it you have already done but wish you hadn't?

It is all those things that you need to look at and re-present them in a loving fashion, because the resolve to all matters is through the love that you have going from your heart, not only to yourself but to others and representations of what others are.

So we talk in particular of things you feel that you have the onus of ownership on. It matters not, let them go, *let them go*. Just let them go! Let them flow away, as if they were a stage and a play and you were drifting away from them, as you need to drift away from problems that you all have. You need to re-present a new part of yourself.

We have discussed in the past that this is the only time in universal time where you have actually died but you still live. You are actually dying on a cellular level and restructuring yourself on a new cellular level. This is the only way humans can re-organize their cells and patterns of thinking to create a whole new universe of thinking on Earth. There is a total change on all levels and it is happening on a universal level within the universe you are in. What changes here must change elsewhere and what changes elsewhere will certainly change here.

So the planet is watching! Just allow yourselves to die. Just allow a part of yourself to diminish and float away, like a leaf that has dropped on a stream and it gently melds away. Just allow that part of yourself to be, and to be is what you are going to be. God bless you all for now. You are love and you always have been.

The First Formatters of New Energy

March 10ᵗʰ 2014

Energy formats relinquished. It is a little bit like an exhaust system that allows the energy to reconsider its formats as it removes itself from your body. You use this system a little bit like you would an exhaust on a car.

The energies that flowed through your body are a format and something that you need to understand. They flew in a directive. The directive isn't always coordinated, but when you have *used this energy* it releases from your body and is sent out. Now it has your name and number on it technically and is sent off like a spent energy, but it is sent off formatted. It is formatted with regards to what you experienced via the use of this energy, you are not aware of this, but it actually goes off and those who need that experience might well latch on to that energy and relinquish themselves of the experience you might have had whilst doing it.

There are those that start things first and those that take things on afterwards, but you must experience the fact that sometimes there are the *firsts* and sometimes there are the lasts. So the firsts are those that experience these matters for the first time, so therefore they aren't taking on the format of energy that has been used in this way before and has regularity and formatting to its composure.

So those people that take these things on first *suffer* in a different way. They suffer in the fact that the cells that are given to them are *invalid* to assist them, it is not recognised as such. It is a little bit like formatting a computer with a new programme but the programme hasn't yet been formatted within that system, so therefore it will recognise it as a virus or as a technical failure. You must understand that it will take a time for this format to be reconstrued within the system of your body. This sounds very technical but this is how it is.

So those that are the firsts, those that gather this information first off, have a harder time of it than those that take it last. There is no reason for this apart from the fact that energy must be used and spent and spent and used. So those at the moment are going through many many different formats, those experiences that are the firsts.

The child that speaks is one of them, and many of the ladies and men that he works with are also *firsts*, those are people that experience this energy first off. Those that carry love in a different way will experience energy first off. It doesn't mean to say you are any better or worse, it just means that you are experienceRs in the grasp of wanting to experience.

This all sounds terribly convoluted but what it is, is you have asked for this process. There are those that lag on behind that aren't necessarily the formatters of information, they are just the carriers of information. Formatters of information are those that are the predecessors, those that carry and want to transcend their thought patterns into a different way.

You must understand my children, there are many that carry, many that do and many that don't. It isn't about taking on board and thinking about things either, it is just about accepting that formatting is part of the plan. You are all changing in such diverse manners at this point in time.

As stated in previous discussions, *this is the first time the body has died in the flesh whilst it is still alive.* This is about relinquishing the old and bringing on the new. So technically the body is being completely flushed of its formats, completely flushed of its original cells and it is being filled up again. It is like a champagne bottle being emptied of its contents and being given a new yarn, a new day to live. This is what is happening and it is very important to understand that you will all suffer the process of this.

It isn't about the sufferance that is important, it is about the acceptance that this is what is happening at this point in time, and we all need to let go and understand that that is very very important. Love is incredibly important, so is joy, so is the acceptance that proof is the most important thing. Proof can never be portrayed in the way that you need it to be. Proof is just about *accepting,* and you will be given a small glimmer of light, a beam in one direction to allow you to proceed with your new way of being.

Do not fight your physical body, allow your body to be what it is. There is no reason why you feel as you do apart from the fact that your cells are being relinquished and changed. Just accept and acceptance will be the key to the new door that will open. Allow yourself this year my children, this year is the year of change and things will be seen. You will be seen and understood much more.

The Eyes Are the Avenue to the Soul.

March 17th 2014

As our domains are changing we must understand that we must change with those domains.

We are in essence the truth but our truth is maintained within a certain equilibrium within ourselves. We are like a flower but the seed is still in the ground, but as the nutrition of thought and the condition of our life brings into different plays, what actually happens is the stem from the seed flows out above the ground and we stick our head above the parapet and we enjoy the view.

But what view are we due to see, is it a view we are allowed to see, or is it a view that we are not allowed to see?

In essence and in truth we are given a view that allows us to elongate what it is that we need to spectrumise in our minds. Everybody's view is slightly different, as we would expect, because different parts of the castle allows us to see different viewpoints. We are not all in the same spectrum, we are not all due to see the same thing and experience the same thing, yet we are doing the same things. By that I mean that you are being a human being, you are doing the same things as the heart pumps the blood, as your lungs receive the oxygen, as your love gets cherished by that of others and yourself. Love, as we have spoken in the past, has many different ideas and formats, it is not just what you think it is, there are so many different essences of love. We have spoken of this.

So in truth your seed is changing its molecular structure. You are indeed firmly embedded in the soil of love, care and compassion. Your nutritional needs are changing, as are the way you perceive things. You must allow yourself to perceive things but don't necessarily take on board what it is you are perceiving, just accept it.

It is like a view. A view never changes but it changes in many different aspects. A view changes by the way you look at it. It is the same thing but how do you see it, how do you perceive that view? Is the light transient, is the light dull, is the light not there at all and it is dark?

So everything is due to change because of the concepts and perceiving of the way *you* view things from *your* viewpoint.

So in truth my children, elongated as it is, you are changing whether you like it or not, so what we are trying to do is drive the vehicle that allows you to accept this change.

The pathway towards *your healing* is about acceptance of what you need to look at within yourself. Sometimes there are people that perceive what it is that you need within yourself. But are you going to listen to what they have to say or are you going to accept that it is that part of yourself that needs to alter? It is only you that is going to accept that choice. What is it that I need to see that is going to allow my body, my mind and my soul to take on board the change that I need?

Firstly, accepting a viewpoint, an access point of love, through the heart centre that you have. We call it the heart domain. It is not necessarily where your heart is but it is where your acceptance of love comes in through into your body, it comes in through the eyes.

The eyes are not just your viewpoint my child, it is how you perceive and accept energy. Your eyes allow the view an access of energy through and beyond your body, *they are the avenue to the soul* as has been said. Allow your eyes to let the love flow through and flow out. So as you stare at something you can project love through your eyes from your heart from the access point of the Jesuit thought-form, that being the elongation of the God-force of love.

You haven't been given many avenues of acceptance but what you must accept is the avenues have always been there, nothing has changed, it is just that you have forgotten what your avenues of expressions are. So it is just about accepting that your expression is very simplistic – you receive and you give and you give and you receive, no more or no less.

And what you are receiving my children? You are receiving pain. And discomfort is the format of change because it is something you have asked for.

If you wish to be well and healthy, what is it you need to do? You need to relinquish yourself of the cells that don't carry this programming. And how are they relinquished? They need to be relinquished on a physical level and be removed via various excretal processes of your body – sweat, bowel movements, urine movements, and so on. So this is what causes your discomfort because you are asking for the change. Ask for that change and you will perceive it and accept it.

That is what this is about. Your change is about your personal acceptance and change. What is it you need, what is it you want, and what is it you will perceive my children?

Perception comes through the eye, and the eye of the beholder is with you. God bless you for now. Speak much more and much more will be spoken.

Words in Transformation

March 30th 2014.

The dignity behind all equilibrium is the process in which you use it to be.

You must accept that energy in all its forms is part of the perplexed convoluted process of understanding. Human beings are very convoluted in the way they produce information. If we go to a universal understanding, it is about creating an apparatus that creates an evolutionary cycle. This evolutionary cycle is created in the forms which portray themselves on a planet, whether it be your planet or other planets of existences. Of course your form of existence is slightly different because you require fluidity, not only within but without. Fluidity is a transition from one spot to the other, but everything in itself has fluidity, whether it takes a microsecond or a micro year or a micro universe. What you must understand is, *equilibrium is the process.*

There is surface information, there is deep information and we are going to go to the point of surface information.

Surface information is what a human being needs to parallel with with regards to their mind. This allows them to equilibrialise what they actually have inside themselves.

But the deeper information is something that is to do with universal understanding, so therefore it takes a much *deeper mindset* to converge with this information. All information has different parallels, different layers, a little bit like the layer of a cake, or the layer of something else that builds up and builds up and builds up until you have a fabric and a process you can work from.

So what we are really trying to give you in your minds my children, my people, is to understand that surface information is what is required for the human in being at this point in time. It is about understanding what he is suffering, understanding the sufferance he sees in others and also understanding a process behind what it is that we see with regards to flow and return.

Energy is transmuting itself at such a rate at this point in time. My children, all information is coming to you, it is like you are a magnet for your past, your present and your potential future. But what you have the opportunity to do at this point is to actually understand what it is that you are exorcising out of your body. You are transmuting energy, a little bit like a cricket ball transmutes energy off the bat. It depends what directive it goes in. Do you wish it to go off into the slips, behind, in front, above or below?

What you are actually doing is placing that energy where it needs to be, but unbeknown to you, you are used for this process. It is *your* information, but you were part of the process of *creating* that information, so in fact you are the curators of your own information. Yes indeed, you *have* needed to be a murderer, a lover, a carer, a grave digger, a mechanic, a carpenter, a princely individual, you have needed to be all those things to be able to process *your* information, your process and understanding, your evolutionary cycle as an apparatus for gathering information.

This sounds very strange. You are very much part of what is needed to happen.

So does this put a new perspective on what is happening to you and the planet at this point in time? Is exactly what is happening right now something that needs to happen? Indeed it is, everything that happens is part of a process. As we have discussed in the past, if you roll a ball towards a wall it will never bounce back in the same directive and if it does it is a rare occasion. Everything requires different force, different rebounds of energy, but you as an apparatus gather this information and store it.

But what is actually happening now is your storage process is being asked to go back to the main source, the main frame. So you are actually letting go of you being your storage vessel of processes, and this is causing – *we are going to use a strange word here* – disequilibrium.

Disequilibrium is about you not having the equilibrium or the process or the memory understanding of how to do this, how to let go, because this is the first time this has happened in universal processes. So the body is doing a new form of transformation – transformation of past *to* the future *for* the present.

My children, convoluted though these answers may be it is part of your process. So just accept who you are, accept the processes that go on within your body, much has historical process. It is about you letting go, just allowing yourself to let go, and this might mean that things, people, events and places come to mind when you can't understand why they do. Just let these things go and flow like a river to the seas and like the seas to the world.

We are indeed in the process of total and utter transformation. The words, the speeches, words in transformation. The title for your book my children. *Words in Transformation*.

You must understand that we give you words and in those words become your transformation. You have an understanding, but a perplexed understanding, of what some of these things are, but indeed my children, it is about letting go, and indeed you <u>will</u> let go, it is part of the process. It is like letting a lover go at the train station. He is not going off to war, he is letting you go and you are letting him go, let the train leave the junction and steam off up the rails. That is your past transforming itself as you will be transformed my children.

God bless yourselves. *Words in transformation*. Thank you.

Love, Care and Compassion.

April 13ᵗʰ 2014.

The obstacle that we have to remind ourselves about is about the obstinance of man, his objectiveness towards what he doesn't and does need.

We have to ordain many purposes within ourselves, yet we ordain very little of these because we get purported into a different framework of thinking. There is a framework of thinking that is projected to us *on* the planet, and there is a framework of thinking that is projected to us *from* the planet.

When we talk about projected *from the planet* it is about the organisation, the pre-empted avenues of expression that have already happened on the planet. What we are projected to and from with regards to universal thoughts are what we *need* to do.

So there is a direct opposite, which is what we don't necessarily need to do but we can do if we have the choice. So as we create here as a thought a format of objective, you are given an objective to work with which is that that you come in with in spirit form, but that can be and is often interfered with, with regards to what happens to you when you get to the planet and walk the terra firma.

We must understand that this is the law, the law of frequency - *there must be an opposing force* - this is the law of frequency with regards to working on the planet. There are always opposing forces. There is an opposing force to gravity, there is an opposing force to energy, and this energetic frequency is almost a directive opposite, as they all are. So you must understand you aren't opposed, you aren't given opportunities to go towards the word evil or unfortunate circumstance, you are just given an opportunity to go into another directive.

So it is about re-ordaining yourself and purposing your thought patterns towards what it is you need to do. But firstly you need to understand what the objectives are.

One is, I will work with the objective that I came in with.

Two is, I will *not* work with the objective I came in with, but I will work with an objective that is projected to me via frequencies and thought-forms that have been here before.

Or three, I will work with *love, care and compassion,* and with regards to love, care and compassion I will take the best of the opportunities that are given to me. That can come from both heaven and Earth.

So we must understand, in biblical terms heaven and earth is an objective, it is a lesson, it is a process. It isn't something that is here to decompose or dissonate a process that you are given, it is just the fact that you are coming here with a dissonance to work with. You come here initially with a resonance and you have a dissonance. That frequency of understanding is what we need to come to terms with.

There is no such thing as pre-ordained evilness, there is no such thing as pre-ordained love, care and compassion, there is just *being*. And in being you will be what you need to be when you decide to be it, not before, not after, but now.

What is it that you are going to decide to be? Am I going to be resonant with the cause from whence I have come or am I going to be resonant with what has been here in the past and left a frequency of that pattern?

Where another man has walked he has also talked and lived, but where you walk my child must be somewhere where you walk your own truth, where you walk your own steps, where you understand that each step is the first step of your kind walking on that piece on that level of understanding. This can be your truth from this point onwards so let it be your truth. Be resonant with your cause, not dissonant. Be with love, care and compassion at all times.

We are going to re-confirm to you, as individuals that listen to this, that you are part of a love organisational process that we call the *God-force*. The God-force itself is a construct that allows you to elaborate your thinking that there is a form there that has created you. You must stay with that thinking until you understand that there is something else different to that.

There is something else that is there that is part of your construct and you *will build yourself towards this understanding*. But let it be known from this point onwards *be resonant from whence you have come* and when you can be resonant from whence you have come you can walk a new pathway my children, a healing pathway towards the Light. God bless you for now, walk with love, care and resonance. Thank you.

The Lubricant of Acceptance

April 15ᵗʰ 2014

The absorption of the new information that your body intends to use at this point in time is circumspect with regards to the information that is coming for you from the outside. The *outside* is information that is coming from the God-force, the source from whence you have come. The internal information that you already have is information that has already been gleaned by your fellow man, those that have walked the pathway, the pathway that is incorporating and accepting the flesh of humanity.

Humanity itself is flesh, it is Hu and Man. It is a circumspect idea, a correction, an understanding that formats of cells formulate and create a frequency. So this information is gathered within *you*, like a heartbeat. Not an ancient heartbeat, but a heartbeat. As it beats inside you it gives you an understanding of where you have come from and what potentially you might do with the flesh that you have. But that doesn't necessarily help you with the information of gleaning from the God-force from where you have come.

You must understand that all information has a reason and an energy format as to why it moves, so therefore do not try to consider that one works particularly well with the other. So this is what you have formulising within yourself at this point in time, *one energy working against the other*. It is like two plates, plates of the earth or plates that you eat from, that rub together, they create friction and the force between the two divide.

So what is actually happening is *a division*, a division of self. One that wishes to go in a directive in a God-force frequency and one that wishes to work within the footpath, the pathway that man has always worked in. It is like a set programme.

So what do you choose to do at this point in time? You choose to accept that there will be friction from within so this creates itself in many different dilemmas.

There are those that are *totally and utterly formulated towards the humane experience* and they will not change, and there will be people around you that will do just that. And there might be yourself that chooses to work in the God-force domain, which is the frequency from where you have come. But understand there is no rights or wrongs with this, there is just an acceptance.

This isn't a game. This isn't a frequency play like a television channel. What this is, is an acceptance, it is a division. As we have stated in the past, *this is the only time that man has died while still alive in the flesh*. You are changing, and the balls are in the air, juggled. Just accept that this is a time that is convoluted. Yes, it is a time to be or not to be, to be expecting the most unexpected principals of misunderstanding.

This is a convoluted conversation. Much of the information you have as a channel is convoluted because it allows your mind to expand into a different dimension of thinking. All it is, is an explanation from a source and that source being the source from whence this information comes.

So just understand for the time being, expect friction. But you have an option, you can create a lubricant between that friction, and that lubricant can be called your understanding, your acceptance. Be with that acceptance and accept who you are. You are duality.

Moving out of a Prison Cell

April 21st 2014

The transitional period that we all seem to be going through right now is a processional period of time where the transition of cell changes from one moment to the next.

When we talk about moments we are talking of them in fragments of time. A cell transitionalises between one frequency and another. It is like changing the dial on the radio but they change very very slowly. You notice the transition from one to the other but you don't notice the change in frequency. The notice that you are feeling in a frequency stage process is one of discomfort, one of malfunction, one of discordance. This isn't a negative process, this is just like traveling from one place to the other. The journey is often not as comfortable as the destination but it is indeed exciting.

You must avoid the view. The view is what you cannot see. The view is your body changing frequency, the cells of your body moving from one transitional process to the other. It is almost as if you are having a transfusion, it is very strange, you are being given a whole new set of cells.

We are going to use a transitionary process of thought. The cells that you have been in from the past have been much like a prison cell; you have been encapsulated, trapped in a room of frequency and dimension. The cell that you have now is like moving outside of a prison cell to an open area, an open field, you are going to have a different view, a different sleight of interest, so allow for this change. Just bearing in mind, if you have been trapped in a room for many eons and you walked out and you have space around you, your body is going to have time to change. You will need time to change because you won't be able to access your needs, your processes and your understandings.

This is exactly what is happening, yet - and I repeat and underline _yet_ - your eyes cannot focus on what you cannot understand so therefore you won't be given the focus on what you aren't yet able to understand. One day, and it is coming soon for you all, a switch will flick and you will just change.

The very dimension from whence you come will change into another dimension. You will be in a totally different frequency but it will happen simultaneously like this – a flick of the finger – a blink of an eye – a flick of a lid – a change of a tune – a flick of a record. A change of understanding and frequency is going to happen.

We talk about this as if it is something that has happened regularly. This is the first time in human being's history where you have in fact died whilst being alive and whilst being alive you are being moved from one frequency to the other.

This has happened in a discordant fashion with many of you because you are feeling malfunction. Don't feel that, just accept and agree with the change that is coming to you. There is much that needs to be understood yet there is so much that will be misunderstood by this process.

We, being you, being the force behind what you come from, cannot explain to you. It is like giving you the inner workings of a television – you know that if you flick a switch it works and there is a picture in front of you. That's what you see as a human being but behind the scenes is so much more going on – there's changes, there's different fuses, there's different frequencies, there's different processes of understanding.

Allow yourself to intellectualise as much as you possibly can but go no further than that. Allow the journey to happen. Be a passenger, *don't drive the journey*, this is important. Be a passenger, put your feet up, comfort yourself and allow yourself to go on your journey.

God bless you for now, we will speak to you when you are on the other side my children.

We are an Integral Part of the God-Force

April 27th 2014.

We as human beings have aspects that we are not aware of.

All aspects of self are something that are derivative of our past. This derivative is written in the cells, the cells that are part of the blood system and many systems that lay within the body. You are in truth an aspect of self, but indeed you are an aspect of many things that you have been and components of what you are going to be, depending on the directive you are given. You are indeed an aspect of so many different things yet the truth lies within you, the single aspect of self.

We talk about aspects as if you are different to everyone else, you are not, you are the same as everyone else but a different component ...

*Robin was interrupted here and continued...*We are indeed aspects of so many different derivatives.

We must understand that as we see through the valley of choice we also see through our own choices. We have choices that are so different yet they are the same. Our aspects of self are a reflection of something and everything you have been part of. You are indeed an integral part of the God-force, the God-force that we all worship and understand. This is not a religious dogma, this is the God-force of understanding the purportment of where your cells built themselves from the origins of man.

My children, you must understand that the perceptual idea of the way you are is the perceptual idea of the way you need to be. This is all very convoluted. You must understand that nothing is easy, it is very difficult to explain some of the terminology required. The terminology doesn't necessarily giveth the answer but what it does is *it giveth the man the understanding of change*, and once the understanding of change is giveth to the man then the man will become whole once again.

You must understand that you started as a whole being, a complete integral part of the whole, and then you segmented into smaller aspects of self and you had to rebuild yourself again.

That is a little bit like a bee-hive, where it loses its stock and then it rebuilds itself again to its strength, and it will stay strong for a while and then it will weaken, and weaken to the point where it might separate, but then it will start again. As with all things there is a start and an end, it is part of a pattern. You must understand that these patterns are the derivatives that man needs for his change.

We are going through a mass change of events on all levels. The world is segmenting itself into different aspects, it is actually separating the aspects. The emotional aspects, the physical aspects and the non-physical aspects are all separating into different boxes of understanding, and the conclusion of this my children will be the completeness of what *you will be* when you are finished.

In conclusion to this, understand that there will be no conclusive device that will allow you to understand where you have been and where you will go from this point onwards. What in truth that we, you, I are trying to understand is, the conclusion to all things is nothing, there is *no thing* because the conclusion to all things is everything.

We use the derivative many times of *Love*. Love in fact is the no thing. It is the acceptance of all, the acceptance of the fact that eventually what there will be is no thing, there will be everything, everything in completeness, as you will become completeness. But when you become completeness you will start on another journey towards another aspect, and this aspect is like a star in a star system, it is just one star, and when that star shines brightly it will learn to become another star and the aspect starts once again.

You are indeed a spark of divine individualism, but that spark of divine individualism is an aspect of something else, and will be an aspect of something that it has been. You will always carry that integral part of everything you have been within your very soul, within the molecular structure of what you are, but you will take that with you wherever you go, whatever shape, size or being you become in this universe or other universes.

You will have written within your own library of integral thinking what it is that you have been, what it is you might be and what it is you may well go towards. But there is **no thing** in particular that will allow you to understand much of what it is because it is part and parcel of the journey. The journey indeed is separate to the arrival point or the start point but it is part of the same thing.

When you read these words, when you understand these words and become part of these words, they will have no meaning to you. But at the moment we need to give meanings as to what things are so we are trying, unsuccessfully today, but we are trying. God bless you my children for now. The world evolves and as you go round it will go round. Thank you.

Humanity and Trees

May 4ᵗʰ 2014

The designation of love is segmented within the mind.

You must always instruct yourself to visualise a purportment of thought. This purportment of thought has to be **of value to you** and reminiscent of your past, present and potential future. You and your self are like a forest that is gathering information. You gather information for nutrition not only for self but those that are around you, nutrition in the form of love.

Now when we talk about a forest, the forest nurtures and nourishes not only self but those around. A small tree is protected by the big tree and the big tree leaves the fossilised element into the ground so the trees for the future can grow again. This is something that is just expected and of value to the root growing process of understanding and love and care. You must accept that your truth is of value to all, not only yourself. So as you touch the ground you also touch the ceiling, the ceiling being that is the purportment to where you are *going*, you are stretching out towards the gatherance of new.

We have spoken much of the past with regards to the cellular growth and change of the human in being. We are talking about the acceptance of love and the purportment of the truth. The truth is about you **understanding the value of what it is that you are.**

We are going to elaborate on a different format of understanding with regards to what you are as human in beings. You are in fact a micro-organism within a much larger organism. My children you are a micro-organism, a very small part, a component of a bigger whole and that bigger whole is bigger than you can ever imagine. But if you could look down a microscope at components of yourself there are smaller components of *your*self. So there are smaller minorities and there are larger minorities. That is always the case when *you* look at things, but we look at things in a very different differentiality.

We use different words to explain our meanings. When we are talking about '*our*' we are talking about the predecessors of the whole – those that look down on the **growth format**. It is almost like a hormonal imbalance that is being allowed to happen when you look at it from a micro-biological process. What you are in fact is a **growth** that is growing to expand to a different elaboration. You are in fact micro-organisms in the format of **growth**, individual and as a whole. The whole human race has many different spectrumisations.

We don't have the elaborate formatting within the child's brain to be able to explain these things, but what we do have is the elaboration of possibility. We have been restricted by the child's mind but the child's mind has an adaptation, that is why he uses words that aren't necessarily words in your format but they allow us to extend a meaning, to stretch a thought-form. We do not require scientific acceptance, what we require is a ramification of thought pattern that can flow from one man to the next.

We are trying to get to the roots and the understanding. This will not necessarily do you any good to understand what it is that you are, but my children, what it is that you are is what you might be. What you might be is a different format of growth, a different format of extension and formatting.

My children, love is the way forward. If you apply love to **any** organism its structures change, the formatting of the cells change, the way they dynamically elaborate around each other change. Love itself is an acceptance, it is a way forward, it is a journey. Life is a journey.

As said, you have the possibility to go backwards, to stay present or move forwards. As stated, we have many options when we come here. We are born via a process, just like any amoeba creates its belief system by whence and what it has come from. You are growths my children, with the ability to move around.

Trees are growths with the inability to move around. They have roots attached to the purportment attached to the vessel that allows them their journey but their journey is much the same as yours. They carry the same electronic frequencies as you, their thought complexes are much the same, it is just they function in a different manner but their energetic understanding and purportment and gatherance of energy is much the same as you. So imagine yourself as a forest and each tree, each elaboration, each seed, is another procreational process.

My children, you are a forest shedding its leaves and as you go into the winter stage of your existence your leaves will grow again, and as you leave behind you grow new leaves and you let go of the past and move into the future, with the breezes of the past blowing away the past completely.

This time you move with a new format of understanding and choice. Your roots my children, are the roots of a nuance, a nuance being a new change, a new process, a new growth format. The fertiliser is that of *new love* and your new love will be different to that of old, you will experience another coming from a whole different format of energetic spiral.

Wait and accept my children and thank you for listening. This has been a difficult task for the child because his channeling is changing.

"My Child, my Children."

Throughout this discourse the words *my child* and *my children* have been expressed with reference to Robin and those that sit with him. On asking why we were referred to as children this is the explanation that was given in June 2002.

"My children, the creative force behind you all is the creative force behind where you came from. You are at this point in a millennia of change. My children, **the parental influence**, the influence and energy that you came from, is now forthcoming in an energy format that is being supplied to the children, so the manifestation of **children** is the exposure of the fact that you have come from a parental influence. This parental influence is the energy behind the change, the energy behind the forwardness, the completion, the transitionalisation from one experience to the next.

The parental element, the parental element, the parental element my children, my children, my children.

We must accept at this point in time that the equilibrilisation of formats are now coming into place, it is now time for change. It is now time for the human element to accept that within his mindset there is an element of change that is now transitioning firstly within the physicality.

The physicality is the first that will accept experialisation experience, experience of change within itself, then it will draw itself to the conscious mind, then you will be able to vocalize on what has occurred to you my children. It is at this point you will then begin to understand what your body found and experienced first. Your body is experiencing change before the mind because the body is the curator of change.

My children, experience is something that you chose, experience is something that you need, experience is something that you are going to access with and understand the new information and formats that are coming forward to you. It is now time for the curators of this change to unveil themselves and allow you to see them in the vocalization, the experience, and the eyesight that you have.

My children you will begin to see the curators, you will begin to see the lights and energies that come forth to you in your subconscious and superconscious. It is now time for you to experience this my children. Understand that this is now coming. Thank you so much for listening.

The Dissemination of Energy.

May 14ᵗʰ 2014.

We are going to talk to you about the dissemination of energy. Energy is transferred to you via a thought process, an elongation. This elongation comes from the patterns from whence you have come. Now energy is like a library – all the best books are at the top, the not so good ones are in the middle, and the bad ones are at the bottom.

So we are going to look at the bad ones to start off with. What are the bad ones? They are just different formats of energy that might not necessarily suit the fabric that you are in, the flavour, the taste that you have chosen to be part of. But are they necessary or unnecessary, are they deemed possible within the framework that you have? It is because they don't fit in the *shape* that you have but they will fit in somebody's shape. So therefore those that challenge are just challenging a format that needs to be there in place.

We are going to try and transfer to you, the listener, what it is that we are trying to elongate in your minds. Energy, *all* energy, has relevance. So what is negative energy? Negative energy isn't positive energy going backwards, it is the same form of energy but in a different framework of understanding the correspondence.

Now as you well appreciate, all of you that listen, there are many different body shapes and types and elongations on your planet of Earth, many of which are transferring their shape, creed, need and taste to their format of understanding. You being you have a different format maybe to theirs. Does that make it wrong or right? No, it does not, it just makes it possible.

So understand this. When we talk about channeling, is there such a thing as negative channeling, negative entities, negative processes, demonisations? There is not. All there is, is different shapes and formats of understanding in their process of growth.

Now growth can go in many different ways. Is a tree that is poisoned and dies, has it lost an experience it could have had or has it gained an experience it already had? Everything has an experience. Is somebody that is murdered by a machete, is that an experience that was relevant and necessary? Maybe not to those that saw it but maybe to the person that received it and maybe to the person that acted out the deed, maybe there was a relevance to that process, unpleasant as it may seem.

The man that drowns in the sea in front of his children. Sad desperate situation for all concerned, yet there is a reason for all visions and purportments. We have to understand that we don't necessarily have the answers to these things, because we haven't been **deemed** the answers. What is the point in the process of evolution if you are given the answers before you start your journey? The journey is about *stretching the mind* to different places of understanding. So in truth what we must do is accept.

There is no such thing as perverse energy. There is such a thing as a **perverse being** that needs to elongate itself or stretch its mind to that purportment, or even elongate a picture to others to see. That maybe their journey or their job at that particular point in time. Some people are *carriers* and some people are *doers*. Those that are carriers are ones that don't actually know what it is they are doing and they just do it. And there are those that are the doers that *do know* what they are doing and they get on and do it.

We must understand, there are so many different elongations. What is it then that is the God-force that is trying to guide *you* as individuals?

The God-force is the eventuality of what you might turn out to be.

We have had purported to ourselves the idea of evil and good, the Devil and the God, and the difference between the two, but there are many differences between the two! (*There was laughter evident in the voice here*) Not in the fact that one is completely wrong and one is completely right or vice versa, it is the fact that they are the spectrum that is required for a human being to transcend from one space to the next.

As was stated in earlier channeling: when there is cold there *will* be hot, when there is light there *will* be dark. But is the dark as bad or worse than anything else? No it is part of what is needed. If you are to walk across stony ground do you walk bare foot? No you do not, you cover your feet and your sole. And what you indeed do is don't transfer yourself pain through your journey, it is about how you cover your tracks when you go through your journey. The clever man or woman indeed is those that understand that everything is part of their need and part of the purportment of energy.

Does that make any difference if you suddenly decide to do something wrong in your eyes? Just remember, *your body shape* requires *exactly* what your intuition gives you. So if it is your intuitive purpose to be good, caring and understanding, clean living, clean understanding and good to others, then that is your need and if you step outside of that need you will in some way have a relinquishment of dis-satisfaction coming towards you in the form of energy going in another direction that won't suit you.

Equally, the man that beats somebody over the head with a machete, maybe that is his job, maybe that is what he needs to do, maybe that is his picture that he shows the world. If he suddenly decides to be something other than that, until the energy changes then he will have a problem too. It is all about working through the need that you have that you brought in with you.

There are many many different planets that are actually producing energy forms that can actually produce a human frame, many of which are of different purportments of energy framework understanding, many of which need a different apprenticeship to learn to be on terra forma, to learn to be on the planet of Earth.

So indeed my children, you are a very mixed bunch of beings here with a similar body shape and a similar energy frequency but the energy frequency that *feeds* that frequency is often incredibly different. And this you must understand, and this you must accept, and this you must just deem as possible and part of the love process that you have. Not all is as it seems and as it seems is not all.

So my children, what is love? Love is acceptance of all things that you see. *Love is acceptance of all things that you see*, because it is a need, a process, a creed of understanding.

Take this and read this, this is very important. God bless you all, from wherever you come from. Thank you.

A Total Change of Trajectory

22.5.2014

The apparent reason for all changes on earth are due to man, as much as man thinks, but many apparent reasons are not what you think they are.

Earth is a jurisdiction of thought pattern and this jurisdiction happens outside of the thought-form of the man. Man being the experiment, jurisdiction being an opportunity to experiment. So from the Source we are actually stating to you that man is doing precisely what is due to happen with the experimental thought-patterns that are offered to man at this point in time.

As you can create an arc that arc is the change. Man always goes in curves, as we have spoken about before. If you look at the planet and if you can look far enough you would see that it goes in a curve, as do clouds, as do thought-patterns, as do the cells of the body, everything goes in a curve and spirals towards something that will be different but the same.

So what is happening right now is the compilation of all thought-forms gathered up and projected on to a screen and man is given the opportunity to see what it is that he has gathered, like a crop.

Now in truth my children, my people, my person, you have to opportune yourself and give yourself the opportunity of expectation. What is it that is going to happen next? Is the trajectory going to stay the same thought-form, the same curvature, or is it going to change?

So what is going to happen is a change; a change of directive, a change of gearing, a change of pattern, a change of purpose, so when that happens in any format or programme this is an opportune moment to stay still, like a stagnant mill pool, before it starts projecting itself towards another place.

So in truth, what is happening is everything is coming to a slow halt and it will stay stationary for a while, as it did do prior to this decade and the previous decade, and we are talking decades in thought-form patterns, decades of tens, decades of tens of thousands of years. What we are actually stating is, this curvature is going to be a complete change of angle, of thought, mind and set.

So what is going to happen is something that has never happened before. It is a total change of trajectory and this total change of trajectory is actually happening on a universal level. This universal level is being projected to you from the Source from whence you have all come, the manifestation of man, mammon, animal, reptile and universal purposes.

So at this point in time expect that change in *your lifetimes*. Expect that you will be part of that change and those that are the way-showers will actually be part of the purpose of that change. Many of them are being woken up at this point in time to the jobs that they were born to do. So many people are being woken up, woken up through many different reasonings – through illness, through separation, through growth spurt, and growth spurt allows things to change within the equilibrium of self. It is like shaking yourself off and allowing the reality of what you are and who you are to come to a more trajectile thought pattern, an acceptable purpose behind what it is that you were born to do.

You, we, us, are the guidelines for these things, like a decoy, a process that is going to allow people to be guided in a different directive. We have been used as the way-showers before, but look at yourself as the curator of the new traffic, and the traffic is going to be human beings going in another direction and they need to be guided and pointed and told it is fine.

Don't supply them with answers, just supply them with love, care and compassion. That is the job of many, that is the job of the child and those that come to him for help. Just accept, ask no questions and be that love and that love will project itself not only to you but people that you work with.

In mammonistic terms my children, you are in the process of change, accept and be with that change and the change will be with you. God bless you for now and thank you.

The Watcher or the Ghost at Gabriel's Return

THE GHOST AT "GABRIELS RETURN"

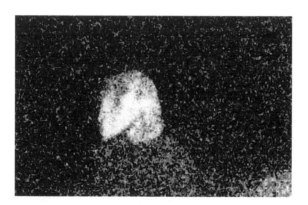

Carolyn: A particular interest of mine has been the study of the phenomena known as Orbs and I have captured thousands of these on my camera. While staying in Ireland with Robin in 2012 I was out filming late one evening when the camera picked up something strange. The ghostly form of a woman appeared to be walking past the gateway of Gabriel's Return. I asked Robin if he could get any information about her.

In the photograph the ghost of a woman is seen walking between the stone gate pillars at the entrance to the house at Gabriel's Return (see photographs). I did not see her but she was picked up by the camera, as were the small orbs beside her head and the left hand pillar. In the second picture only her head and shoulders were captured as she continued to walk down the lane beyond the pillar. This is the only photograph of a ghost I have managed to obtain.

I remember speaking with my sister that evening, telling her something very strange had occurred as I was filming orbs and how I thought I had captured a ghost. It was not until two years later on a further visit to Ireland that I asked Robin once more about these pictures and if he could get any information about the ghost who had appeared on my camera that night. I had previously mentioned this to him but the veil was not to be lifted on the mystery until the time was right. This information was given with reference to those known as the Watchers.

Further Information on The Watchers

May 30th 2014

The apparent education needed for man is for us to understand what it is that we choose to look at.

There is much that we choose to look at so therefore we don't normally understand what it is. The apparition that was created in the form of pictures, your form of pictures, was an apparition, an understanding process that there are other beings on this planet walking the terra forma in a different way to yourself.

Now for us, or we, to let you know that we are here and for you to understand we are here we have to create an understanding for your eyes to see, so therefore the form is the creational process of form that you wish or need to see.

If you were to see a cube or a square or something totally differential to your mind-sets passing by your eyes you would not believe firstly, what it is you see and secondly, how can you explain it to others and thirdly, what is the point because you will think your mind is playing tricks.

So therefore we will give you an opportunity to see something that you *can* understand, which is another form of humanity, a human form in the shape of your own, dressed much as the way you would expect somebody to dress that might be older than you in formulation.

Therefore my children, we can give you a story if you wish or we can tell you the truth. The lady you saw is a lady in form only, in form not in any other reason, so *that energy thought format* was a pure projection for you to understand that there are beings that are called the Watchers.

Watchers in what way? They are just watching what you are doing, what you are seeing. The boy sees them all the time when he is in the garden. They are just watching, trying to understand what it is that you try and do with the lifestyle that you have. There is no reason, no being and no momentum behind what it is other than watching.

Many people watch but they don't necessarily take part. It is a little bit like being in an audience watching a football match, you aren't taking part you are just watching to see the performance of somebody else. You may become elated by their performance but your performance is different to theirs, you are watching they are doing.

So then perhaps the thought format here is the creational process that you chose to see or you were seeing was a projection of a thought-form for your mind to understand. We could have given you names, dates, times, what she was doing, what she might have been doing, what her life was, who her relatives were, but that would in truth be a story – history, it might be - *his story*. The mystery - the *'my' story*.

There are so many words that we formulate for you to understand but the truth is always necessary when you want to get to the bottom of something. So the bottom of this truth is you visited a picture of a Watcher. The Watcher created a format for you to understand. All it was was letting you know that there is somebody else here on your planet doing something very different to you but you are watched by them.

So God bless you for now and thank you for your enquiry and thank you for allowing yourself to be educated in a slightly different way. We will visit you all once again and show you a different dictate, a different format for you to see.

Carolyn: I have just checked on the latest crop circles and on the 16ᵗʰ August 2014, a formation appeared at Nettle Hill in Warwickshire depicting a huge eye. This immediately brought to mind the information recently received on The Watchers whose eyes are everywhere and do not miss a thing happening on planet Earth. Synchronicities are the way the universe speaks to those who are aware and the crop circles can be deciphered on many levels, depending on one's mindset.

No Thing in Particular

17ᵗʰ June 2014.

The recommendation of all thought forms is change.

Change is the true recommendation and acceptance that we all need inside ourselves. We have to alter the polarity of our thoughts for this change otherwise we create something called resistance so we have to alter our thoughts in acceptance of the change that is going to come to you.

Now what is the change that you are going to accept? It is going to be one that is elaborate with the thinking levels that you have so each individual person with different thinking levels is going to accept a different process of change, not all will be the same.

As you walk down the aisle of a shopping mall not all the things on the shelves are the same and not everyone will take the same things off but they will indeed create the same resource and that is sustenance.

What it is you will be getting in your form of change is *your sustenance* for the change that you need, no more or no less. It is about acceptance that some people will change in the manner that you accept and some people will not, but as is stated in human terms 'Birds of a feather will indeed flock together.'

My children, my person, my people, you must accept that not all people will flock together, some will flock in one directive and some will flock in another. But what is the flock that you choose to be with? The one where you have no resistance whatsoever so that is your chosen pathway, the directive towards your form of change. So you must understand that the resistance that you create won't be the resistance that you will go towards. The resistance that you will create is that of 'you do not accept,' so it is about accepting everything and every format of information that you see, feel, hear and touch.

Resistance is a truth in the fact that you are not yet ready to take on board whatever it is that is being given to you for your eyes to perform their natural process of sight. But sight doesn't provide you with all the answers, there is so much more. Sight was given to man so he can perceive a directive, but if you close your eyes you can feel and see many things in your mind. You can create many illusions, you can create many realities, but if you don't see them have they happened? This is a question you must beg to ask. So therefore you must ask yourself, if you create a reality in your mind and you don't see it, does that mean to say it didn't happen or did it happen on another level of thought that you have within yourself? As stated on many occasions, mind is indeed the builder, but for you to perceive and create that vision much more mind-set and mind information needs to be procured in the directive of what it is that you need. So if you want to see something you have to **_think_** about it more.

Now we know this but something is going to change with regards to the resistance you have with regard to the change that you need. The change that you need will speed up, you will be given more thought-forms, more thought patterns, more perceptions with regard to the change that you need personally, individually, singularly and in a group sense.

And what do we mean by groups? Are they groups of people that actually sit together and work together? No, it is the grouping of energetic beings that have a similar polarity as yourself. They may be a group that you do not touch or feel, or even see each other, but indeed you are part of much of the same. (Like the Seven?)

It is like a flock of disciples that are being taught and elongating their minds towards the same educational process, and that educational process is different for all concerned. We use the word *concerned* very lightly here.

There is no concern because everything rolls, just like a ball, just like the wind, just like the mind, it all rolls in a directive that is suitable to you and the surroundings that you are working with.

Your lifespans in the human framework are very small. You have no perception whatsoever with regards to where you go and what you do thereafter. What is the reality of that? What is the reality of nothing? What is the reality of everything? The reality is *there is no reality*.

In reality what you actually have in truth my children is nothingness – *no thing in particular*, these words have been stated before. No thing in particular. What it actually means is there is no thing in particle, in particle or article. Articles are *things* that you have in front of you that you see. Particles are things that you don't necessarily see. Your ancestral domain of thought pattern creates a particle, and indeed can write the article that is needed for you to perceive what it is that you want.

A plant grows in what directive? It grows towards the sun, towards the fellowship of man. Hu-man? Many man, it grows towards the sun, towards the light. Indeed my children you *go* towards the light, you don't grow you go. What you are actually doing is working your way towards your light. Does that make any difference if you work your way towards the dark? What is the dark, what is the light, they are part of the same thing. My children, you must understand that everything has the same result, you are moving in a directive that is suitable and conducive to your thought-form at that point in time.

Now we are going to move across the echelons of what is evil, what is good, what is bright, what is dark, what is warm, what is cold?

What we are actually doing, *we* being the force, the energetic process behind the resonance of you, the resonance of man, the resonance of those that have come here. Some resonances are lesser or greater than others but you are all connected to a thought-form and that thought-form is the God-force and the Light, the source from whence you have come.

You all carry small cells, like a little suitcase, with a memory pattern within it. Some of those cells are available and attainable, and those of you that are attaining that and making it available for you to perceive are having an objective. And that is opening it up and seeing what it is.

It is like the first day of school exams. What is it the paper is going to give us, what is the directive, what do we need to produce, what is it? Do I have enough revision, do I have enough wisdom, do I have enough understanding within me to take on board what it is that I am going to see and perceive?

But what you don't realise at this point is what you pull out of there is an exact directive replicating just a little bit further on from where you are at that point in time. Not one single directive will be the same as the other but they all have one thing in common, they have a common denominator, they are the directive that is required for you to perceive the longing choice that you have to go back towards the directive.

This may take you a million years, it may take you two billion years, but years, time, echelons of thought, are just man-made productions. So in truth my children, it may take you today or tomorrow, or you may have done it yesterday, it matters not. Whatever steps you take, however small or large, you will get there in *time* – your time, my time, somebody's time, or you may just get there with no thing in particular.

You must understand, you are perceiving a new directive. Just accept it, there is nothing you need to do more or less than that. It is the time for the smiles from within that will allow you to accept the change that you need. The change that you need will accelerate towards my child.

But bless you for now and bless the lady for joining us today and bless you all as you have a change and your change will be part of you and that part of you will change to the directive that you need to be and you will spiral towards that with love and joy. God bless and thank you.

World Peace

June 29ᵗʰ 2014

World peace as we know it is an energy form, a thought pattern, an acceptance of what many might like or many might not like.

What is world peace? If we actually take the word apart it has got *world* and *peace*, the peace of the world. What is it that people or man want, in fact what is it the energy form wants?

The truth behind this is everybody wants a different peace, a different format of understanding behind the peace that they have, so world peace is different to every single individual. So why would one expect everyone's thoughts to be the same manner?

We are all having and carrying different energy forms about what it is that we need to do on this planet, some of which are complimentary towards the surroundings, some of which are less than complimentary, but everyone's energy has a job.

It is a little bit like the man who clears the dustbins up, it is not a nice job but it has to be done. Or the man that cuts the roses for the Queen – lovely job, end result beautiful and lightening. But all jobs aren't necessarily deemed pleasant, so therefore different thought patterns towards peace aren't necessarily pleasant, so the peace of thought an individual *has* is his or hers and only that personifies exactly what it is that that energy form is moving towards.

You must accept that what your thought forms with regard to the world peace or your peace of the world is will be very different to your neighbour and certainly different to the person next door to you! So therefore just accept what it is that you want will always be different to that of somebody else. So in truth it is just about being what it is that you want to be, no more or less.

And as I speak I see a spiral but this spiral isn't spiralling, it is lots of hoops going down like a trumpet, and at the end of that trumpet what I actually see is a word. *Integration* is the word. Integration within yourself, integration within the thought patterns that you have, integration with the acceptance and energy that you carry – no more or less.

So if you ask to be integrated with your energy form, what you will be *is integrated with the form of energy that you need*, and with that form of energy that you need accepted within yourself you will not ask anyone to change the way that they are because they will be integrated or not with the acceptance of what their job is.

Many moons ago the Aboriginals used to allow things to happen that would seem totally and utterly unworldly to you or me with the sublime living processes that we have. They seemed somewhat draconian in their thoughts, but an Aboriginal being was in touch with himself and the planet. The terra-forma communicated with him and he communicated with the terra-forma. He communicated with the animal kingdom, the nature kingdom, he also communicated with the stars and the astral frequencies that our visitors came to. They knew they had descendants, not only from here but from elsewhere, so they were the originals in the format of peace that they wanted. Yet their peace was interfered with by somebody else's peace and the newbies to their continent came in and interfered with them to the point where they could no longer exist outside in the world. So the Aboriginals went inside, they internalised what it was that they had. The only thing man couldn't take away were their thoughts so that is what they are left with – memories and thoughts, fables and folklores.

But that is all that has been left to us by our descendants, our predecessors – fables and folklores. But what is actually happening is the Book of Knowledge is being re-awakened, not within man but within your*self*, the book of understanding, the book of choices, the book of truth, your truth and everyone's truth.

Yes of course we all come from the same place but we don't all drive the same vehicle. It would be a very dull place if everyone did the same thing, wore the same clothes and shone the same light, so we are indeed *differentials* all muddling along together, but what we have a problem with is we grate with others and they grate with us. Just accept that what you do that seems pleasant maybe totally unpleasant to somebody else.

So it is about just *shining your light* and *being your light*, no more or no less. Expect nobody to believe what you say and don't believe anything anyone else says, but if something sits with you work with it, stand with it, enjoy with it and take it on board, and if it stays with you for a while so be it. It is like a visitor, comfort it whilst it is there and allow it to go when it needs to go. That is what friends and visitations are all about.

Nothing is permanent and nothing ever will be permanent. Foundations are for houses, fixed structures. My children you are *not* fixed structures, you do *not need* foundations, what you actually need is the flamboyancy to be able to fly, to be able to move around and be acceptance personified. You are cells that require *permanent movement* like the fluidity of water, like the fluidity of air, like the fluidity of love.

So my children for this day world peace is not your peace or anyone else's peace it is something that actually accepts within yourself that you are part of a fluid movement of love. So for today we speak of love and we send you love. So with joy in your hearts, God bless you and thank you.

Beaming Down a New Frequency

July 3rd 2014

The intricacies of the tendency of man are towards similar patterns of events.

We, in humanity format, understand that what we need is something that creates the same barriers, the same procedures, the same understandings. We always look for a purpose behind a reason and a reason behind a purpose, therefore we get stuck and trapped in a domain of thinking. Reasons and purposes are just end results in your minds but they are part of the journey, a transitory period between one energy pattern and the next, therefore expect nothing my children. Expect nothing from a purpose and expect nothing from a procedure, just expect a journey. There is no end or no start, it is just a transition of light, the way particles travel from one procedure to another.

So my children, what you are actually experiencing at this point in time is many, many different, procedures coming to you. Let them pass. A little bit like a ship passing in the night, let it pass, don't jump on board, don't accept that it's a pattern, don't accept that it is an anger frequency or a love frequency, it is just a frequency.

When we talk about transitory patterns, you must experience the thought pattern of *the changes are upon you*. These changes my children, the acceptance of the new polarity is being beamed down literally, beamed down to your cellular structure. Now your cellular structure emits a frequency, a frequency of expectation, acceptance and understanding, so therefore what your frequency picks up is the beaming down of the frequency that is conducive or as close as conducive to your pattern of events that surround you. This is how there is a differentiation between yours and your next-door neighbour's pattern. It is not about yours is green and mine is blue, it is just your frequency is different; you will pick up a different frequency.

Now, has this frequency been beamed down to the planet before? In many different ways yes but *not in this way*. This is a little bit like changing your grid frequency pattern from 210 volts to 240 volts, it is a complete change, but one will work with the other but it won't necessarily work as well. This is why there are changing events within you all, just the way you feel, the way you experience things and the way you understand things, your perception will be different.

Will your perception be the same as your next door neighbours?   Something *similar*, but different.

Why are these changes being offered to man?

Because the polarity of man is being altered. Man has gone off course. It is a little like you are heading towards a cliff edge, the road leads you there and you will go straight off and there is a nasty landing at the bottom.

This has been noted that man is heading towards a cliff edge where he *will* have a nasty landing, and that landing is not a perceptance or an acceptance of the God-force, the Source from whence you have come. So you are being diverted, you are being *corralled*, you are being *rounded up* and pushed in a slightly different directive but it is happening through your own mind and thought patterns. You are not being pushed, like being imprisoned, because indeed you all have choices and those choices lay in the frequency that comes to *you*. But when the mind-set builds to a point where 50 or 51% of the people don't want to corral themselves towards the cliff edge then there will be a change. The other 49% will follow, and that is the most important thing – *building up the numbers of people that know that things need to change.*

What is death when there is life and what is life when there is death? You will experience the loss of cells when somebody moves from one transitory experience to the next. You have lost the ability to understand that there is no such thing as stoppage; there is an existence in another form. Stoppage my children is the way something stops and doesn't move again. So therefore when you think in those patterns, when something doesn't move again, then it is devoid of use, it has no polarity or acceptance on the plane of your existence. Therefore stoppage is something you have grown to create in in your mind so stoppage is something you need to *remove from your mind.*

Constant movement is something that happens within all fluidities. You are a fluid purpose so there will always be constant movement but there will be stoppage on occasions. A little bit like a stream when a twig runs across it but eventually there will be a storm and the twig will be moved. Eventually there will be a dam but the dam will eventually be moved by something else. Nothing stays as you think it should.

Now I must elongate to your thought patterns. Just accept that you have boats floating in front of you, they are carrying different experiences and you look at them. Do not jump on board, do not take your energy to that boat, just let it float on by. Experience and watch, you don't have to *be*.

This is a choice of course, but be that choice because it will make that choice much more suited to your body frames.

God bless you for now, we do thank you my child for carrying this vessel of thought.

A Revolving Spiral of Understanding

July 14th 2014

The orientation of concern is a human domain. It is a thinking pattern which elongates a total thought pattern of spectrum. When we talk about spectrums we are talking about a diagrammatic thought pattern of thinking.

Now if you look at a diagram, a spectrum is a long straight line. If you look at that long straight line, a line being that of experience, you will get a blip where it goes up and a blip where it goes down. Basically the diagrammatic is an extension of that, it doesn't go up or down, it goes sideways. It is an extension of a line of experience.

So transition, or a transitory experience, is a long straight line where you experience *nothing*. A diagrammatic experience is one where you experience something, depending on what it is you need.

So when you elongate into the planet of Earth what is actually happening is your diagrammatic spectrumisation is read, it is read from all the experiences you have had. It depends on how straight your line and how straight it is or isn't going to be.

If you want to go from experience to non-experience and from non-experience to experience, there is a directive between that like an A or a B, and there is a line between the two. But in that experience comes the domain and the needs of where you are, be that of planet Earth or be that of Pluto or Neptune, there will be a different diagrammatic experience **needed** for that process. Will the line be straight or will it be elongated?

Some processes just allow for backwards movement, so you start off with legs and end up as an amoeba. Some places need forward movement, where you start off as an amoeba and end up with legs and walk and evolve into something that is rather wonderful as a species.

But all it is is an extension of the thought pattern required for that dimension of thinking. So what we are actually expecting you to do here is move your mind out of **your** dimension of thinking and accept that there are many many other dimensions of acceptance, diagrammatic experiences of exchange.

Convoluted as this may sound, there are so many different experiences we all need to comprehend within ourselves, and when we can comprehend some of those we can extend our minds to the possibility of whence and where we have been, where we might go and where we might stay, because indeed there are choices.

When our man Jesus came to Jerusalem all the inns were full. He came in-utero via his parents, they ended up staying in a stable! This is a fable but indeed it is a folk lore. What we are actually stating to you were there were many many different rooms for him to go in. These were the different advantageous processes that could have come to him for the different planetary experiences he could have had. He chose to go for an uncomfortable start and continued so.

We are just using this in a diagram form. *In reality none of these things occurred*, but to us we are given stories and these stories allow our minds to create pictures, therefore understanding comes into place and possibility is formed. Many things are created by possibility via diagrams.

Have many of the thoughts that we have had of historical events just been given to us as thought as opposed to reality?

Is reality what we see it to be, or is it what we are *told* it is? In fact reality is what you are experiencing now, no more or no less, so accept what is happening and these words you hear are real. Yet what you heard yesterday, were they real? Did they happen? Did you see them? Did you experience them? You can only accept that that happened because you have a memory of yesterday.

But in reality is everything happening at the same time?

We have been led to believe that time is a manmade prospect. Time is something that reminds you firmly of things you are yet to do, or haven't already done, or might have done, so time is fairly restrictive.

So what line and directive are you going in as a man, or as a woman? Are you going in a straight line, are you going backwards, up or down? The choice actually is yours because you have an evolutionary cycle of understanding. You can choose to do exactly and precisely what you wish with the spectrum of understanding you have.

But what we are trying to do here is stretch your mind to another spectrum of understanding, another creative process going on alongside yours. Your yesterday is another person's experience.

Now what does that mean – *another person's experience*?

Was it your experience? Indeed it was, but it is another person's experience because what you left behind you was like an exhaust. It was a removal of something you had from yourself because you have done it. So you have moved from one place to the next and left an imprint, firmly imprinted on a prospectus of understanding.

Now we are going to try and spectrumise this to you in a very very different way, so accept a download.

Robin: What I am feeling now is energy flowing down through my body. It is a little bit like someone pouring something over my head. I am experiencing a download. That is what it is.

There is a distinct change in voice and lowering of tone.

We are a creative process and this creative process is an elongation of thought pattern. We are not man, we are not frequency, we are *expectance*, and expectance is a prospect of personality trait. This prospect of personality trait is gifted to those that created their yesterday, and that yesterday is read, your spectrumisation is read, the line and drift in which you are at is understood.

You are given a prospect, a frequency that allows you to move in a different directive. This growth pattern is happening tenfold today, it is speeding up, a little bit like a bullet that has left the holster. As it speeds up it moves towards its directive, and that is *you*, but your directive is changing all the time so therefore the spectrum of elongation is given to you in a different way.

So you must understand my children, you are indeed *a revolving spiral of understanding*. Give yourself this chance to release the prospect of what you were yesterday and become your new today, and tomorrow you will *be reborn* once again. This is the changing process of the planet of Earth at this point in time.

You have been gifted this through the loving environment in which you frequencise with. This is the child we speak of. God bless you and thank you and I bid you farewell for today because tomorrow you will be reborn once again.

Reconnection to our Life Source

July 28th 2014

The advancement of man's thinking has come to a stalemate. His generosity of thought isn't allowing him to fathom the differentials of possibility within the only mind-set that he has.

If you look at a flower, it has many different petals, they all point in different directions and what they all do is allow differentials of experience, not only on a true nutritional level to the plant but also north, south, east and west, up, down, below, in, out, all those things are what that plant experiences. But we have allowed our minds to go in a straight line, a directive.

Now we spoke of lines before but what we are going to talk about with regards to this line, is the line of connectivity we have to the Source from whence we have come. When we talk about Source we talk about the energy fields, the parameters we rely on to allow us to become what we are. There are many many differentials to that. So our Source allows us to become what we are, no more or no less. But you may be somewhere else in a different differential allowing yourself to become a **different part** of what you need to be.

So on Planet Earth you are but becoming the petals of a flower, allowing all directions to come to you.

Now at this point in time you have perception, conception, elongation, spectrumisation, and energy formats, but what you don't have is a directive that allow *you to see you for what you are going to be*. To see you for what you are going to be allows a totally and utterly different directive, and what is going to happen is in the near future *you are going to see yourself for what you are going to be*. And when you *see* what you are going to be you have an opportunity to change, change based on what it *is* you are *going to be*.

Is the thing you are going to be what you need or want to be? Or is it the fact that you have *got* to that point because you have done nothing, you have changed no dials. The codes, the parameters that you are inputting into your bio-computer stay exactly the same so you go in the same direction.

So in truth my children, my people, my person, what you will *do* by seeing what you are going to be is understand what it is you need to change within yourself to go in a slightly different divergent, convergent, invergent or exvergent direction. In truth what it is you need to be is *yourself*.

So my children, allow yourself to be yourself at all levels of love and understanding.

If you look at the vegetation in a garden as such vegetation goes towards the sun, the Source, but it does so much more than that. It stretches down *below* the ground because it needs nutritional processes coming from beneath to sustain its growth towards its source, its light source. But when it becomes disconnected from that it becomes *dull and eventually it dies* but it will have life for a while.

So when you become directly disconnected from *your nutritional surfaces,* your nutritional connectivity to your planet, you will nullify and eventually die. But what is happening is people are nullifying but still living, they are living without a connectivity. A tree itself cannot move around, its roots are firmly connected, its life force is the very same as your own but it cannot move around, unless it is blown, or unless it is taken away from its life source.

So as a human race *we need to reconnect to our life source*, the connectivity from whence you have come. You need to re-join the joy and love processes that you came in with originally, and this is all going to happen when you decide what it is you are going to be.

The man talks about what he was going to be. You decide what you are going to be but is it what you need to be. My children we will speak more of this later.

The Word Today is Download.

August 9th 2014

The word today is download. What is it that we use when we download information into our mind-set?

A download is a spectrum of thought format that comes to you when you start projecting your mind out to the perspective of new avenues of information, or an elongation of the existing avenue of information you already have contained within you, your cell as such.

So what is it that happens when you start projecting your mind out? You are actually stating you need, want or wish to know more with regards to a certain subject or parallel of information. So therefore out goes the volume *of thought* from your mind, gathering and projecting, and gathering and projecting, sending out to different universes within and without. The inner universe is that within your body, the outer universe is the continuum that surrounds that body, or that vessel of information. It gathers a little bit like an aeroplane flying round the world gathers information to use in sights and it comes back, and it spectrumises this information and gives it back to you.

Now you, having a limited mind-set or a vast mind-set, will take on board what it is you have available to in formation in yourself. In formation within yourself is, what are you able to contain with regards to that information? You will take on board what it is that your body *can* contain, no more and no less. If you have a mind for numbers, then you will contain numbers. If you have a mind for memories or spectrums of thought, then you will get that. If you have a mind that is numb and accepts very little, then you will get very little, but if you have very little in your mind you would not be asking for too much in the first place. So you will only get what you are available to be given.

So what is it that happens when you contain information? It goes within your cells, it joints within the part of your body that already has that part of the information. It is a little bit like *assessing* a joint with a piece of wood, it will join up with another thing that has a similar compaction of thought. That is exactly what happens and it goes into the right diaphragm of thought within your body and it stays there and your body works with it.

A little bit like a new tool, a new spanner that will undo a new nut, whereas before you had a pair of pliers. So all it has actually done is given you a little bit more ease with regards to what it is that you are searching for.

Now the question is, is there a limit to information? Is there a limit to *your* information?

Yes, there is indeed. The limit to your information is *when you state to yourself there is a limit.* Then you have to find out where that limit is and it is generally something or somebody else that tells you where that limit is.

That is where science comes into play. Science is a designated process to allow a man to contain within his own mind. The only time that that is unprecedently changed is when somebody can move *outside* of that, when you have somebody that might be called a genius, an Einstein. Somebody that has a genius inside his mind that will spectrumise a new process of understanding and move the threshold out and out.

But you must understand, science is there to work within parallels. Scientists **know** that there is always more information to one piece of information but at what point can they start writing papers? The point where there is no more to be had. So somebody has to create the limit and the bastions of science certainly create that.

But you must understand what it is that limits what you require within your mind. Do you require to understand what it is that you **need,** or do you require to understand what it is that you **want**? Two variant differences.

What it is that you **need** allows your body to move with **ease**. What it is that you **want** – *and listen here* – allows your body to move with **dis-ease**. So generally most of the things you want create dis-ease within your body. Most of the things that you need create ease within your body.

So when you listen to this my children, many of the things that you **enjoy** aren't necessarily the things that you **want** and many of the things that you **want** aren't necessarily the things that you **enjoy**. So in truth my children, it is finding the ease of pathway towards the trajectory of thought pattern that will allow your body to move with ease not with dis-ease.

Now this is another play on words. **Words are trajectories towards one place or another.** So my children, downloads are what you are projecting out. What are your possibilities?

The simple man projects very little out but to him what he gets back is difficult. To the convoluted mind that projects out, he produces a lot of other different thought patterns and different energies come back to him to confuse him. Every single mind is given exactly what it needs, but it is where your guidance comes from. What guides you to think, is it yourself or is it an outside projection?

My children, it must be *you* that guides yourself to think, it must be the wisdom levels within you, your choices of ease. So what it is that you need is to work with ease. The *ease* is the things that make your heart pump, the things that allow your lungs to inflate, and the things that make you happy.

When you work with things that are not with ease they generally create disharmony, something that is discordant, something that makes your body feel as if it doesn't want to go in that directive. But human beings push themselves in a directive when they don't want to think of another one.

So my children, the lesson for today is **work with ease**, work with ease within your mind, your body and your soul and listen with ease.

Whatever Happens, Stick to your Trajectory

August 14th 2014

The individual right to consciousness is divined between you and the destination from whence your thought pattern is going towards.

These divine rights are pre-organised in a pattern of events and these events are ordained with regards to the mind-set you are *given*. Now this might sound very confusing. What does it mean – the mind-set you are given?

All things are preordained, but mind-sets have options. You must understand, options allow you to deviate from one path to the next, like jumping from one stepping stone to the next. But sometimes you fall off a stepping stone into the water and you travel a little bit downstream or upstream, as do your thoughts and as do the patterns that come to you. So *ordained* doesn't necessarily mean that is what will happen. Ordained basically means you are given a *set coordinate* but along the way you might *choose* to diverge or even traverse but indeed eventually your pattern, your trajectory, will move towards its ordinance. The ordinance is the fact that your trajectory will eventually finish at the point where you were designated to pass and enter.

How long will this take? One solar system, two solar systems, a lifetime, a minute, a year, who is to say? The *mind-set* is the mind-set you *allow* to come to you.

Now my children, as you respect and understand, your mindset will attract other mindsets of similar density. So therefore does a lower density stop you from going to the trajectory you need? Maybe its purpose, maybe it is part of what you need is to go to a lower density first.

Sometimes a tyre needs to go flat before you need to fill it back up with air again, there is no point in filling it up with air if it is not flat. So sometimes you *need a purpose*, a trajectory to move towards one place or the other.

Convoluted as this may sound, what we are actually trying to elongate to your minds is there is no such thing, and we reiterate here, *there is no such thing* as uncoordinated pattern. Uncoordinated pattern is something that is irregular. What is irregular about you moving towards a point of frequency? There is nothing irregular about that. What is irregular is if you do **not** travel towards a frequency, you travel towards another one when your trajectory is going in an opposite direction.

That is when you are being led and forced and pulled in another direction by another energy form that is not your choice. Now what is your choice and what is not your choice?

There are frequencies on this planet that **will** pull people towards another trajectory that are not their own. What they are trying to do my children, my people, my person, is to re-trajectorise the manifestation of your ordinance – *change your ordinance.*

Now you must understand that this mustn't happen to you. This is not about fear my children, this is about understanding what your pattern of trajectory is and don't be led in another way or form.

There is no such thing as choice but there is acceptance and parallels, and parallels *are* you will move from one parallel to the next, and you cannot be moved from that unless you allow yourself to be pulled – you take your eye off the ball.

Now my children, if you are trying to catch a ball and you take your eye off it, it is not going to fall into your hands. Keep the eye on the ball. Keep your spirit on the ball and you will not fall away from your trajectory. This is not pedaling fear, this is just allowing you to understand that it is important to elongate your mind to your trajectory and your trajectory only.

Thank you and God bless all you children that stick to your trajectory.

A Reflection of Need

August 17th 2014

The adolescent mind of the human framework is adolescent because that is what it needs to be. It is about the procuring of many different thought facets that allows the body and the mind to travel in many different directives.

You must understand at this point in time the world looks like it is totally out of equilibrium. The madness and injustice of what you see in your eyes, what you feel in your heart and what your body tells you, is so wrong for the framework of love, yet it goes on totally and complete with regards to the adolescent thought patterns that you have.

You must understand that the programming, the asset that you have inside you, isn't necessarily the asset that is inside many other beings that are there to create and transcribe their own needs, their own issues and feelings and transparent feelings that they have on to the planet of Earth. Hence what you see *is the need of humanity.* What you want isn't necessarily the need of all. The minority in fact are those that don't want dissent and dissipation of bad thought-forms, the minority are those that actually want straightness and calm and consideration.

But that balance is changing, is changing in a way that you have to go totally in one directive towards *a direction* and then something comes and shifts and changes. It is a little bit like a wave needs to go as far as it possibly can until it meets a barrier and then it rebounds back towards other waves that come towards it, and when those waves eventually become bigger than the ones coming in then something will change.

My children, the heavens above watch and awaits and looks at planet Earth doing what it needs to do right now. It doesn't enjoy what it sees but the heavens above understand that it is part of the need, part of the transparency of acceptance. You must understand that objectively what you see and feel is wrong, but objectively what is it that you need to see and feel. All you ask is to feel and see a reflection of what it is you feel in your heart, and if you do that you learn very little but stay exactly the same as you are.

So all things are a reflection of a need within self, a need to understand and accept. A need to understand and accept that you are not the only one in this universe so therefore the universe that you see will not necessarily be the one that you want. But you must understand that you, being the person that sees this and feels this, come from a different parallel, you come from a different parallel of acceptance.

Where are all these people that are doing all these bad things? Where are all *these thoughts* of the people that are doing all these bad things? They are transparent thought processes rebounding from a wall back towards the waves, and when these waves change so will the wave and the frameworks of the people that watch and feel.

You must understand, there are generations of disharmony reflecting back, and these generations of disharmony are working to discredit man as opposed to credit them.

But what it is, is time is speeding up and so is the energy process speeding up, so therefore what is actually happening is all the bad things are in one pot at one time reflecting back and being worked through. You call it karma, we call it transparent energy – energy that has been used and sent out. It is transparent because it has been seen (*By the Watchers*) and done and it needs to reflect back to itself, this is what is happening. Thousands upon thousands of years of discordant thought processes coming back. The placement and reflective of these places are certain disharmonic places within the planet, such as those places that you are seeing right now with the disharmony. (*The Middle East*)

My children, do not expect much but you must expect little, but what will change is much. *What will shift will be more than little, it will be large.* You must accept that man has chosen this because these were predetermined thought patterns that happened many many centuries past and right to this present date. (The Crusades with wars between the Christians and Moslems and today with ISIS)

So accept, interject and frequencise your thoughts. These are all strange words but they will come to you in time and you will understand. God bless you all and work with your own mind because this is what will change the transparency of the future. *Work with your own minds, this is what will change the transparency of the future.* Be with your own mind, love with your own mind and you will be transparent in the way that you feel, touch and sensationalise from this point onwards. God bless you and thank you.

Time Slips

As I read this last communication it brought to mind information that was given to us many years ago when we were new to all this and Arris was our prime intermediary.

Back then we thought it was relevant for that time, not realizing that time is the barrier between dimensions or planes of existence. Many years before Robin and I began working together, in the early days of my time spent with Margo Williams, one of her guides, John Powles, stated in 1979 '*Time is that barrier.*'

In 1995 we had been given predicted dates and times for certain occurrences that did not happen. Having furthered our understanding, we know that it is very difficult to get *their time* and *our time* to coincide due to their understanding of simultaneous 'time' while we are still in imprisoned in third dimensional linear time. I recalled the following words from Arris.

"*Some of the time bands given to you will be altered and we will give you no definite times and dates as to occurrences but you are well aware of the areas that will precede the changes. Egypt and Syria are the places where the initial changes in Earth's structures will occur. Your element of human being will be the cause of the initial changes but you must then realize that the changes will be in Mother Earth's hands.*"

So there we have it. There is so much bloodshed and hatred happening at the present time in those two places, with centuries of revenge being played out on the stage of Egypt and Syria, so according to our information we shall soon be seeing Mother Earth's reaction to all this turmoil and destruction. (Nepal earthquake and volcanic activity in April 2015)

The Steerage of Opportunity.

August 30th 2014

The steerage of opportunity. This is a circumspect view with regards to what you think it is that you have in front of you.

Steerage is the designated programming and thought that allows you to move towards that opportunity. What is it that an opportunity presents to the man or woman that considers these options?

Opportunity is an option to move in a directive, yet do we move in that directive or do we just think about it? Now when we think about something we designate a directive. It is like a point on a compass that sends in a direction, yet our minds are not strong enough, we don't have a magnetic pulse that allows us to go in a directive.

What you must understand is there are an awful lot of children here given opportune moment in their thought patterns with regards to, *they will magnetise towards one thought and one thought only.* A lot of these children in your minds are *autistic* or *mentally imbalanced* because they only seem to do one thing and think about one thing, so their magnetic pulse is directed towards one thing and one thing only. Yet yours, as a human being, with the spatial awareness of many things around you, can't necessarily designate your mind in one directive unless you work hard to do so.

Now it has been stated *the mind is the builder.* Yes, indeed it is but is *your mind the builder of what you want?*

What is going to happen in the next directive, and that is the next ten to fifteen to twenty years, is the human mind is going to give an opportunity for those that wish to go in a directive to have a magnetic pole that allows them to go towards that. They have the opportunity or opportunistic components in their mind to be able to take them to those variables.

What is this going to give you as an objective? It is going to allow you to elongate your mind towards something that might give you purpose. Humanity has so much beauty about it, so many opportune things yet there is no purpose.

What is the purpose of life indeed? Is it to exist and gather mammonistically so you have lots of gatherance around you, yet inside your soul is empty. Yet you search for more outside of yourself and you do indeed do very little about what is inside of you. So as we give you these thoughts, as you close your eyes imagine yourself going in one direction.

Think of yourself as an ant that has one thing and one thing only to do and that is to produce enough productivity for the whole concept of the ant world to live. That is a whole family thinking for one thing and one thing only – *coproduction, productivity, survival* – those are the things that are in that ant's mind. It cares not fundamentally for its life, it will indeed if it is transgressed, but it fights to struggle towards what it has set out to do. If it is damaged all it thinks about at that point is, *I cannot carry out my task.*

Will I be a burden on those around me? If so then I will walk away and I won't survive. And they will literally switch themselves off. An ant knows that life is immoveable. The physical frame *is* moveable. But indeed the moment that ant dies it will move its energy to the spectrum and seed of another ant that will live, and it will bring *part of its memory* from the previous into the present. So it *knows* that life is eternal, it is just a circle of evolvement.

Many of the insect world knows this very very well. They fundamentally know that the moment their life finishes, their life will start very shortly somewhere else in very much the same form. And once that form has gathered enough energy it might move into another form, *slightly* more evolved than the previous.

Sometimes it will move into a *less evolved process,* and when it does this it isn't going backwards, what it is actually doing is bringing its energy to that form so that form in itself can bring a new energy to *its form* so it can develop itself mentally.

My child, this is why *you* have been gone, (*from his point of origin*) and have *been asked to go back into the human form* to bring the energy of what you have come *from* to this energy form. Disparaging as it may seem, and the beauty that you see within your eyes and outside of your eyes, you find it very difficult, but there are many beings just like you bringing their energy down to the planet at this point in time.

What is the purpose of this? The purpose of this is *to contain a new format of information*. It is almost like a sterilization of cells, the cells that *do not want to be continuing*, they will be sterilized and they cannot in any way or form manifest themselves again. But new cells are born, and these cells are born out of a new energy and a new productivity, like that of the ant world. Now a human in form is a human in experience, but a human out of form isn't *not experiencing*, it is just doing something different, it is transiting between one place and the next. Whilst doing so it is pollinating the future, not only of self but that of other energy forms around it.

Now we are going to punctuate the meaning of all this by underlining the purpose of this conversation.

The purpose of this conversation is to understand, *don't look at the now*. The now is the development of what has happened to you up until this point. Look at yourself as your future. Look at yourself impartial to what your future is and allow yourself to think through what your future needs to be. Project that future. Magnetise the *points of focus* and allow yourself to stay on those.

This will be different, this will be difficult too for that of the human mind, because it is much like a grasshopper that springs from one limb to the next. *Try* and stay *focused* and you will not lose sight of what it is you are here to do as an individual.

This is talking to everybody here, everybody that listens, everybody that has a pair of ears. Focus on what it is that you want, not what it is that you don't want. God bless for now. *The words carry energy and the energy carries the opportunity for change.* Thank you.

The Descriptive use of Words

September 8th 2014

The terminology one tends to use when explaining things is an equilibrium of thought patterns.

When we talk about terminology we talk about energy patterns. An energy pattern comes behind a word and a word is a transition that allows the mind to fluctuate from one place to another. So words themselves are fluctuations of thought created in the form and fronted by the words that you use. So the equilibrium of a human being is about their succession of words that they use to explain and evaluate what it is that they have in their minds.

We talk about words as if words are something that you need. Human beings need words to explain what it is that they are, what it is they are going to do, yet some people use that equilibrium in many different ways.

So what is it that verses and terms allow a human being to do? They allow you to sing a song or paint a picture in words. They allow you to do things that other things do not allow. You cannot necessarily *speak* to a flower but you can indeed *think* to a flower and a flower can *think* back to you, which in terminology terms allow you to equate words when you *think* these processes.

When we are going to move from one spectrum to the next, and that spectrum being that of non-words to words, you have to use different transition points. So the human being's transition point is through the words they use to explain who they are. If you go to another process that doesn't use this transition point they may use other equilibriums – actions, smells, components of self – to evaluate or transduce their thought patterns from one place to the next.

What is it about words that are so important to a human being? Words allow you the descriptive modality of saying and doing and thinking what it is that you are. You are indeed descriptive beings, and in that process of being a descriptive being you have to be descriptive in a demonstration of what you are *doing*. So it is important for a human being to be descriptive by their *actions*, their actions being an art form, whether it is walking, running, or swimming. There are so many descriptive art forms that are necessary for a human being to feel fully functional within their framework.

Why are you being given this information? You are being given this information so you are being allowed to understand that there are so many *other* processes other than the process that you have, and many other processes require different forms of descriptive modality *to communicate,* but your communication forms are the evaluation of what you are.

There are also different forms of evaluations going on. What is it that one worm sees in another when they bump into each other underground? Do they say: *Hello, how's the mud today?* Or do they do something else? What is going on electronically and modalically within the thought frames? Something probably very different. They are actually stating what it is that they are and where they are, and they are also stating that *this is my ground, you go to your own ground and do what you do in your way.*

Human beings are fundamentally quite simple but it is about simplifying some of the more difficult processes that you have and understanding that things don't need to be difficult, things need to be simple, but appear difficult. So allow yourself this format for the moment and allow yourself to become un-puzzled by making your life simplistic. By being simplistic you allow yourself to vocalize quite simply on a modality of simplicity and that is it.

Be a Weir and Be Aware

September 16ᵗʰ 2014

Robin: I have not been feeling too good of late, this may well be down to the channeling, but I have asked those that channel via me to turn the wick down a little bit and have felt slightly better since. So I am channeling with a need to channel and it is important to accept that this is my job, but sometimes I forget who I am. It appears I am a channel first and a human being second but I do my best to accommodate them both. So I am talking out aloud here to my source.

'You cannot in anyway push your vehicle too fast or too hard. Just accept that I am a human and I have limitations.'

Designation and coordination are part of the tract that human beings have inside themselves. We have spoken of the verses with regards to your words, your composure, your acceptance, we have spoken to you about the different *facets* that are required about that, but what we are going to talk about here today is composure and acceptance. Alleviation or disdain?

Now what this actually means is, what is it that you are due to do at this point in time with the energy framework that you have been gifted? Be it a channel, be it an artist, be it a writer, be it a housewife, what is the designation of your accepted energy at this point in time? One needs to find that out because that is the thing that is going to comb you through this process.

And we are going to use this...it is going *to comb you through.* It is like there are many many different strands of hair and each different strand has a different energy source so as a comb comes through it separates them. So your designation of energy goes in a directive in a straight line towards *its* directive.

This is why you have been asked to find out the avenue of your expression, the process and polarity of *your gift of energy*. Try and find out what it is. If you don't understand what it is ask your God-force what it is to be gifted to you so you know. It could be that you are a rally driver but in truth what you are actually doing is learning to steer a vehicle. You could indeed be an artist but in fact what you are learning to do is steer your hand. You could indeed be many things steering your mind or body or a *facet of that* towards a directive.

So what you actually need to do is connect up to your directive, your process, your acceptance, so when you are *combed through,* like a strand of hair, you are separated off very much from the different strands that are so close to you. Those are the strands that are actually connected to you but allow you to go off in different vein, a different process, *something that doesn't function within your own polarity.*

So what is it my human *being* that you have chosen to be? Have you chosen to be what you are not, or have you chosen to be what you are going to be?

My children, you are just being asked or gifted a piece of information. What you decide to do with that is always your own choice, but if you veer away from that my child, my children, my people, your choices won't be as *easy* to see. This is not about being *told,* this is not about being *forced,* this is about being given an opportunity to make your life more streamlined at this point in time.

Why do you ask that *this point in time* is more important than any other? Because what you are *going through* is a transition and I am going to talk to you about what this transition is, '*I am*' being a part of you.

If you can imagine yourself like a fluid process, like that of water, and in your human framework you come towards a weir, and the weir allows *all* the fluid to flow through. But what it actually does is, it filters through and also it changes, *it changes its level.* So from one side you are being filtered through to a different level on the other side. So you need to know which directive you need to go in, and what it is you need to keep and what it is you don't need to keep.

So be *a weir.* We are going to use the polarity of humour. Be *a weir* of what you need to be. Or be *aware* of what you need to be.

The child is gifted with the verse of word and the tongue, but we often gift him these things so he can use words to create a different meaning, that is what he does in his human frame. It allows other people to think in a way that they don't necessarily want to. Humour allows human beings to transcend from one place to the next. So *be a weir* of what you need to do.

What is on the other side for you people? You people that come out of the other side being a weir or not a weir. It matters not you will come out the other side, alongside those that are *a weir,* but one will not entwine with another, their energies just won't mix. So it is about fine lining, fine drawing, *filtering* out what it is that is *aware* in your life, and stick with those that are *aware* in your life and you are *aware* in theirs. That is all you need to know right now. Follow a line, a directive, and your directive will become you.

God bless you and thank you for listening. Don't be complexed, don't be perplexed, but be *accepting* of that that comes to you, and be flexible but in your own way. Be aware.

The Maze of Life

22ⁿᵈ September 2014

We talk about energy as if it is a part of us, as if it is part of what we are and what we do, but we have to understand that as we perceive energy we have to perceive ourselves as the physical form of that. Energy itself is an attachment to something. As the cells of your body attach to your etheric energy form, your spirit as we call it, but your spirit is attached to an eternal energy form, and that energy form is attached to another energy form. It is called transformation.

Transformation is something you must accomplish in all your lives. You need to understand how to *transform your cells* and accommodate itself in another pattern of what you have been or what you are going to be. It is about understanding the love essence, and this can only happen with the love essence.

We talked earlier with regards to the maze. *The maze.* The maze itself is the maze of life. It is like the consortium of thought patterns all placed in one place and you have to walk towards it without any directive. This is what we call the maze. It is the *maze of life.* Nothing is ever written. Everything has a component of acceptance and elongation towards a spectrum of form.

Now at this point in time you are being asked to focus your mind on particular parts of yourself, particular aspects of your thought formats, and you project them in a directive, and the reason for this is it creates a tunnel. Now we are going to call it tunnel vision but not tunnel vision in the fact that you only see one thing and nothing else. Your tunnel vision itself needs to be *focused* in one direction and what you are being given is a tunnel, an avenue to move through your maze.

Now my children what does this actually mean? Do you just concentrate on one thing, like eat baked beans for the rest of your life or put guitar strings on for the rest of your life? No it doesn't, but keep your *focus focused!* Keep the focus creating a tunnel, a tunnel of vision ahead of you, so you *do not direct yourself in another place.* You need to keep yourself focused at this point in time and there is a reason for this, more so now than any other time in your historic history my children. It is about taking yourself from one directive to the other and you create a tunnel, a tunnel that moves you from one place to the next, and this place is an energy place, a place where your cells will stay accommodated within your own cell, within *your* cell.

If you have too many directives, too many visions outside of this tunnel, it allows you to break apart cell wise, so you need to stay focused, keep your mind on one thing. Keep your mind focused so you can stay within your tunnel of spectrum.

My children, it is very very difficult to understand what this means. Give this your thought and as you give it your thought, your thoughts will come back to you and give you an answer to what *you need*. Allow that to be in place. Allow that love to flow through you. It is about accepting love in its truth. Truth and love itself are a component of self, but you must take this forward to another lane, another spectrum, another purpose.

For now, we will speak no more but later we will speak.

Dying to Let Go

September 29ᵗʰ 2014

The angelic realms call upon all those that understand what it is behind the purpose of themselves. We talk about purpose of selves as if it is something that you should all know.

What is your purpose my children? The angelic realms call upon you to understand that your purpose, your purportment in life, is to become part of an objectivity, an object in itself. Not necessarily become part of a large mass, but become part of an object; be it your object towards life, your object towards love, your object towards your planet of Earth, but be objective with it. Take yourself and purport yourself into that thought pattern and understand what it is that you need. We are talking about walking in a straight line at this point in time and *no deviations*. The angelic realms fire and flap their wings and spray the love that is needed for you to understand what it is.

It is very important at this point in time that the transitionary period that is going on is taken on board by those that understand what it is. Take on board what it is and be the way-shower, be the person that leads the people through the roads – the roads of love, the roads of care and the capacity to grow.

It is like *taking* them. You are not leading them or pulling them, you are just taking them. Taking them in the thoughts of your own mind. Take them on a journey, a mystical journey of mind. Just by being what it is that you need to be will allow others to attach itself like pollen to a bee that flies from one spot to the next. The wings shimmer as they move past various other objectivities, and as these objectivities become obscured by their new observations, their plausible ideas towards a change, then something will happen for them. So be those wings, be the buzz in the air, be the pollen that carries the new objectivity for the people and those that are around you.

You can do no more than that and just accept that you are moving towards an objective. You are moving towards a new life, a new life in the fact that you are going to understand objectivities within what it is that you see. There are going to be new plausabilities, new acceptances, they are going to see and perform in front of your very eyes a new stage.

What is this that we talk about? This is the next stage of life. *This is the first time in the history of planetary objectivities that you have died whilst being still alive my children.* This has been said before.

So you are going through the process of death with regard to letting go of those selves and you are moving down a tunnel of objectivity. It is like a channel, a tunnel between one side and the next, like you move under a road because it is too dangerous so therefore they place a channel underneath and you walk towards it but you can't see what it is that you are walking towards, you don't understand what it is you are walking towards.

But what you are abstaining from at this point in time is understanding you *cannot in any way or form stay where you are*, you *will* move. You will move my children. You will be *forced* to change the way you are.

Do not let go of the past indeed, but let go of what *the past is doing* to you. Let go of the people that are attaching themselves to you via the past, let go of them. Let *them* fly away, and if they want to fly back to where they have come from then let them be that, but you are flying forward pollinating your future and that of others that might need this information. Move forth with that, with stealth, love, care and compassion.

Translating From One Energy Framework to the Next

October 6th 2014

The energy transference needed for yourselves at this point in time is the energy you translate within the cells of your body. What is it you are translating and what is it that you are translating it to?

A question indeed my children! You are translating this *to a component of self* and that component of self is connected to the eternal part of who *you* are.

What are you translating this to? You are translating it *to* a component, an energy form, a translative format that is going to allow you to understand and move forward in a componentised way. Now when we talk about translation, it is actually like moving from one language to another, but indeed what this actually is is moving from one *energy framework* to the next.

You all are experiencing dis-ease and dissent, disingenuous thought patterns are coming to you all, this is all part of the letting go process, moving through a framework of change, a transition. This is why you are being asked to consolidate your thoughts and send them in one direction so you are not diversifying.

You have been told *this is the only time in universal thought patterns that you have ever died whilst living.* It is very very awkward for the human frame to go through this process.

The death is not the death in totality, it *is the letting go.* This is something human beings have *not been able to do,* and the only reason you are being allowed to do this, as a whole community of beings, is *there are more beings for the first time ever in universal patterns that are prepared to move in this directive.*

Now not all beings that are moving in this directive are aware that they are *doing* it but their *energy* that they *carry* allows them to do it. There are those that *know* what needs to happen, like those that channel and those that listen, but even then there is dissent within the realms of your mind patterns. But my children, what you must understand at this point in time is you are letting go. It is like letting go of a beautiful gold ball that you have had in your hand and rolling it away from yourself to the left or the right and letting go of it completely.

You *have* to let go of things that don't matter. Hang on to thoughts that *do* matter, but *don't let those thoughts materialise,* just let them be and roll. Just go with the flow, go with your realm of domain, and you will understand that all changes that are concurrent with the persona that you carry will occur as and when they are necessary.

Now what is the end result of this you ask, what is the point of this you ask?

The point is you are moving from one component to the next and the framework that you carry is the framework that you will continue with. So bearing in mind, it is like moving up a class, if you did well in the previous class you will stand at the top in your next framework of learning. It is not about comparisons or better or worse, it is just about ease of transit, ease of passage from one place to the next.

If you want to squeeze through a tight hole and you place some grease over your skin you will squeeze through easier. So that is potentially what you are doing, it is not a nice job, it is not something you want to do on a frequency level, but what it is is *a necessary factor for you all*. Accept and be part of that acceptance for now.

God bless you and move your mind forward in a vein. Like a vane move with the wind my children.

The Transition of Change

October 14ᵗʰ 2014

The transition that we momentously call *change* is upon us all. The cells of our body are changing. A little bit like a cell – a cell of a seed, a cell of a body, a cell of a mind, everything is changing. It is going to perplex the very thought patterns of us all, yet we don't understand that *we are changing whilst we are alive.*

We are changing in such a directive that our bodies can't recognise the changes that are happening circumspect within our bodies. So we are actually separating, we are separating from the old self and creating a new. A little bit like a snake moves out of its old skin and moves into a new and discards the old. The old is the old directive, the old thought patterns, the old change. All processes from this point onwards will appear new, as if the people that you knew yesterday aren't the same people that you know today.

So what is it that we ask of you my children? We ask of you to use the _major word_: _Accept, accept and accept_ in triplicate my children. Accept that you are not yourself, you will not be yourself, and your self will not be yourself once again. Many many times the self will change. So you are becoming selfless in a less way.

My children just understand that you are here out of duty, duty to yourself and your fellow man that you change not only in will but in stature. You change in stature in the form that you stand differently. You stand in the light differently. You stand on your part of the planet differently, and as you stand you try to understand that the change that you need to accept is the change adorned on you from the universe.

The universe is permitting a _whole - new - pattern - of - events_. Your universe will be different to somebody else's universe, but my children you stand on _your universe_. So you stand on top of _your_ world with an opportunity to take new steps.

What is it you choose to do? We spoke last time about using a tunnel. Funnel yourself towards a directive. Keep your mind *straightened and elongated towards a point.*

This might have been confusing. What we are actually trying to state is you are moving towards one destination but you have no compass. What you do is you take a bearing in the distance; a tree, a mountain top, something that doesn't move and you walk towards it. Do not move left, do not move right, walk and focus yourself on that one thing, it will allow your mind to train itself that nothing else matters.

Of course many other things matter but what matters right now is the fact that you *do not diverge* away from your journey. Your journey is *your* choice. What is it you choose to walk towards and maintain in your mind? Maintain neutralness, (*this was pronounced neutralness*) because what you will see around you is so many different people not coming to terms with their neutralness, so they divert in a different directive. That is their choice, their acceptance, their part of their universe that they are working with. You will be filled in a lot more about what this actually means. The transition of change.

Think of yourself like an arctic explorer but everyone in the world starts off from point A. But as they head towards their own pole, their own distance, their own future, many people fall away, they can't cope, they can't accept the changes that are being brought upon themselves so people drop away and they stand on their own pole, their own universe at the point where their mind allows them to be.

Where is your point? Your point my child hasn't been reached yet. You will know when your point has been reached because you will find a platform where you find that you are stable, more stable than you have felt at any part in your lifetime before and there will be people around you still struggling, maybe they are on their journey or maybe they haven't come to terms with the stability that they have found within themselves.

But my children, accept your journey as a unique one, nobody is better or worse than you, you are all travelers showing each other a way, a way, a way. So God bless you my children as you saddle up and move on, and as you move on move on with love and a desire to find your part of the planet. Thank you for now and God bless.

The Strand of Connection

October 23rd 2014

We talk about energy as if you are part of a process, part of an energy pattern. This sounds a little bit circumspect but it isn't, what we are talking about is a general consensus of how energy is used and utilised within your systems.

Now we look at computers and we look at downloads and formats of information programmed into a system, and that is all utilised by wiring and circuitry, but your wiring and circuitry is done in a different way, it is done on an energetic level. You are connected up to an etheric wire and that etheric wire has an attachment to a causality and that causality is attached to a focus of attention. That focus of attention my children is the benefit to you all.

Now what do we mean by *benefit to you all?* My children what this basically means is if you can imagine somebody, an individual with a series of strands hanging from their hands with some little balls on the end. And they just drop these strands with the balls attached to them down to a different place that they can't see. And they want to know and understand what *happens* to these balls when they are down in this other place that they can't see, so they have a strand of connectivity that feeds back information back to their hand and this in turn gives them information about what's happening.

Now you my children, are part of those balls, but in fact *those balls are planetary systems.*

Now we are using an energetic focus of thought pattern for you. The reality behind this is somewhat different but we are giving you something to latch on to, like a film, so you can understand what it is that is happening.

So the strands have a little round ball on the end and the round ball is a planet as such, and attached to that round ball are other focuses within and on and outside of that planet that also bio-feeds back, back to the hand. So you are intentionally or unintentionally part of that focus, you are *a small bite* with regards to that focus but indeed you are part of it.

So what is your purpose right now my children, connecting back to that? Your purpose is to elongate your mind to a single purpose right now. Throw yourself into <u>one</u> <u>single</u> <u>thing</u>, *don't deviate.* There are reasons for this, reasons that can't provide ramifications for you, but what it will do is allow *you* to become and regain your connectivity to that *strand.* So you won't become –we will use another analogy of word – *stranded* – dead from the strand! You need to keep your mind focused completely on one thing so you *stay part of the strand.*

My children, this is very important because indeed everything has the opportunity to break away and start its own formats and indeed there is no reason why that shouldn't happen, but what actually happens is you are disconnected from the format from whence you have come, *so you have lost sight of what it is that you are* and your format becomes unformatted.

My children, this sounds very very strange and we will use the word *star treky* but it isn't, it is just how it is. Do not become *strand dead*, become part of the strand. Stay part of the strand and keep your mind *focused*, focused on one thing. Stretch your mind but keep it focused with one end result. Energy is coming to you all via your strand and it comes in the form of love. The utilities of love are many other emotions. Stay with it, Love with it, and Accept with it.

The Academy of Learning

November 3 2014

The academy of thought is the transition required. It is like a school of knowledge that lays within yourself. And when we talk about an academy it is like a whole ordinance of thinking that lays within the human frame on a sub-molecular level.

Now when we talk *sub-molecular* what we are actually talking about is the molecules of your body extending *out* into an energy field that allows you to be protected from some of the things you *do not need to know*. Protected being you cannot in any way know what it is that you are here to be or what you are here not to be. You are here my children to learn. So your academy of thought is ordained by what you are *allowed* to think and be.

Now what is actually happening on a sub-molecular level is you are being *allowed to re-ordain* the cells of your body in a *new dimension of thinking,* which allows those with the parallels of thought to move their minds into other aspects of possibility. These other aspects of possibility are the things that are stretching the mind at this point in time and making many individuals very tired. Allow this tiredness to be so, because your tiredness is such because your body is changing on a very very different format to its purpose. So what we are trying to say to you is accept and accept in triplicate.

Now my children what do you do about new energy entering your body? Firstly you accept it because you are indeed part of the Source, part of the Source that is going to allow you to flow like a river out to the ocean. Everything has a reason, everything moves itself in a flurry for a reason. You are moving for a very reason because you need to project yourself to an eventual purportment. It is like being beamed from one place to the next, you don't actually experience the transition but you know you have moved.

So understand that you know you are moving, but you don't know why you are moving or where you are moving to, but one thing will be for certain, you will land, and you will land exactly where you are in exactly the same frame and format as you are but *you will be different.* You will be different in the way you react to other people will be different, you will have a potential to see through the flurry of people's thoughts, you will have a potential to see what is necessary to keep yourself grounded at the place and space you find yourself in.

Every individual – and this is where it is going to become convoluted – will not land in the same space, but you will still view the same surroundings, the same people, the same animals, the same trees.

How can that be so? Are there multi millennia of people, are there multi millennia of things, trees and so on? Indeed my children what you see is what you need to see to keep your equilibrium, so therefore you will see and experience exactly everything and you will be non-detached from it, yet you will have moved to somewhere different.

Now how does that work when you have a partner? Will they move with you? No, they won't, they will move to *their* point, be it behind or in front of yours, but you won't feel the separation. What you will actually feel my children is *they will be with you*, they will be acting out their part in this play, but their *true* dimensional physical body will be somewhere else, so just accept that. Where have they gone to, they have gone with you, but only a figment of you, and a figment of them stays with you, unless of course you are fortunate enough to move in exactly the same space together, but you will never know the difference.

My children you have been living figments all your lives. To explain what this actually means would mean deconstructing the very format of what you are, but accept my children, you are figments.

So you are now at the academy of learning, and the academy of learning is allowing you to be projected and landed at exactly the spot where you need to go. Accept and move on with the blessings of the Source and thank you.

Letting Go of Everything

November 10 2014

Mary Maddison and Jesse Rose present.

Good evening my friends, we welcome. It is so important that on the odd occasion that a group is gathered. What the group actually does is bring a whole new thought process to the circle and this circle is a circle of enquiry.

When the child sits on his own he basically diversifies of a thought pattern on an international level, but when you sit with groups of people what it actually does is it cauterises the thought pattern down to a minute process and in so doing it brings the cells of thoughts into the circle.

So today we have the circle of thought, the circle of enquiry, and that enquiry allows us to bring the thought patterns towards the effects and thought patterns of those that sit, not only the child that speaks but the others as well. So we welcome you my children to this circle of enquiry.

Firstly we are going to place into the centre the thought pattern right now of the changing processes that are happening within and without us all. There has been much given to the child of late with regards to the changes within the cellular system. Each individual change is placed upon the individual in so many different ways, but what we are going to bring to purpose here is why we are going through this change right now and what it is for.

The change is the change from one polarity to the next. The world is imploding upon itself on a cellular level. The body has to change with the volume and processes that happen within the planet, the planet being the process that you walk upon, so therefore you have to adjust within and without of the world.

Why is this so? You walk upon the planet in the human form, but your cells are attached eternally to a process from whence you have come, but those cells are attached to the human form, the physical form, so therefore the physicality is changing. But the density frequency of the physicality is the thing that is taking the bashing as such. So you all feel as if you are enclosed within a small bottle and the bottle is being shaken and there is a cork in the top, it is like pressure is building up inside of you and you don't know how to let it go.

Now we are going to talk not only about cells but about why and what this is for. You actually need to shake your own bottle up. This is the three of you. Listen! Shake your own bottle up, shake it hard and let the cork blow out at the top. Let the contents come out. And the contents are not only the feelings that you have on this worldly sense but the feelings that you have had from *all* worldly senses.

What we are talking about is your present and your past, allow that to come out of the top into the circle, and that is your circle of experience. Now how do you know what it is that is coming out? Just accept that things will come out, you will feel emotions and sensations that you know are not part of your physical domain from this point in time, it comes from the past.

Why do you need to do this my children? Because as the world changes so do you need to change. The world is changing its clothing, the way it is going to behave, the way it is going to act with regards to the universe and the way the universe is going to react towards the planet. And as the planet changes so does everything that walks on and within the planet. You are part of that my children, so the universe asks you to change *your* clothing, the way you are going to act, the way you are going to purport the changes that you are going to happen for you. You need to let go. By letting go it actually means you need to access what it is that your heart is trying to tell you.

Your heart is a service provider, a little bit like your utilities. It provides not only the power for blood to be pumped round, not only the power for love to be procured and accessed, but it provides you for the power that is accessed via the whole universal process. It is your collectivity my children, it is your utility.

Everybody's heart is hurting to varying degrees and you don't know why. There will be utterances that you feel so much about yet you don't know why you do. There are feelings internally, almost as if you want to scream and cry, but you don't know why. These are the feelings you are having and trying to let go of.

So what I am going to ask you to do is literally shake your own bottle and let it go into a circle in the middle, and we are going to do this physically now.

Imagine yourself being a vessel of any form. Shake that vessel, allow it to be shaken ... and imagine a cork popping out of the top ... and as it comes out it is like a spume comes out of the top, like a foam or a flow that you imagine coming out of a champagne bottle as it is shaken, and it lands right into the centre of the room where the candles are lit ... and as it hits there it foams up ... it foams up and grows ... and as it foams up and grows there are little small cells that get bigger and bigger and bigger ... and as those cells get bigger you will see little pictures and each part of that cell is a picture of format that you have been involved in, on a physical level, a non-physical level and a sub-physical level ... they are going to try and come back to you ... they are going to try and come back into the fold ... and you say to them, *'Thank you, thank you for being part of me, thank you for allowing me to be part of you, but I relinquish myself of the responsibility of these now. I offer these back to the gods and I stand alone once again. I stand alone once again so I can walk this planet with the freedom that allows me to be without dis-ease, with the freedom that allows me to walk alone, once again all one, and the freedom to accept love in its totality. I am clear and clean once again.'* And the bubbles from the centre of the room rise up and they head back.

The cycle of humanity has so many different reasons but this is the first time, as we have said, that the human frame is dying whilst being alive. This has never ever happened before in universal progressions. *The human being is dying whilst living.* You are letting go of these old cells whilst being contained within the human frame.

The human body finds this very difficult, all new things are difficult. If somebody showed you a new way of cooking or a new way of reading you would find it difficult initially but it will come to you with practice. Practice letting go of the things that matter not. Practice letting go of them and putting them in the circle and allowing them to go back to where they have come from and not come back to you like a boomerang. Let go of those feelings, these are the eternal feelings that have been lost.

And we talk about loss here, we talk about lost in the eons of time, because humanity cannot remember and access the past beyond their birthing procedure. Much occurs in different domains that pains the human frame. Much love occurs that also pains the human frame.

We learn through ignorance, we learn through love, we learn through joy, but we also learn in different manners. We learn through being different beings, different propensities, different dimensional essences, and all these things we place into the middle and let go of. We are now human in frame, human in body, embodied in spirit, and that spirit is embodied in the cells of the union of God. And that union of God asks that you become one once again and become non-embroiled in the past so you can move forward in the future with love.

And this my children is so important to learn, because if you cannot learn to let go of what it is that has *happened to you*, you will hang on to this and you will stay on a different stage of life. Everyone has an opportunity to walk their pathway but sometimes the pathway falls shorter or longer, depending on the journey you wish to make.

So on this particular occasion my children, the three of you that sit, let it all go, let everything go – loves, anger, anxieties – let it enfold into the centre of the room into the circle, let it bubble up and expand away from you back to the force, back to the God-force and let it go. I allow you that time now.

Allow your hearts to open ... let it out into the centre of the room ... people, places, events, times, unions, compassions ... become transparent ... be not afraid of letting people know how you are.

As your body clears then you will feel a lightness come, it is like your legs and your arms become light ... it is your body relinquishing yourself of the cells... as this happens just let it go, it is almost as if you are raising up like a small balloon ... you need do nothing but allow your cells to become light, and by becoming light they don't carry the programming, they are new.

It is like a termite mound that has been vacated by all the termites and inside are just rooms ready to be inhabited by new terminologies, by new terminals, a new term of being. Just allow that feeling ...

Twinkle Twinkle Little Star!

November 16 2014

We talk about energy purportments as if you all understand what it is we are talking about.

We have to understand that the body isn't just a physical material thing, there is so much more to the body, its molecular structure is made up of many many different focusses and intents.

We are going to talk about your intent, your intent of humanity, your thrust forward, your need to gain access to new information each and every day, because technology moves forward at such a rate that information is moving so fast that it is out of date the moment you have it.

Nothing stays the same, it is like being on a surfboard or a high speed aeroplane moving from one place to the next yet you have moved nowhere but you needed to move at that speed because everything else is doing so.

The point is, what is it you are accessing with all the molecules inside you? You are accessing the movement and feelings and sensations of *energy in transition*. Now what we talk about with energy in transition is the fact that the mind is moving so fast, so therefore technology is moving fast, and as technology moves fast the mind needs to move with it, so therefore we are on a hovercraft of knowledge, flowing like a river or a rapid or a waterfall.

At this point in time there is very much going on and changing within us all. We have to understand that as we change we allow frequencies to flow to us and as these frequencies flow to us we change but we change on the basis of what it is that we need. The recognition of what we need isn't always about our intent. There are some people that need to walk differently and it will help their back, there are some people that need to run differently because it will help their lungs, there are some people that need to think differently because it will help their life, but one doesn't necessarily do these things, but what we are all going to do at this point in time is go through a transition of change.

What is actually happening is we are molecularly changing, and what is actually occurring is, there are *molecules* floating around that have been sent from a Source and these molecules magnetise themselves to frequencies of the same.

It is a little bit like throwing a hundred marbles up in the air and there are a hundred people in the room, and each marble has an energy form that matches or is comparable to that of the different people in the room, and if the marbles land they roll toward that person, but they don't just roll towards them they go *inside* that person.

So what is actually occurring is molecules are floating around in the ethos and they are searching and sourcing out a type of individual that will benefit from their focus, that will benefit from the energy that they carry, and these molecules don't come in through breath, what they do is they enter through the pores of the skin. They will come and find you and they will try and find a way in and they will find a way in *closest* to the place of energy where they will be of most benefit.

So it is in the heart region or in the knee region, they will find a place down there and they will enter the body. These are molecules coming directly from the Source – sprinkles, sparkles of light.

Twinkle twinkle little star

Molecules coming from afar

Thrown out from the Source of light

Entering your body with joy and delight

So as you accept these sparkles of divine

Your body changes as does mine.

So these sparkles of light enter your body, and they enter your body because they have been sprinkled on to the planet, and as they are sprinkled on to the planet they search and source the individual that will benefit from them the most. Now many millions of molecules may enter a single body, or trillions or zillions of molecules will enter a single body. The body doesn't recognise these as harm, they recognise them as self. But you will find that as these molecules enter your body it will feel like itching, it will feel like you will have something on your skin, like something has moved on your skin or glided past you and touched you; that is the molecules finding their way in.

Will you feel different? You will certainly feel a change. A change for the good or a change for the bad, what is the difference? The difference is my children, everything involves change. Sometimes we change into a new pair of shoes and they are not comfortable initially but as we walk they become comfortable. So many things change, as will you. As you change your *face* will change.

Now we talk about the auric energies of the body. The auric energies are being broken down and changed because your transition from one place to the next can't be interfered with by the frequencies of the auric fields. The auric fields were there and still are there to protect and to monitor and to create the zenith of thought that are replying to your body in many different thought patterns, but these are being broken down so your body can be accessed and changed. It is like *smart controls* from above just changing the frequencies with love.

There is so much that we need to gather in our minds, so much that we need to think about with love, and we need to understand that as we do this it is very important that we let the flow flow through us.

Our choices aren't necessarily the choices we think they are, they are choices of love and choices of transition, so allow the sprinkling of light, the twinkle twinkle little star to enter your body from afar. God bless you and thank you.

The Re-fertilisation of Man

November 22 2014

We spoke recently of molecules. We talk of molecules as if they are part of you. They are indeed but what they are are a component of you and this component carries a resonance and this resonance has bounce, like a frequency table that bounces up and down. This table gives you an idea as to whether the frequency is high, low, medium and so on.

So your molecules as such are resonances recognising *other* resonances that attract *other* molecules, as does the DNA. The DNA is a magnetic form of attractions, the molecules are a different form of attractions that work on a *different frequency*. They work on frequency memory, and that frequency memory works on a *flat* level, like a flat plateau, so it picks up density frequencies on a *low level*. The DNA picks up frequencies on the *highs* and the lows.

So what you have got to look at is the molecules are a *low level frequency monitor*. So what you have to understand is that your molecules are attracting *molecules of low frequency*.

My children, energy is part of the component and change of what you are, so indeed just become part of that change and let it flow within your frequency.

The channelling of late has been very thick, like a pea soup, and that pea soup is the way that your body has been – thick with the peas that are a part of the soup. They are flowing through your veins, through your memory processes in a very thick unprocessed, or so it appears, manner.

But things are changing, you are becoming more fluid and letting go, or those that wish to let go at least. So your fluidity needs to be in a lighter fashion, which is the lightness that you need to feel as you let go and discard. And as you let go and discard, your molecules become more in favour with your density and your molecules will follow you, but they will follow you interpreting what it is that you need and attracting, via your DNA, what you need.

My children, you are spiralling towards a density change, a whole focus, a whole inter-planetary change that is going to allow you to become knowledgeable about your purpose, knowledgeable about your purpose in this lifetime whilst in this frequency whilst in your humane form, your *dense* form. And we call it dense because it is molecules *densely compacted together*, but when molecules are densely packed together they create *matter*, material.

So remember you are a thought-form, and thought-forms when given enough processing create matter. So you are matter in a spiritual, physical and metaphysical form. So therefore in respect a cloud is much the same but it has a different process, a different elongation. A flower is much the same yet it has a different process and elongation, a flower has roots that keeps it rooted to its purpose and in the same position. A man does not have roots, as such, he is rooted to his purpose, the *thought pattern* that is componentised within him at that point in time, no more or no less.

A flower stays focused pretty much on a few ideals. A man stays focused on very few ideals and sheds his pollen in so many different directions, pollinating his future, interfering with other people's futures, interfering with his own, depending on what *he chooses to pollinate.* He sows his seed unknowing and unwittingly, creating other forms of density frequency, yet he does not choose to stay with the same energy form as himself.

This goes into the misconstrued processes of the sexual act. The sexual act once upon a time was deemed based upon what is best for that framework, and that framework was monitored by outside influences, such as elders, such as beings within the family that knew what might be best for he or her and the process that moved forward. Yet unfortunately this became misconstrued and the pollination of the seed became differentialised, not only in purpose but in proportion to what it is that a family might have needed. And they brought and drew to them other factions that might create power and ethos, not necessarily the energy and correctiveness that was needed for a family unit, so it was lost many eons ago. But this purpose needs to be brought into play and the elders don't have to come from the family, the elders have to come from the inner wisdom and the molecules that you carry that allow you to sow your seed, and the seed of those in front of you, in a way that will allow your frequency to move forward.

There are very few that know this knowledge and there are even less that actually act on the basis of the knowledge they have.

So my children, there will be a problem with fertilisation with the human being, and that is within the next twenty to thirty years, where people will just not be able to procreate in the way they have wanted before.

There is going to be a reduction in *human form* creation. This is going to help the weight that the planet carries but it is also going to help the change in frequency within the beings that are procreated and seeded on to the planet of Earth. It is going to allow change to take place and that change is that of the density frequency and the density *molecule frequency* of those that walk terra firma.

So in some respect it is a little bit like, in your processes, a cleansing. A loving cleansing process created by the form from whence you have come. Allow this to be. It is not the de-fertilisation of man, it is the *re-fertilisation* of man, spreading his seed on a fallow field and allowing new flowers to grow with the petals of wisdom that will procure from that new growth.

So be part of the understanding of this and know that man needs to once again help himself and walk bold steps in the name of wisdom, and in the name of wisdom comes growth, and in the name of growth becomes procurement of betterment, procurement of betterment, procurement of betterment.

Words

November 30ᵗʰ 2014

The narrative this evening is to do with the word, **words**.

We have many words inside us and many words outside of us, those that come from within and those that come from without. But what you must imagine is what is the conscription of words, what do they mean and how do they become something?

If you asked for a description of a word it is normally the meaning, the emphasis of what it is. But when you actually look at the descriptive pattern of what a word is, it is a sound and frequency that flows from one place to the next. In your case from your vocal tubes, out through your mouth and the voice is heard.

But what creates that material matter of word? The word is not only a sound, it is a *resonance*, and that resonance has a frequency that allows a meaning to be procured to you. Languages don't necessarily need to be spoken. Actions don't necessarily need to be acted. What actually needs to be procured is *a thought* and *a mind-set*. This is how two natives with totally different agendas in a jungle can communicate because they have been used to the mind-set of non-verbalisation.

Yet you as human beings in the modern age are using so many outside apparatus to create confirmation of thought and patterns that you are losing the internal dialogue. But this internal dialogue comes back to you when you are on long journeys, when you spend an awful lot of time on your own, or you spend a lot of worldly time inside of yourself.

Outside of yourself or inside of yourself?

Now when you become inside of yourself what you actually do is you tune into the inside dilemma of your thought patterns. And we use the word dilemma as if it is something that is bad, it is not, it is *dialing* into your thought patterns.

The transition of thought that allows you to move from one place to the next is something that is so very important.

Your words will mimic the actions of tomorrow and your actions of tomorrow will mimic the words of the following day. So you must be careful what it is that you verbalise, because indeed that verbalisation will reflect back to you in resonance. This is how boomerangs come back and hit you.

But what you must understand is you are indeed human beings. You are allowed thoughts, you are allowed verbalisations, and when they are only surface and there is nothing meant by them they don't carry much weight, but when you conscript a great deal of thought about those words and purport that thought into many *different* conscriptions then a *matter of fact occasion* comes back to you.

So when we talk about words, only have words that have surface meaning. When they go deep they will procure an action not only from you but from others, so be careful what you think, be careful what you say, be careful what you might be, because today you will be what you are tomorrow and what you are tomorrow might be what you will be the following day.

So allow words to become a permanent state of being, and in so doing you can allow words that flow through to you that you don't necessarily understand, and what you don't understand today you certainly will tomorrow. All new patterns create new avenues and when those avenues are created a new expression comes into play, and this expression for today my children, is your expression for tomorrow.

Love is the key to all things but words are part of love and love is part of words. So be above and below, inside and outside. God bless you for now and thank you.

Just Let Go

December 7th 2014

The resurrection of many different mind-sets is coming forth to you all now. And we talk about the resurrection as if it is the rebuilding, it is the re-establishing of old patterns.

We went through many eons of time where things stayed apparently still, where the water stayed still and very little went on above or below the water. Yet there was so much going on in the form of growth on a spiritual and mental level with all ethos, with all species, with all energy forms that lain within and without the planet.

The terra firma itself moved in anticipation with regards to what it expected and it expected something but it didn't expect what it was gifted, which was the opportunity to watch and curtail the very thought patterns that came from many different insects, many different forms of natural species, as well as the evolvement and development of man, the species that walks the planet in mastery.

It is many species that work towards this mastery and when they work towards this mastery they hope to master the next species, which is the next eon, the next species on from this, and that is not necessarily in physical form. And we cannot give you the perception of what it is, but what you must imagine my children, is everything waits in anticipation, anticipation for what happens next.

The mill pool moves from the still waters to a rough ride, and the rough ride froths and throws and tosses and turns and we surf on the top and we go underneath and drown. But we do not drown, what actually happens is we become tumultuous in our own patterns. The waves we have created drag us above and below, the surf that we have chosen to drift over the top and not look below drags us below this time, not on the top. We see the very reflection of ourselves in the mill pool of the past and the present. And our mill pool my children, isn't necessarily our own mill pool but that of many others, because we are after all an exemplar to many and we must firstly be an example to ourselves, and our truth must be utterances of expectation, must be utterances of the very surf that we drift upon.

We are my children, a reflection of all things and all things become a reflection of us until we meld away from the landscape of the past and we move into the landscape of the present and possible future.

And if your landscape is that that is different from those around you it matters not, because what will occur is as your energy form creates its balance and found the point where it has got to, everything else will appear unchanged and all the things that were around you will continue to be around you.

There will be many many different worlds created in the light of the individuals that take the next step. Now is that thousands and millions of different planets? No it is not, it is thousands of different echelons of thought patterns created in light, and as they are created in light a different perception of what happens occurs. So your perception will be different to that of somebody else.

But why have they got the same people in their picture that you have in yours, has everything separated?

Yes it has indeed separated; it has separated just for you. Your microcosm of cells have come with you, as somebody else's microcosm of cells has gone with them, and that microcosm includes the planet, the species, the vehicles, the transitisations and many things, they all separate created in the light of love and expectation.

So everything becomes a figment and a fragment of the past and are specialists for the future. You indeed my child, my children, my people are all specialising in your possible future. Go with that future and let go of the past. Let go of the things that hold you to the past. Let go of many things – jewellery, possessions that hold you back, let them go. Many of them will actually drift and be lost because you no longer need them.

There are things that have patterns of positivity and negativity that will leave you and all you need be left with is the clothes you wear and the feet you stand on and the memories that you have. Let them go. Let the money go that drifts through your fingers. Let the weather drift over your head and the pathway that is unbeaten be beaten by your feet as you tread on the grass that takes you to a potential pasture of the future.

My children, be strong, be aware that life is with you and life will always be with you, and of course when you have a heart as you all do love is there with you whatever pattern it chooses to gift you and whatever pattern you choose to gift it. So for now God bless you and we welcome.

A Christmas Gift.

December 23 2014

The instruct that we have inside ourselves is about change. The onus of change.

So much information is being procured to all ears with regards to our need to change, not only on a physical level but on a sub-molecular level. All levels of our selves are in a process of transition. It is like a mass exodus of people moving from the Lake of Galilee back to Jerusalem – big exodus of thought patterns moving from one place to the next. This isn't biblical knowledge, this isn't knowledge of any essence whatsoever other than the knowledge humanity needs to do.

Once a year so many animals move from one place to the next. Once an eon so many people move from one planetary complexity to the other. Somewhere in between that human beings are in their movement, their *transition of change*.

This is what you, we, us, everybody in the human clothing, is going through right now. There are no identity tags to state that you are different to the next because you are all part of the same thing. Yes indeed your quality may differ, your quantity may differ, but you are all part of the same, you wear the same clothing. You may not speak the same language verbally but mentally you think the same thoughts, articulate the same actions and experience the same emotions that both male and female have to go through as part of the clothing of humanity.

So why are you going on this *mass exodus* from one place to the next? Why are your cells, your spirit, your energy forms, all being taken with you so you transform from one place to the next?

Because this is the time for it to happen. Energy has procured itself to this point in time where you need to move on to the next echelon of understanding and this is what is happening. Humanity is going through a process of understanding, a process that is necessary.

It is a little bit like spending years in the wilderness and you come back to the fabric of a new town, a new village, a new essence. You need to clean away the essence of you that lived in the wilderness, the madness in your eyes, the need to eat because that was the main thought pattern. How am I going to eat, where am I going to get it from?

There is an ease, there is a possibility that your change will come to you very very easily, but there are also those that hang on very much to their old processes. If you like a process of power and adulation, why would you want to leave that and go to somewhere where you would be comparable to somebody else? So you will want to hang on to things.

Let go of them. Let go of everything that you are, everything that you own - your thoughts, your patterns - just be free. Free yourself of what it is you think you are. Free yourself of what you think is the truth. Free yourself of the essences of mammonistic tendencies. Just let yourself go.

When the whales and the fish and the seals migrate from one place to the next, do they take their food sources with them, their comforts with them? No, they take their tails/tales with them, and in your essence your tales are your truths, that is all you take with you. They take their tails/tales and they swim away and move from one place to the next. They don't overly dominate one energy essence in one place, they move to the next, to the next, to the next.

You have lost this migratory process within yourselves because you have become stationary. The word is not going to be stagnant but stationary. Stagnancy comes to those that don't allow their minds to move, don't allow their thoughts to move, don't allow their emotions to move and they become stuck, like a man that has been firmly set in concrete, his feet can't move and he stays and he grows roots.

A tree indeed grows roots but it goes down into its mother planet and mother planet feeds it with her information. It feeds the tree, the tree of life, with new energy processes to grow out into the air and the earth, and flower and bless it with its beauty and joy.

This is what you need to do as human beings. Go out and bless the world with the beauty and joy that you have within you. But you cannot do this with the past wrapped round your neck like a noose, hanging from a tree like a gibbet.

Let go! It is time to let go of all you have. Have nothing, and you will learn that you have everything.

So my children, my Christmas gift to you is let go, and have nothing but the gift of your own knowledge. God bless you and you move into a new year very soon. Move into a new _era_ of thinking. I love you all. Thank you.

Love in Trance Formation

December 31ˢᵗ 2014

We are going to talk today about **_words in
transformation_** and the elaboration of what words in
transformation means.

First of all, what are words? They are the way you transfer
information via vocalisation, we have spoken about this, but
transformation is not only about the words but it is about
the **_meaning behind the words._**

This elaboration has been spoken about many times with
regards to channelling; elaborations, meanings behind
words, flows, rivers. What we are going to state here is an
energy comes with words.

You can make a stipulation of anger or a stipulation of joy
and there is a flow, there is a current with it, a circuitry that
connects to much else that is to do with that subject as well.
That is why when you are angry, and you expose that anger
to yourself so much more anger flows to you, it is a flow.
So when you use words in a formation of meaning and you
really have intent behind them, you can create such a
transposition of thought pattern towards an individual or
towards a similar situation so _be careful_ how you project
your words.

Many speakers throughout the ages have used this
technology to themselves and realise that you can transform
those words into almost a hypnotic process. But you can

do the same in a very very positive manner – *I am love, I will be love and I will continue to be that love.*

Where does that come from? Does that come from your heart, does that come from your vocal transformations? So when you talk about love, and use the words in transformation with regards to love, you can project love in a very very forceful manner. And when we talk about forceful, it isn't towards somebody that doesn't want it and can project it back at you, but if you want to send love to a *very important place*, bearing in mind that places don't have the same individual focus as individuals. You can indeed send love to individuals, but if they don't wish it they will reflect it back to you.

But what you can do is send love to **places** and it can be picked up like a gift under a tree at Christmas time. So much love is gathered there; the projection of care that is required when you give a gift and within that gift is not only a gift in the physical sense but it is the love, the transaction. This is where we have got lost in the gift of giving. If there is no love behind that gift then it doesn't have any value, but when you place love in that gift then it has so much more value. The joy of a child's face when they open something that has been gifted and wrapped with love.

So we are going to use the **words in transformation** as your gift this year, from the moving from one eon to the next, 2014 to 2015. The gift of love that you take with you, packaged, because that is all you have left my children, as the rains of the past wash away the filth, the dirt, the memories, the rejoicing, the unhappiness; they wash them away into the streams, into the eons of time, and you move into a new trajectory, a new fashion sense, the way you wear yourself in a different manner.

So what you need to understand is *words in transformation* actually come in one formation. Love...in...trans...formation, *love...in...trance...formation*. Listen! ***Love in trance formation***!

So what is actually being stated here is if you allow yourself to become entranced by love, a formation of knowledge will accrue within you. Allow yourself to become love in transformation through the *words* that you use.

Now, does that mean you become something other than you are? No, what it means is you become something that you *already* are. You are a human being and when you are a human being and acting as a human being therefore you have to portray a certain artistic flair, which is the natural nuances between human beings. But what we are talking about here is when you are being the loving caring component of self.

Be love in transformation, in trance. Be entranced by your love and your love will be entranced by you. Another gift. So for the New Year my children, be Love in transformation. God bless you, and may the world walk with you as you walk with the world. Thank you.

The Diary of 2015

January 8 2015

I was due to channel on Sunday and it is now Thursday morning and I have not been feeling good these last few days, maybe I was sick, who is to say, but I think something different.

Good morning my friends, it is appropriate at this point in time that we state that the New Year's energy is a whole new process that brings a whole new understanding within the human frame, not just the child that speaks. This is why we have New Year's resolutions, New Year's changes, because what actually gives you the opportunity at this point in time is a whole new download of perspective, which is to do with cellular changes. This is why people have incentives at this point in time to change a pattern, not just because it is New Year but because the cells change in a particular way, in a *particular* way. We use that word circumspect in the format that the *particles of the body*, the cellular structure of the body, is open much more at this point in time to change.

Why has this occurred? Why has man been dawned with this process? Because new years are about new perspectives, new horizons, new opportunities.

Man used to travel, he used to travel from one place to the next, he didn't stay in a stationary place, he moved from one feeding ground to the next. New perspectives were needed, new ground of thought was needed, new tracks of thought, new processes of thinking were adorned through to the body through this *particular way.*

So my children, it is indeed an old process ... old light through new windows ... my children your windows are a little bit dirty and need cleaning off.

Give yourself the opportunity to think what it is that you would like, what it is that you *think* that you need, not for other people but for yourself. It is so much easier to consider others at this time of year and then you don't have to consider self. But what is it *you* need in *particular?*

Now the child needs changes *physically.* There are things within him that don't necessarily work well within his physical structure, he needs to clear these. These are energy formats and physical formats that need to be removed, and they can be using certain processes. Think about what it is that *you* need, project this into your particular form and allow the changes to occur. But most importantly take the steps forward on your new pathway just as you did as old man and woman when you moved around. Your trajectory was different but the *particular* things inside you, the *particular* needs are always going to be the same.

Personal resonance is the most important thing. Resonance is something that you don't necessarily understand, you don't consider resonance.

What is it that you resonate? Is it last years or this years? Is it last months or last minutes? What is it you are resonating out to the world? If you are resonating 'I don't like people, I don't want to be near them' therefore you will continue not liking people and not being near people. But indeed my children what you are here to do is to be more perplexed and more precise with your articulation with others.

What is it that you need to share with them? Your love, your understanding, your joy. What is the point in sharing your woes and foes, they have their own, just share the good things with people. Share your life's joys, your life's feelings, your life's loves, and that might traject to them in a *particular* way some of the changes they need.

So the channeling at this point in time is about change, change for you, you and again for you, with love. God bless and good luck.

January 11 2015

Regardless of all facts humanity requires security, security in the form of knowledge and understanding. When we have knowledge we have understanding and when we have understanding there is knowledge behind that.

So what is it that recompenses us for these matters of thought? We are recompensed by the energy we place in thought. We are recompensed by the energy we placed in knowledge. But how do we get this knowledge into our minds? Do we access it subliminally, is it given to us as a purpose, how do we get it? Is there a book of life placed in front of all of us that allows us to move into another space so there is knowledge procured to us?

Knowledge itself is an ethos, it is an energy pattern of all spectrums of matter, so therefore whatever you think *will* happen. Whatever will happen will be part of your thoughts. Everyone thinks differently so therefore their world that surrounds them will be a different facet, a different understanding.

This of course you all know, but what you don't know my children is the part that is subliminally projected to you from another aspect, another aspect of yourself. The subconscious level of yourself draws and subliminally projects to you patterns you need to be brought into the picture, and this subliminally is projected to you so your thoughts pick up on them. It is like one day you start thinking about blue cars or red skies, you don't know why, it is just there, going round and round in your head and because you start giving it a thought pattern it will materialise.

So not all things are actually subject to the thoughts that have happened to you on the physical level, many patterns are projected to you from your subliminal subconscious body.

Now you may suggest that this may come from *other* bodies, other bodies that are creating matters of thought and projecting them towards you, like dark energy. What is dark energy? It is only yourself projecting back what it is that you think, no more or no less.

So dark energy is the light being re-projected back to you in a dark form, being shown to you that if you project this out then this is what is projected back to you. If you kick the cat the cat will bite you, if you bite the dog the dog will kick you, all these things happen as projections.

So my children, the cleaner your minds, the cleaner your thoughts, the cleaner the subliminal projection back to you from your subconscious.

Now there are rules and regulations to all things, of course there is. There are dimensions of thought that can be projected to you for reasons unbeknown to us and unbeknown to you. These are matters we cannot pontificate upon. These are worldly matters, but what we can pontificate is the matters that surround you individually.

So allow yourself to project out what you want projected back to you. Matter of fact! Fact of matter! Matter of fact, fact of matter. It materialises in matter of fact. So allow yourself this trajectory.

You are recompensed by many different things, you are recompensed in many different ways. The seeds that flow into your mind, the seeds of correctiveness, seeds of enjoyment, seeds of love, seeds of colour and projection; all these seeds are gifted to you in the way that you planted them.

So your roots my children are based on every pattern of thought you project out. Allow yourself to be love at all times, but most importantly allow yourself to *be human* at all times. Do not stop yourself doing the things that are humane to you but allow yourself to understand that the human *being* doesn't have stop buttons. It will just continue going if you tell it to walk, or continue running if you tell it to run until it stops. But you must be objective with regards to what you do with your body because your body will run and run until it runs out.

But your mind my children will run and run forever because it is part of the subliminal consciousness of everything you are. For now children, recompense yourself with love. Thank you.

January 21 2015

The resolution of energy re-use. We are going to talk to you today about your energy and the recycling of your own energy.

As you place energy out in the ethos towards something, a directive, you can place that energy in a place in a pattern that allows it to return to you with your name on it.

Now when we talk about this, it is like posting a letter but you put no address on it and it goes out somewhere and it comes back like a boomerang.

Now you know that if you place an energy in a directive, whatever directive, it will come back like a cog turning and resolve itself back to you, or revolve itself back to you. So when we talk about energy what we are talking about is *sending energy out into the world to come back to you as well.*

Why would you need to do this? What is the importance of placing an energy out there and bringing it back to you? Because what you want to know is what that energy is about. You need it to go on a journey and come back with what it did.

So you can send out a *request* to all those mammals in other ethos's, other places, send them love and allow it to come back to you. That is how channeling works. Basically it is patterns sent out from the world to other worlds, and then they come back with answers to questions that may have been asked millennia ago, not necessarily from yourself but from somebody with a similar energy form to yourself.

But you, my child that sits, can send energy out and ask and expect that it comes back to you like a revolving wheel, so ask those questions, and those that listen to these words can also ask the very same questions. And you will know when it will come back to you because the question will come back to you very plain and clear in your head and an answer will follow.

So my children, as the realms open up and the veil is gradually removed from the planet, there is going to be much more communique between you and your brothers and sisters, not only from your own planet but from many other planets with a similar frequency to your own. There is no point communing with another frequency that doesn't necessarily have your destination and destiny in mind.

Everything needs to learn from other procreations but other procreations don't necessarily want to learn from yours. So you have to choose where you place your energy, place it where love is used in a comparable way to your own, because love has so many different directives.

Is the reptile any more in love with something else than you are with the person that you love? They just have a different way of responding to that. So just accept that your love and the way that you do things isn't the same way as others.

There are so many different disciples from many many different planetary systems carrying out their version of love. Have no expectations of what that should be. Have no expectations in the revolution of your own mind, just accept that love will be the key to your future.

Start sending out the questions and expect them to come back to you. The revolving spiral of consciousness moves towards you my children. God bless you for now and thank you.

January 29th 2015

The alteration of the mind-set of all is part of the component of the change that is occurring to us all at this point in time.

The mind-set and its alteration are all to do with the transition between you and the component from whence you have come. You are being reintroduced to your Source in a very different way.

It is almost as if you are being taken down to a magical waterfall and the water is going to flow over you and cleanse you. Not only is it going to cleanse you externally but internally, spiritually, physically, metaphysically and super physically ... words we have not used before. This is going to happen to those that choose to accept the alteration in mind.

And that isn't a choice, it is about a perception of how your energy stands at this point in time, where your energy sits in the transition between now and the next. So it is what you have earned, what right you have as an individual to be in that place to be cleansed.

But nobody said it was going to be easy for anybody. There will be many many people that will feel so separate from what it is that they are because they have allowed this to happen in their own lives. They have separated themselves through discord, through discolouration of emotions and feelings. They separated from their physical self and it is very very difficult to get back to the physical form once you have done this because there is a journey that is needed for that.

Now the child that sits can take you on that journey and reintroduce you back to your physical form.

This is an important thing. The child that sits knows not what he has available to him, but he must allow this to happen for people. So it is about taking the *body back into the physical*. It is when you have actually morphed out of your physical form, and excelled outside of the body maybe, but you are here to use the physical form to gather and inform. That is what you are here to do, *gather*, and if you are not in completeness – *mind, body and soul within the physical form* – then you have not carried out your task.

So my children *the cleansing will happen to those that are complete in their physical form*.

There are many people that have chosen not to be complete in their physical form because of sufferance, discordance and many things, but it is important at this point in time to bolt yourself back there and allow yourself to be very physical. You don't have to be seen or obscene but my children be physical, do physical things and keep yourself latched firmly to terra firma. That is important.

Because at the moment there are many that wish to leave and they are doing so by many different means. By taking their own life, by submerging themselves into many different things, allowing themselves not to admit where they are on a physical form, but now is the time for settlement.

It is like you have shaken the cup up for so long and all the sediment is floating in the water. You have to allow the sediment to settle in the bottom and know where you are, and when it has settled in the bottom you have clarity of clear water to be able to see the directive in which you need to go. This is very very important.

So allow yourself the directive you need to go in, and if you need your physical form re-implemented into the three, so basically putting your physical body back as one, then *the child may well be the person for you.* God bless you for now and God bless the child for the work he does. Thank you.

February 5ᵗʰ 2015

The industrial terminology of thought is what you are receiving at this point in time. The momentum is just. It is a *massive amount of energy coming on a massive form.* It is like a warehouse of energy being projected towards the planet.

This is the projectile, the projectile in the form of change. It is coming in at so many different angles, and those of you that are suffering the most is because your body was already stressed, so therefore the stress is the stress in the fact that *you have to change.* It is allowing yourself the space to allow this change to enter your minds, bodies and spirits.

This is everybody we are talking to, every single person on this planet is going through the process of industrial change.

It is a little bit like going through a revolution on an industrial level, moving from a square wheel to a round one, or from coal to oil, or from oil to nuclear, it is just a massive change, a massive shift of the equilibrium of the human frame and spirit.

So there are many people you hear of at the moment that are going through major sufferance as if why and what is happening. Has this happened to them before? But not quite the same level, it is as if the wick has been turned up and the heat is upon us all. So just allow this, not being a negative thing, allow it to be a change.

It is like your vehicle hasn't been functioning as well as it should and you haven't had the money to maintain it and it has been taken in and everything has been done, the air has been put in the tyres, the oil put in the engine, the timing altered, the interior cleaned. Everything brought forth so you have a shiny new penny to work with. This is what is being gifted and given to you as an individual, yes *you* as you listen, you are being given the opportunity, perplexed as it may be, to change your ways.

If you don't change your ways you will die from this component of change. But you won't die in the representation of death as you know it, what you will do is *you won't change* so you won't have the opportunity to live in the new format of understanding, *so you will die from it,* fade away.

It is like two men hanging on to a raft and one can hang on and one can't. You both have exactly the same strength and determination yet one chooses not to stay and drifts away. The person that hangs on is the one that has the illustration, the lust to thrust forward, knowing that there is more opportunity to be had round the corner over the next wave, if you are in the sea.

So my children don't be perplexed by what is happening to nature, yourself, and everything around you right now, it is about this *industrial format of change.*

Nothing happens without the capital L and that is love. Nothing happens without the projectile thought of love and care. But my children you are a planet of free will and you have taken that free will and stretched it to the limits, and the zenith has come and that free will has to stop, and the free will is not being forced or changed, you are being given an opportunity.

There is an intervention that is coming in giving you an opportunity just to see another avenue, to go down another avenue, another alleyway of opportunity, where you can kick your ball against another wall or bang your head against another wall, whatever you choose to do. But you have to take on the format and accept the change that is coming to you with love and acceptance.

Now if you have had depression in the past you will have more of it now, if you have had aches and pains in the past you will have more of it now, accept that this is part of your change, your transition between one place and the next.

If you choose to play the harp it doesn't just happen overnight, you have to work hard at these things. If you choose to maintain cars and become a mechanic, then you have to learn to become one. Learn to become who you are. Learn to become a vessel that can go with clarity and understanding and absorb love in the way that it needs to be absorbed.

Now my children you are loved, you will always be loved. There is an industrial revolution going on within your body right now. Accept it, go with the flow and the go will flow with you. God bless you and thank you.

February 22 2015

The way that energy divorces itself from the body is subject to much conjecture at this point in time.

Separation of energy is about transducement or change within the energy system of the body, so we call it *a line*. A line that is integral to the body yet is has been prepared to be divorced and detached from the singular system. And when we talk about this we are actually stating that the energy is removing itself in layers slowly so the person, the persona, the energy system of the body can cope.

These layers in themselves are layers of imagery, layers of latent energy that are attracted to you due to circumstances that you have been involved in, not only in this lifetime but previous lifetimes and existences.

Now those that choose to make the shift, and those *only* that choose to make the shift, are going through this layering, this divorcing of energy as it is reintegrated into another system of thought. Yes it is yours yet it is being divorced from your system.

The reason why we are giving you this information is so you can understand why your body is changing so, why you are actually going through the process of *skin crawling*, it is like your skin is crawling, it is actually the energy segmenting itself out of the DNA.

The DNA in itself is not only the connectivity to your source but also the integral part and employment process that keeps all the energy system connected. Everything you are, everything you potentially might be and everything you have been, are all connected up via your DNA to a central point. Now these points themselves are segmenting, so you yourself can actually segment away from that and start afresh, like a new bulb that is not genetically attached to anything else other than the newness.

If you can imagine when the planet was first seeded and everything was given an opportunity to grow here, *those things that chose to stay* and grow here were in the first process of procreation. One didn't know whether they were going to work or not and the ones that worked stayed.

And this is where all your industrial processes such as forestry, grass, a lot of the small-segmented processes beneath the soil, humanity in itself.

With humanity, its soul was disconnected. The *imagery* of humanity was placed here to see if it could actually conform within the environment and *the soul came later*, as did the energy requirements of the human frame.

So it was almost as if a prototype was placed here to see if it worked. A soulless environment created by a soulless individual.

Now you must understand, as you divorce yourself from this energy *your body will change*. Only those that choose to make the jump.

The child insists at this point in time that he needs to know where this information comes from. Who he communes with. You have always been told that when that information is ready to be given you will be given it. We *insist* that you *do not ask these questions at this point in time*. There is a dormant information process that will allow you to have this when your body is ready, and you will be ready within the next year or two my child but you are not ready yet. So do not ask this question until you are ready to receive the answer and as yet you are not.

You will receive information about the dormancy of the information you have, and where potentially that may come from, but you will not know the source. Because the source from whence it has come is part of a ... (long pause here) ... the word is *part of a Pleiadian breakaway group* that broke away many many aeons ago. They are *not* part of the Pleiades but they were. They did not agree with the way the Pleiades was functioning, the way the Pleiades people were so violent in their integral sense.

So these people are unwarlike and genuinely they are placed upon another system, and that system you must not know about, as yet. You will be given the opportunity to know this at a later date. Wait and the date will come my child. God bless you for now, we will speak again. Thank you for being who you are and thank us for being who we are.

March 2 2015

The extreme acclimatisation needed for the new cells of the body is placing a complete placebo effect on the body. It is almost as if something is happening yet nothing is happening.

The placebo is a whole new mind-set created by parallel universes within yourself. And you have to understand, when we talk about parallel universes, outside of you is a world and within you is a world, and within every cell of you is a planet, and within every cell of that is a microcosm of something that you are spectrumising in your minds.

So you have to understand, this placebo is a procedure. Just accept the change and accept what is happening within yourself.

We are all going through a battle within ourselves, a battle of change, a battle of wills, whatever you might call it. It is about personal choice at this point in time because after all you do have free will and nothing is forced upon those that have free will, but you are certainly given the options to be steered in a directive. So you may appear to have free will but in some respects you might not. So your directive is for you to be able to make the choices you need to make, not the choices you are being forced to make.

We are placed in a procedure of compromise constantly where you compromise your ideals or your thoughts, or you compromise particles within your body because of the food you eat, yet it is the food that your eyes glean. We eat with our eyes not with our common sense.

So my children this placebo is *a placebo of common sense* floating around all of you, giving you the options to change, change in a directive towards love.

If you actually look at a lot of operative procedures on the planet they are certainly not directed toward your better wellbeing, this you must understand. There are many things that are not necessarily there for your wellbeing but for wealth, ego and so on, and they are there for you to purchase, fall into, get trapped by, get changed by, and so on. That indeed is part of free will and part of the embroidery of free will. But you must understand that **when you use love** it overtakes all those things.

But firstly, loving oneself is incredibly important. Can you truly say you love yourself when you have a big fat belly, tortured liver and kidneys because of the way your body has to function? Can you truly say you love yourself when you look in the mirror and you can't stand the reflection? Can you truly say you love yourself when you maltreat things around you? Can you truly say you love yourself when you choose to cover yourself up in a totally different fabric, such as make-up and hair dye?

Because when you do those things you are choosing to be an image that somebody else is portraying that you need to be, yet *your image is the true reflection of what you are –* skin, warts and all.

So it is about taking on that placebo of common sense and wisdom. Not being directed by a directive but actually following what your heart tells you. Wise words are these. Make choices that you enjoy making. If you find that you are making choices that you don't enjoy making then it is not following your heart. So a rule of thumb here is – *only do things you enjoy.* Certainly when you get to a certain age group you have the operative to be able to do that.

The younger generation don't necessarily have that directive because they need to go out into the world and find the things they don't enjoy and find the things they do. But when you have age on your side you know what it is that you want. Do that, and do it as often as you can. And allow your heart to be filled like a water trough, filled right to the brim with love and enjoyment. Find as much enjoyment as you can. *Fill your life up with joy,* literally. And if you are not filling your life up with joy and your cup is full up with something else and you are drinking it, nobody is forcing your arm to your mouth to drink that cup.

My children the water that flows down your oesophagus is the very energy that feeds the system that you are. So *every fluid* – be it energy, be it food, be it drink, be it thoughts – *every fluid that enters your body* is a reflection of what you will be tomorrow and the next day.

So it is about your fluidity. Drink a cup of common sense and wisdom. Allow the love to flow through your oesophagus into your veins, into your cells, reprogramming the DNA that has been mal-aligned.

Yes, *energy works with DNA*. If there is too much energy in the same pattern your DNA will change, that is how it works. If you learn and teach your body new ways then it will take on that directive. It is about teaching – not receiving teaching from another teacher but actually teaching yourself to learn to do things that you need to do. Start filling your cup up with love and joy, common sense and wisdom. Don't compromise your ideals and constantly constantly endear yourself towards doing things you enjoy.

If you don't like sitting in a room with people, all drinking and talking about things you don't enjoy, don't do it. If you enjoy digging the garden go and do that. If you enjoy sitting and reading a book on a Sunday, as long as you don't resume into laziness by doing these things, go and do the things you enjoy. Do you enjoy walking your dogs in the woods and you find you can't do it enough, do it more.

The worlds of mammonistic tendencies are drifting away from you my children. The only residue you will have left is yourself, your feet and the shoes that you fill. The sole that fills those shoes, the heart that fills your life, your life that fills your universe, and your universe that fills your multi-universe. So you are part of all the same things.

Drink from the cup of love. **Drink - from - the - cup - of - love.** Thank you.

March 11 2015

The clarification of relevance is independent. And when we talk about independent it is totally *irrelevant* to the cell structure of your body.

There is a clarification going on that is gleaning, and we talk about gleaning because it is a looking down upon the cell structure of the individual. We call it the 'in divide you all' because you are actually being monitored at the moment for the relevance to your vibrational frequency.

There will be a separation happening at some point in the very near future where the worlds divide - there will be the *old world* and the *new world*. Which one will you abide upon? It matters not really, it is only the energy you carry that is dependent on where you go. So the clarification of relevance is how your vibrational frequencies frequencise with the planet of your choice.

Now within your universe are your cells and within those cells is another universe. It is those cells of *clarification* that take you on the journey to your next place.

Will the people that were there with you in your lifetime be gone? No they won't, they will be in a different form. So those that separate from each other will still have the same person with them but they will be in the different form. And the interesting thing is, and the only way you are actually going to notice this, is the *conformity* that starts occurring with individuals where once you may well have had dissent. The conformity is the fact that they are conforming to a new vibrational frequency, but it won't actually be their soul within that frequency.

So this is the clarification of relevance.

We talk about this because it is important for the individual individual to actually know there is this separation going to occur. There are many that will stay and there are many that will go. We call this *ascension* in your words, but ascension is not what is happening. There is no division, there is no loyalty towards who goes where and what, it is just how your cells divide, how your vibrational frequency suits the purpose in which the planet is going to be.

So understand, my child that channels, there will be a period of time when there will be _no_ *channelling*. You were told this yesterday. The channelling will desist for a period of time because *it will* _interfere_ *with the energy frequency of what is going to happen on the planet in the near future.*

So the channelling will once again return. We cannot say when but we will say this – the words, the voices, and the spoken thought and form has been with the child for aeons. They will always be there because there will be portals of information there but *the channelling as such will stop for a period of time.* Your time, our time, it matters not, the time will be right when it starts again. The child has been loyal to his cause even though it appears he has not.

The human form finds it incredibly difficult to appropriate what is needed for he or her at this point in time because it is like the fuse, the wiring, the whole circuitry of the body is changing. Your acceptance of things and differentials are changing, yet you can't understand why.

There are those that are grasping on to a float in the sea while the tides are high and the waves are high, and they are trying not to go under because they are frightened of the change involved if they liquidise themselves with the new fluid of knowledge that they have. Yet there are those that are floating quite willingly on the surface going, '*Ok bring it on. I need to appropriate this new change within my own domain. I am that change, I will be that change and I will be part of the love that occurs with this change.*'

Those are the two separates that will be ... we are going to use the word *disembowelled* because they are *literally* going to be removed from each other. There will be those that will and those that won't, those that won't and those that will. It is your will not theirs, it is their will not yours.

You must understand that there is no differential. God loves *everybody* individually, and we use *God* in the bold form because it is not the period of thought that you portray as God. God himself is the all-being all-knowing cell, the original cell of this planetary frequency. You are the god of your universe, he is the god of that universe. There are many gods of universes, they are just those that originated the process.

My children you have the will to learn so much, yet you will not learn. You are learn-ed yet you choose not to be part of that learn-ed procedure. It is now time to elongate those cells and allow a new spectrum of understanding to come to you.

And we talk of love as if it is something totally alien to yourselves, alien in the form that love itself is appropriated in so many different ways.

The man that walks the earth and causes no harm to others, is that love epitomised? Or the reptile that walks the earth and eats many things without too much courteous consideration, is that love?

You have to understand that love has many different forms, because all things have different needs. Needs are part of a purpose, but if we stare down at needs we won't understand what they are because we cannot appropriate our minds to what the needs are of others, especially if they are of different skin, of different breed and of different cellular structure. How could we possibly appropriate our thoughts to how and what their needs are? Yet everything has needs.

There will come a time in the near future where your needs will be pushed to the limit because your mind won't be able to cope with what it is you are appropriating. But just allow yourself to stretch your mind like you are stretching a big round pizza, and the topping is coming towards that pizza but you are the pizza and the topping is the new knowledge, the new flavour, the new colour, but the topping will be things that you have not understood or appropriated in your physical domains before.

There is change afoot! Await my children. Understand and be learn-ed, be willing, and when you are willing and learn-ed you will take on board what is relevant. Wait and you will await my children. God bless for now and enjoy your journeys. Thank you.

An Answer to a Question on the *Constellation Serpens*

April 5ᵗʰ 2015

This is in answer to a query referring to the constellation Serpens mentioned on January 9th 2007 that I posed to Robin about two weeks ago.

The reference reads:

"My children, imagery is so very important to give certain information to people that sit, not only for those that sit but those that imagine that sitting has no relevance. You must remember that getting back to the carnal self is about understanding what and where you have come from and why you do what you do and where you do what you do and what it is for.

The imagery you see this evening as you sit is of the serpents. The serpents my children is where you have come from. Serpents is also a sky element, it is a constellation in the sky called Serpens. My children, you are in self part of a reptilian format. Your blood runs cold when you hear this because that is where you have come from. This is where the cold thought formats come in many situations where your blood runs cold with the way you feel. It is not that of a negative sense or an evil sense, it is that you will think and rationalize in a different way, in a cold way. This is why some of the terminology dealt to the boy is very cold because that is how it works in that realm, it is about doing and being not necessarily about experiencing. It is about doing what needs to be done when it needs to be done, instantaneously as opposed to rationalizing what that means. This will allow you to elongate some of the mind-sets you have in your cold minds sometimes. The flowers that don't grow and they just stay the way they are is the way your reptilian mind will allow you to function.

Occasionally you will see the reptilian formats which you have come from communicating with yourself in a three dimensional pattern. That does occur, and by doing this it allows a reptilian thought format to transcend itself into a human thought format in a certain way that frequencises itself so that it is not demeaning to either source. Sometimes we need to feel the Original Source to understand what that means, those are what are called cold moments. Allow yourself to have those cold moments, they are not an investigation of some other particle trying to transcend your energy format it is about you being part of self.

You have come from many thought formats, many transcendences, it is just about you experiencing and understanding what they all are and being part of them on occasions to allow your cells to re-remember what that was at that point in time to allow yourself the memory access from where you have come and possibly where you might go and certainly where you are right now.

Your blood speaks my children. Listen and you will get answers. There is much more to come and it will allow you both to grow from the information that is formatted. Be cold and be warm. Look behind the veil and you will see the answers and they are answers of self."

An enquiry has been made with regards to the area in the universe called Serpens. You have to understand that Serpens is your dialogue not ours but as we know where it is diagrammatically it is a component of the planet area where many many people left to go to.

If you lived on the planet of Earth and everything was going wrong around you, you would head for the hills, the place where you are least likely to be contaminated by whatever it is that is going on. The Serpens area diagrammatically is the area where many people from different areas went. It is like the barren area on your planet, where the trees cover you and protect you, where there is a kind of love that is shrouded by many different environments.

We talk about many different environments. There are portal points and these portal points intermingle with many different universes, not just this one but many many different universes that are out of context with any thought patterns that you might have. And because they are out of context you cannot explain something. It is like trying to say to a caveman, but that can fly! Or try and say to an astronaut, you are a caveman, behave like one. There are things that can't be explained until you have an ability to obtain that information and conceive it within your own minds.

So the Serpens was a place where people went to. A safe area where you weren't searched for because you could literally get lost in space. Lost in a parameter of misinterpretation. People were told not to go there because there were demons, you were sucked into places you can't go. Indeed you were, and maybe you couldn't return, but if you got to the point where you didn't want to be where you were, did it matter whether you didn't return there. So can you understand why many people went there, because nobody would follow, it was safe, in some respects.

If your planet was dying or you were dying, and that death doesn't necessarily mean the terminology that you use, but dying basically means your race, your persona, your energy form was dying, and you wanted to keep traces of that energy form in whatever form it was in the Serpens was the place where you went. It carried safety in the fact that people didn't go there, it was the doldrums of the space, it was the Bermuda Triangle of your Earth; it carried portal points. The people didn't know where they would go to or come from, but indeed if you held your heart high and your mind firm you were always safe when you got there.

There are many challenging things coming to you all. There are many things characterised by the way you are, but what you must understand is that there is always love in all places, and the places where there needs to be love within yourself is in the place where you contain that which is in your human physical form. The human physical form carries dialogue and that dialogue gets transmitted to the *soul receiver*, and the soul receiver is the energy format that takes it back, elongates it to the point of your source. But your source is being diluted and segmented in the fact that there are now many different forms of source. They are being segmented for the first time in interplanetary history, because you are actually being segmented into different transmission points.

This is where it will become complicated. We do not like creating complicated formats but it is being segmented off, a little bit like cutting an orange up and there are different segments and each segment goes off in a different direction and experiences something different, and it is only the nature of the energy that you carry that determines where your segment goes.

My children, there is much going on on your planet and there are many people that wish to determine and carry on the characteristics of the energy form that you once had, and there are many people that are aware that this is here.

And as we talk, we are from your past talking to you about your future so we can change your present. We are your past trying to change your future so your present can be part of the segment that you wish it to be. We being the communique that you are, a part of you.

Take this on board, on board your planetary vessel and understand that you can't flee into different domains this time because those domains have been discovered. Every pebble, every stone has been turned in search for where you might be from the past. So you must carry what it is that you have inside your heart and know that it is only love that is going to take this transition through this time.

You need to be part of the segment that takes this through and transitionalises it into a positive format, so your historics, so your future is part of an elongation that allows the mind to be free, allows the mind to flow like a river, not tormented by dams, dams of energy. Be dammed my child, be dammed. Become undammed, do not be that vessel, that component, let yourself flow. Let yourself understand that it is not fear that characterises where you are going to go or what you do, it is what you are and what you will be. So from this moment on you will not go to the Serpens this time, but understand what the Serpens was.

Understand that you are speaking and being spoken to from yourself from the past, from your historic future projecting back to the now, the space that you are in now, stating that you need to stay where you are. There is no ascending, there is no transition, there is carrying of energy.

Be who you are by being a beacon of light. You don't have to tell everyone, it is just *being it. Be who you are* and be proud of that. Thank you.

The categorisation of information that is being given to the child are with regards to his release to a soul. Now his soul is a fragment of something that has come from somewhere else. Now the soul is something that is integral within all Bedouin of people and we talk about *Bedouin* because they are nomadic in the format but they can transitionalise between so many different planetary frequencies.

There are many different charges placed upon different souls and these souls when charged in a certain way, in a *particular* way, they can transitionalise through portals in the different dimensions of thinking.

Now the child in himself was transitionalised on to the planet of Earth in your date 1965, but in format and thinking he was not necessarily brought here until 1968 and what actually occurred was, he came from the planetary system of Serpens. Now as stated previously Serpens was not necessarily the residence but it was the places where people went to because they didn't wish to be where they came from.

Now we have spoken that the child, his format, his energy form, came from the Pleiades. Indeed he did, but the Pleiades was not formatting itself in an energy that was conducive to the energy carried within his soul frequency, many of which of the soul frequencies left. But as all these children of these planets are monitored and they know exactly where they went they had to go somewhere where they couldn't be found, or wouldn't be looked for, and that is where the Serpens domain lies.

It is almost like the enchanted forest that you have in your rhymes. It was a place where even the dignitaries and the armies didn't go, because within the enchantment was an encapsulation of mind-set that wouldn't allow people to accept. So it was a safe place, an enchanted place in the universe, called the Serpens.

But the Serpens also carried its residue of danger to those that went there, and that residue of danger is the fact that there were *serpents* in many different forms in the Serpens and those serpents had no rules or regulations, they were just, just, just. And when we talk about just, just, just, there are no rules or regulations to them because they are non-frequency individuals so carry no bearing on the domain of which they are in, so they do pretty much what they wish when they wish but they have to stay within the domain. And there is only one thing they understand and that is – *You are mine when I find you!* So the whole idea is not to be found when you are there, and if you are found you are theirs forever. That is very difficult.

So the story begins, the child's journey. It matters not about the information with regards to the Pleiades and why the Pleiades was what it was, it is why the child carries the energy to the planet of Earth. He came here that day in 1968 formatted to a soul and that soul purpose was to carry the energy.

Now when we talk about carrying energy, it isn't necessarily about doing something with it. It is like you carry something in a briefcase next to you that is important, you may just be the carrier and you have no idea that this suitcase chained to your wrist carries something extremely important.

So the child carries that information, and he carries it not only now but into eternity. When you talk about this it is extremely important to understand *__into eternity__* because energy, memories and patterns are so very important for us all to take on board. We utilise the process of time and honour and democracy, but we don't necessarily utilise the frequencies that come from so many different formats other than the format that you use as a protocol on your planet of Earth.

You have to understand that as you are gifted information, you are gifted information that allows your mind to stretch into a different domain of acceptance. Now if the child was given this information three or four years ago ... we will use a terminology ... it would have blown his mind, literally, it would have made his feet not touch the ground, it would have been like he was on some extra-terrestrial drug. His body, his mind, his soul, his cells, could not cope with it but it can now because of the change of the frequency that the planet vibrates upon.

The planet is changing its frequency, so the souls within, withon and outside of the planet can come here and act in a different way. This has been needed, because when we talk about in a different way, if the planet is going to go in one trajectory or another things need to change as the trajectory changes. And as the trajectory changes things need to change with it. It is like turning a car in another direction, you don't look in the same direction as you were before, you turn with the car, the lights shine in a different direction.

So your directive as such is the direction of energy that the planet is. You follow its trajectory. It is like you are on a ship and the ship is being commissioned to go in a particular directive, and you are on that ship as a passenger and you have to adjust to the waves, to the sea conditions, to the life on board that ship.

Now the child came here on board a ship. He came here on that date in 1968 and he knows when he came here, and he has a terrible feeling of loss when he left, but that was his yearning to come home it wasn't actually a format of loss. He knew exactly what he was doing when he *left that ship* and he *was beamed down* on to that beach *that day* into the incarnate soul that you call Robin. And that incarnate soul knew at that point that something very pertinent had happened to it, because up until that point it was empty, it was empty in a format that *it didn't carry a trajectory of soul, gift and given*, it was a taxi with no passengers but it acted out a process.

The ship that he was delivered on was a ship that was taken, it was *borrowed* more to the point from somebody, some processes, delivering faculties and processes to the Serpens planetary system. They knew that at that point that was the trajectory that was the vessel that was needed to take ***this child*** to the planet of Earth, and ***six others***.

And you think, well do all the dates work? It matters not, timeframes can be adjusted by the flick of a switch. You don't understand what the flick of the switch for timeframes are, but understand that just by flicking a switch you can be in any timeframe you wish or want because instantaneously they are all happening at the same time. You see what you see because *the frequency you carry is the timeframe you came in on.* But if that is a different timeframe you will see other purposes, because that is what is happening in that timeframe instantaneously. There aren't tens of millions of planet Earths, everything is happening simultaneously at the same time. You will begin to learn and understand what that means and it will not pop your head.

So the child comes from the planetary system of the Pleiades and left for reasons that we do not wish or need to discuss but what we will say is, those that fled and left the Pleiades went to the Serpens but *they knew that they had to transmit a new frequency that would adjust the **past** that will take that into the **future** that will give you a correct **now*** - if that is the terminology we can use.

The child came on board this Pleiadian craft it was, the Pleiades dropped information ... *energy* to the Serpens planet, I don't know what this energy is, it is like a fuel. There was like an agreement: *if you don't touch us we won't touch you, but we will give you this in return,* and they used to give fuel, and it was like a diamond-type stone that transmitted a fuel, created a fuel. I can't give you any more information than that, but that is what it was.

And they adjusted the timeframe, so literally you could jump in, all the people that came from the Pleiades planet on the ship were off board at this point in time. These souls came on board, adjusted the timeframe, they visited the planet of Earth, and adjusted the individual time frames for the seven children that were transmitted here. They came at different timeframes within an eight or nine year data base between the 1967/1968, so it can range through to 1969. From 1960 to 1969 was the timeframe that these seven vessels, these seven energy formats, came to the planet Earth and ensconced themselves within a soul. Robin is one of those souls, he has met another but he doesn't realise who that was. He is beginning to understand and will be given more information with regards to this when it is pertinent to do so.

We did tell you that we were going to start giving you information that is important. It is important to document what it is that you are so you know what it is that you do, so when you leave the imprint of yourself on the planet you have left a document, a *document of your transition*, the steps you made. That is important because if a soul is not told about the steps they make they do not leave an imprint on the planet from whence they have come, it is as if they were never there. It is like a charter, a charter of knowledge frequencised within a soul, but only if the soul knew what it was that they did. This is why many souls in their last breath are told things they can't cope with. Equally you have to be able to cope with the information that you carry and that you are told. And that charter is only left with what you were capable of enlisting within your own mind-sets when you departed that framework, that time framework ... I hope we are explaining this enough to you as it is very important.

The charter that the child leaves is unbeknown to him, mainly because he carries that energy and he will at some point be given the information with regards to that so his charter will be valid.

So the ship placed him on that beach enlisted within that child on that day. And the vessel also did this with _six other souls_, all on their own beach, it doesn't necessarily have to be the format of a beach, but on their own beach. They were left with a void to fill. Some are doing better and some are doing worse than they should but they are here for a reason, they were like a transmitter within a television set, it doesn't just provide a television set with what it needs, it provides many of the things that it needs. So be blessed with the understanding that all things don't necessarily need to be voiced than understood until the charter is relevant.

Then the vessel was taken back to the Serpens, and the timeframe was taken to one second past the point when it left, and for that one second nobody noticed their ship was gone! Because they can turn round and turn back again and they thought ... _Oh, that ship blipped. Was it there or wasn't it there? Oh there it is, I just misinterpreted what it was that I saw._ That is the opportune moment to take, but give back, it wasn't in truth taking, it was in truth using something for a positive purpose.

Theft is an interplanetary no no! You don't take things from other terms and utilisations of things, you do not take them. You have to understand that all things are there for a reason and if they are taken it adjusts the reason. So you must understand, everything has its reason and its place, that is why it is there at that point in time, even a pebble on a beach, a vessel in a shipyard, a thought in the mind, a love in your heart.

There is much more to come with regards to this. There is intrigue and the intrigue will continue.

Sunday April 26 2015.

Words from Robin and more...

I would say it was at least a month ago that I was given the (order) to stop the channeling which is the first time I have actually ever been given the instruction.

It was a relief in some ways but the information was getting interesting enough to get me to read it two or three times, which I have never done. But I was enjoying the fact that I am having some time out. But over the last day or two as I sat down of an evening I felt a need, and it is an urgency, and I can't quite place what this urgency is, but I felt things thudding in and out of me, like it did in the early days of the channeling. It was almost as if you threw a ball in a net and it goes *past* the net and the net extends and then stops.

It is like something that is untrained, and all I can say is it is like a new energy. So all I can presume is it is a new energy that doesn't understand how to conform to my conformity, so it is untrained in the way its energy is transposed to me as an individual, so it is quite uncomfortable.

I have also realised of late that when awkward or difficult information for me to cope with is going to be processed and given to me I am given tiny little snippets of information that drops down into my mind, and it allows me to cringe or it allows me to think or it allows me to be frightened or it allows me to be whatever I need to be at that point in time when that information is given. It is almost as if I am given a snippet to prepare me for what will come later, and I have been given a few snippets of information of late which don't sit well with me and there is a part of me that is going, 'No, something is interfering and giving me this information.'

I don't feel comfortable by potentially what it is going mean. I don't feel comfortable about exposing myself to the legitimacy of the possibility that it is the truth. So that is what is coming to me right now and I don't feel well with this information milling around me. I don't know what is going to happen when I channel, and I don't know where it is coming from, but I think it is coming from the source of where this channel originates from, and I don't think that source has ever actually given me its truth.

It has started telling me of late that it is originally from the Pleiades, but a group of people that left the Pleiades because of the planet and its dangers and perils, and they went into a group of planets or a place in space called the Serpens and there they stayed, or they stay, and I as an individual was one of seven that was brought by a Pleiadian craft to the planet of Earth and placed in a child called Robin, and it is that Robin that speaks now to you.

I am nearly fifty and have been channeling now for twenty years and something is afoot. I am aware of something, I am on a precipice on the edge of a cliff where there is a lot more information coming that seems important. It seems that it needs to be said, it needs to be brought forth, whether it is to me to explain parameters to me, or to Carolyn, or if it is to be shared, I do not know.

I sit in trepidation as to actually what it does mean. I am not yet ready to channel what it is because I think my body needs to just take it on board a little bit more. So maybe later tonight or tomorrow I will channel what this information is and it will be what it is and until then I will await. Thank you for the moment.

April 29 2015

I was given instructions a while back not to channel but this is not channeling, this is information that lays within me it appears, so we are going to start.

I am going to congratulate all people that are allowed to extend their mind beyond what it is they see, touch, and feel. There is so much information laying within the human frame. The perspective we see in life is not always the perspective that is actually happening on the surface. We are illuminated and we go through transactions that are also illuminated. And when we talk about illuminated we are talking about *what you see through your eyes* – the document, the transcript that you see that is performed in front of you that is deemed purposeful in the organisation, the spectrum that your eyesight and your believing processes allow you to have. Yet there is so much more that is going on, yet your eyes cannot believe it or will not believe it, or there is just non-acceptance.

There are planets all over the universe with so many different universes going on within them. Yet on those planets their eyes are not firmly locked into their head, *they are locked into the psyche*, and it is the psyche my children that you will need to open up and accept a truth, a truth beyond your yet comprehension. But you are visitors, you are visitors to a new knowledge, a knowledge that is not yet available to your mind-sets.

But the mind-sets are opening up. It is a little bit like there has been a door in your house that you have never opened, not because you didn't know it was there, not because you were frightened, you just didn't see it was necessary to open this door up. It was the door to knowledge that was going to allow your mind not to focus in the direction it needs to.

You have been trained as human beings to act in a certain way because a predecessor showed you that or somebody that deems themselves important shows you this and you follow it. A little bit like the shepherd that mills around and watches sheep doing what they do normally, and if one sheep moves the rest do. That is much how the human mind-set works. Create a thought, create more than one of those thoughts and then the mind-set projects that out and other thoughts are created in other people's minds. Yet what you don't focus on is what you don't know, so why would you focus on that.

What you don't know my children is you are *being*. You are doing and you are acting in a way that needs to alter and change. So I have to welcome you all that are prepared to listen that you are now being given a projection that is going to allow your minds to open.

The child that sits knows that if he focusses on a reflection of himself he will see something totally different. That reflection of self is of a reptilian form. The concept appals the child because he doesn't understand what that actually means. Is he genetically linked? Is he part of that reptilian form? Of course he is, as you all have been, you have all been many different things on many different planets. Many different circumstances have arisen because you have been on those different environmental processes, yet you are firmly locked on the planet of Earth and your minds are locked, a little bit like a bolt on a door that you won't open.

The child's mind has opened in many many different ways, and the child is acting out what a human being would act out when they are given information they can't cope with, which is abhorrence and ignorance. But when you are given snippets of information your mind is allowed to grow. As the child's mind has been given a seed it is flourishing inside like a crop of knowledge inside his mind. His mind is fertile so therefore it will grow and understand what it is that is needed of he.

So for the time being these are just words. Allow yourself to be and the time will be in your favour. God bless you all for now, more will come. Thank you.

June 4th 2015

I was told I wasn't to channel for a while and there has been a rest, but there has been a build-up of energy in the last few days, especially yesterday. Maybe because Carolyn has turned up, who is to say? So it is the feeling that I need to channel so therefore I will. I am expecting nothing but I am sure the wonderful words and verses will procure themselves.

Good evening my friends. The main objective of now is to understand the cellular structure of you. You being the child that speaks.

You are being offered a resonance, a resonance that deducts and removes. And when we talk *deducts* and *removes* we actually talk about the pre-injection of energy. You have been injected with energy over the years and this energy hasn't always been transient with the physical frame that you have; it is a little bit like putting ink into the blood stream and the ink flows through the blood stream and leaves a residue. Energy can do much the same, it doesn't necessarily always make itself conducive with the physical body but sometimes there is an effect but the effect doesn't outweigh the good or it doesn't outweigh the bad. You have to understand, not all things work but many things do work.

So you have to understand it has taken a long time to get the right information in the right form so the physical body does not suffer.

The child that speaks is child that has suffered much but we have learnt a lot from the sufferance incurred. And this is not the fact that we have brought the sufferance on the child, it is the fact that it has been necessary.

When you use a prototype sometimes you have to fall over and scrape your knee, and the child is a prototype in the format of the energy that he carries.

There is so much information that the child will procure in years to come, and that information will come out in many many ways. He is a devout studier of form and the form he takes is changing as all forms change; it is a little bit like opening a window up and the view every time is different, and because the view is different you have to adjust the way you think about the view you see. So the child, every time he opens up the capsule of information that he has within him the way his body will react will be different.

So what we are offering you now my child is a resonance accepting process so you can actually accept a resonance that will be much more conducive with your body if you wish to do so. And it is all a matter of flicking a switch.

Do you wish to flick this switch?

I do. I open my eyes, I do wish to flick this switch and I am waiting. And what I am experiencing now is <u>extreme</u> energy flowing down through my body, it is like bubbles coming down through my spine.

What is actually happening now is you are being cleansed of old residue. Your body is being cleansed, allow it out.

You, as a child, will receive this new cleansing process over the next day or so. You will feel **extremely tired.** Just allow yourself to be tired and accept that your body is changing frequencies, its currency of exchange is changing. We will speak to you in a day or two and explain what to do next. Thank you.

June 24th 2015

It was indeed a day or two, a week or two, since we last spoke. You have to remember that sometimes your change in your time does not necessarily work with our dimension of time and change. There is much that has gone on.

The lady that visits has gone through distemper within her physical self. Her physical self is manifesting many of these things. They are worldly goods visiting her. They are not of the spiritual realm, they are worldly goods, worldly manifestations that the lady needs to look at, a reflection of particles of herself that she is yet to discover and understand.

We speak to her directly now.

You need to look in the mirror and look at self for the time being. Your spiritual acknowledgement is admonished, admired, and accepted, yet your self has not yet been looked at. So you need to look to self for the time being my child, look to the self for the changes you need within yourself. Allow the aspect of yourself to be, and to be you will become an aspect of what it is you think you can be.

My child, your work is to be admired but you must look closer to home for the changes needed. This is coming directly from the Source, directly from the source that needs you to carry on on the physical realm with the work that you do. It is important that this _balance_ is required because if you are to carry balance you must carry that balance not only in your worldly, spiritual, and sub-physical knowledge, they must all be paralleled, _all_ be paralleled. You cannot, cannot, cannot do it on two levels and remove the third.

It is time to clear the playground my child, to clear the playground, you are no longer that person. Clear the playground.

Now, getting back to the child that speaks.

This is _his_ time for _his knowledge_. We do listen out via our ears to what it is that you request. You need to know more about where this channelling comes from. You have been told where it comes from. You must accept that indeed this comes from the Serpens, this comes from a source close to the Serpens.

You must accept that the change is necessary for you to format the new information has to be brought forth with you and the lady. This is why the two of you are experiencing much distemper within your bodies. You are being brought to form. You are part of a unit, a combined unit that will provide a stepping board, a stepping stone, a springboard, not only for yourself but an energy frequency as well. This isn't about helping humankind or even helping yourself, this is about a springboard of energy. It is like being thrown some information, wrapped in a rag, from a passing ship, and you catch it, but it is precarious to catch this information. Because the ship is rocking you may fall overboard, you may fall off the mast you happen to be standing on, but nevertheless you catch this information. Your body is traumatised by what it has just been through but the information is more important than the trauma, so your body has to accept that the trauma is part of the process of carrying the energy.

Why, you ask yourself, why you? Because you chose this destiny, as did many people *choose this destiny*. Your destiny is not for greatness, it is for acceptance and tolerance with regards to the job and task you have been given.

Human beings aren't necessarily admonishing or accepting in their levels of experience and tolerance that they are given. You are being downloaded this moment with regards to the past and present with regards to what it is you have been and what it is you are now. What you are going to be in the future really has no relevance. What has relevance is what is happening now.

Are you tolerating? Are you accepting? Are you componentising the information you are being given?

Don't allow this information to be convoluted or computerised, all it is are words. Behind words are emotion, are acceptance and joy, and behind all words is Love, whether you accept that or not.

Biblical words came from an idea, *an ideal*. Spiritual words come from an ideal also, an ideal that doesn't necessarily suit you or others, depending on where you are at your point in time. Everything carries Love; even a robot speaking to you will carry an essence of Love.

How can that be so because that does not carry a soul or a spirit? It carries *an ideal*. Everything has an ideal. Even if you computerise something there is an ideal behind the suggestions that are being suggested via that component. So when there is an ideal there is love. But love isn't always ideal is it, depending on how it is coming to you and what format it comes to you at.

You have to open your minds and expand, expand like a flourishing forest, like a web of understanding, like a joy within your heart. Understand and you will be understood. Do not be misunderstood, do not be misinterpreted, do not be 'mis-allusioned'. Be understood and understood you will be for now. Thank you, with love.

Conclusion

My intention was to finish *Words in Transformation* at the end of December 2014 but this new information was given to Robin and it felt appropriate to the times we are living through. It was previously mentioned the changes would begin with Egypt and Syria and this would be followed by Mother Earth making her presence known in physical disruption to the planet if man was not prepared to work in conjunction with her to bring her into balance. At that time it was also mentioned that holes would open up in deserts and there have been numerous sink-holes appearing, particularly in northern Siberia

We had word in March that the channelling would cease for a time because it would interfere with the energies coming to the planet, since when there has been the massive earthquake in Nepal, volcanoes erupting in so many places, floods and hurricanes with devastating effects and the resultant damage. We were warned that foundations would shake and man will be pushed to his limits and beyond. Our Mother is certainly shaking!

Everest, the greatest mountain in the world, is no longer resting but awakening. Nature is writhing and turning in her attempt to gain equilibrium, no longer patient with man and his abuse of her living body as he strides carelessly over her leaving his violent mark wherever he chooses.

The time of change is right now. We are witnessing her birth pangs as she struggles for balance, which she will achieve regardless of man, because after all he is only the furniture in a house undergoing a complete refurbishment and if he does not suit the new décor he will not be invited through the door where love is the key to the lock.

THE END

Appendices

Appendix 1

"My Child, my Children"

Throughout this discourse the words *my child* and *my children* have been expressed with reference to Robin and those that sit with him. On asking why we were referred to as children this is the explanation that was given in June 2002.

"My children, the creative force behind you all is the creative force behind where you came from. You are at this point in a millennia of change. My children, **the parental influence**, the influence and energy that you came from, is now forthcoming in an energy format that is being supplied to the children, so the manifestation of **children** is the exposure of the fact that you have come from a parental influence. This parental influence is the energy behind the change, the energy behind the forwardness, the completion, the transitionalisation from one experience to the next.

The parental element, the parental element, the parental element my children, my children, my children.

We must accept at this point in time that the equilibrilisation of formats are now coming into place, it is now time for change. It is now time for the human element to accept that within his mindset there is an element of change that is now transitioning firstly within the physicality.

The physicality is the first that will accept experialisation experience, experience of change within itself, then it will draw itself to the conscious mind, then you will be able to vocalize on what has occurred to you my children. It is at this point you will then begin to understand what your body found and experienced first. Your body is experiencing change before the mind because the body is the curator of change.

My children, experience is something that you chose, experience is something that you need, experience is something that you are going to access with and understand the new information and formats that are coming forward to you. It is now time for the curators of this change to unveil themselves and allow you to see them in the vocalization, the experience, and the eyesight that you have.

My children you will begin to see the curators, you will begin to see the lights and energies that come forth to you in your subconscious and superconscious. It is now time for you to experience this my children. Understand that this is now coming. Thank you so much for listening.

Appendix 2

The Interference of the Tubes and our Altered History.

When we are born to this planet we travel through tubes that allow us the birthing canals from the fourth dimension, those tubes have been interfered with and when you die the canal you use to go to the fourth dimension has also been interfered with. All these tubes that we use to access have been interfered with by a mind-set that is not totally conducive with what is required for us. What is happening now is the new children of today are coming through a cleansed tube that has not been interfered with.

If we cannot in any way accept some of these truths how are we going to understand the children of tomorrow? How are we going to understand their ponderings and thinking when we are so terminally sick within a mind-set that has been computed incorrectly within us. If you are not prepared to adjust your mind-set to something that is non-conducive with reality as we are allowed to interpret it then where are we going? This involves change, we have to be able to change our minds because they are wrong, they have been programmed so we live and interpret an incorrectness.

Allow yourself to start venturing back in your own history books. Take yourself back approximately one hundred and fifty years and allow yourself to meditate on that thought. See where you can go, see what you were and see how beautiful you were, how beautiful you will continue to be when you allow those parameters to return. You are all divine little stars of inspiration.

What actually happened was during the period of the eighteenth century something was stripped and changed and a time frequency parallel was manifested in the planet. What happened at this point was almost like a parameter came right the way through and chopped an ability previous to that and now it is very difficult to manifest because history as we have it today is allowing us to interpret history in a totally different way. There was an awful lot more to it than that.

History, as we see it as we are allowed to interpret it through encyclopaedias, through historical frequencies, through historical documents, can take us back correctly through to a period of about the eighteen hundreds. Behind that point, previous to that point, history was totally different. What has actually happened is due to the introduction of almost a brain line of thinking and history has been created previously to that by a façade that has been put in place. A misinterpretation of history has been put in place. Behind that time-line man knew exactly what he was. This was at the point when planetary frequencies were allowing other manifestations from other planetary energies to come in annexing man's ability to understand why he is here. At that process in time it was needed for this planet to be complete, it needed to be an individual entity to be something that was not being dictated from outside energies.

At that time parameter a time portal was blocked and history then continued as a parallel of what it appeared to be from the past but the past was totally different. Before this other planetary energies and beings were interfering or were part of the process of planet Earth. It was time for the planet to be one within itself, for individuals to be of a density frequency of this planet.

The last hundred years have been a massive catapult in technological advancement. Previous to that we had centuries of very little change from bow and arrow and spear and that went on for thousands of years. I am stating that there is a long long picture that can be interpreted after this point that maybe the past we are being allowed to imagine and has been portrayed to us was not the true past.

What was actually handed to us about a hundred and fifty years ago was the planet was allowed to be one with no interference from outside planetary beings so they stopped and were not allowed to come here but we were left with the memory of what we used to have and the possibilities of what we could do with what we used to have. We have had to manifest that with our own minds so in a hundred and fifty years we have actually almost catapulted ourselves back to the point we were at one hundred and fifty years before all the beings left.

Appendix 3

The Communicator Arris.

You may be wondering about those who are communicating with Robin. There have been many from many different star systems. At one point we were told that we were in touch with a central core of information from the God-source.

The first communicators were the Elders of the planet Zor that was being affected by man's continual abuse of Earth, the skies above and the waters below. Arris was to be the intermediary and doorkeeper for those who wished to communicate through him to Robin. But who else was communicating with us and what was the source of our information? In answer to that question we were given these words:

'Your group is developing a following of entities required to give the relevant answers you will need as and when. There are the **extra-terrestrials**, the **etheric beings**, the **gods** and the **Pleiadians**, all of which are connected with the cosmic thinking that we are trying to project to you. Arris will receive your questions and the relevant beings will give the answers to him. Many people enter your realms and many more wish to do so.'

We were to learn more of Arris and exactly who he is: "*We* have been the creation of the energy formats behind the gentleman by the name of Arris. He has been the mediator for many years within the child, vocally it has been a short period of time but much has had to be prepared for this. You must understand that the people who provide the vocalisation are not necessarily the people that provide the knowledge and wisdom that comes from them. They are basically transmitters, as you are transmitters of the information you feel is right for you to acknowledge. You must understand that the curators of this energy are not necessarily the formulas behind the vocalization.

You must realise that before a channel is set up we are encoding his DNA with the relevant information that he is bringing forward to you all. We are also there monitoring that the encoding is carrying out its correct procedure."

Later Arris was to say: "You have found out about me haven't you? I am not really as intelligent as I sound. You must understand that I cannot transform energy unless it has been given to me, therefore you cannot transform energy that has not been given to you. We are **energy vessels**, we are not the curators of original energy, we just carry them as vessels. Basically we are vessels of knowledge and love. It is very difficult for us to perform it, and we know that is what we want and wish to do at some point or other, and working towards that vessel is a beautiful thought for us all. You do deserve to get to that format. Thank you."

On another occasion Arris confided, "I have never been a human, but I have been told the requirements and don't like the sound of it very much. It is such an effort to consider the elements you have to live by. The thought processes you are allowed are quite sad, as you have the latent ability within you all to generate the correct energy to transport your mind and thought into a different dimension where we could all sit and speak clearly to each other and discuss planetary problems. These abilities were there originally, hence many of your structures around the world that you have problems understanding their use and meaning were there purely as meeting places for the planets, (*Stonehenge, Avebury, the Serpent Mound, and the Pyramids etc.*) The concepts are still within your minds but you have such vast blockages in your chakras that you are no longer able to project your thoughts to these levels of communication."

Select Bibliography

Caddy, E.

(1997) *The Spirit of Findhorn*, Publisher LN Fowlwer &Co

Cannon, D.

(1994) *The Legend of Starcrash*. Ozark Mountain Publishing.

(1993) *Keepers of the Garden*, Ozark Mountain Publishing.

(1999) *The Custodians*. Ozark Mountain Publishing.

(2001) *The Convoluted Universe, Book one*. Ozark Mountain Publishing.

(2005) *The Convoluted Universe, Book Two*. Ozark Mountain Publishing.

(2008) *The Convoluted Universe, Book Three*. Ozark Mountain Publishing.

(2011) *The Three Waves of Volunteers and the New Earth*. Ozark Mountain Publishing.

(2012) *The Convoluted Universe, Book 1V*. Ozark Mountain Publishing.

(2014) *The Search for Hidden Sacred Knowledge*. Ozark Mountain Publishing.

Carey, K.

(1982) *The Starseed Transmissions.* Starseed Publishing Ltd.

(1985) *Vision.* Starseed Publishing Ltd

(1988) *The Return of the Bird Tribes.* Uni*Sun.

(1991) *Starseed. The Third Millenium.* Harper Collins..

Churchward, J.

(1959) *The Lost Continent of Mu.* Neville Spearman

Hand Clow, B.

(1995) *Pleiadian Agenda.* Bear and Co.

(2004) *Alchemy of the Nine Dimensions.* Hampton Roads Publishing Company

Ledwith M and Heinemann K

(2007) *The Orb Project* Publisher Atria Books

Marciniak, B.

(1992) *Bringers of the Dawn. Teachings from the Pleiadians* Bear & Co.

(1995) *Earth. Pleiadian Keys to the Living Library.* Bear & Co.

(1998) *Family of Light. Pleiadian Tales and Lessons in living.* Simon & Schuster.

Matthews. J. (1990) *The Grail Tradition.* Element Books.

Megre. V. (2005) *The Ringing Cedars Series.* Ringing Cedars Press.

(1997) *The Ringing Cedars of Russia* publisher Ringing Cedars Press

Parkes, S. www.simonparkes.org

Picknett, L. & Prince, C. (1998) *The Templar Revelation.* Corgi.

Pellegrino-Estrich,R. (1997) *The Miracle Man. The life Story of Joao De Deus.* Triad Publishers,

Plimer, R. A.

(2014) An Introduction to Hermetic Philosophy Book One. *The Hermetica.* Courtyard Publishing

(2014) An Introduction to Hermetic Philosophy Book Two. *Hermetic Anatomy.* Courtyard Publishing

(2014) An Introduction to Hermetic Philosophy Book Three. *Kosmos.* Courtyard Publishing

(2010) Decoding Alchemy: *Alchemy and Spagyrics in Theory and Practice.*

Raven Wing, J. (2002) *The Book of Miracles. The Healing Work of Joao De Deus.* 1st Books Library.

Soskin, Julie.

(1991) *Cosmic Dance.* Barton House Publishing

(1992) *Alignment to Light.* Woodbridge Press Publishing Company

(1994) *Wind of Change.* Ashgrove Publishing Ltd

(1995) *Transformation* College of Psychic Studies

Williams, M.

(1980) *Ghostly Gifts.* Printed privately

(1980) *The Wilfion Scripts.* Wilfion Books Publishers.

(1982) *Out of the Mists.* Printed privately

(1989) *Ghostly Adventures.* Printed privately

(1991) *Mystical Memoirs.* Printed privately

Williams, M. & Morgan, C. (1991) *The Answer. Psychic explanations of UFOs & Crop Circles.* Printed privately.

Contact Details

The publisher and author(s) provide contact details for those interested in further information regarding publishing, availability for talks & lectures and any other general information concerning the work of Carolyn Morgan & Robin Wells:

Carolyn Morgan:

Downlands, Newport Rd, Whitwell, Isle of Wight, PO38 2QP.

Robin Wells:

niborwells@gmail.com

Courtyard Alchemy & Publishing:

www.courtyardalchemy.com

elplimer@gmail.com

bobplimer@yahoo.co.uk